Walking through Rome

A Guide to Interesting Sites
in the Eternal City

Margaret Varnell Clark

iUniverse, Inc.
Bloomington

Walking through Rome
A Guide to Interesting Sites in the Eternal City

iUniverse books may be ordered through booksellers or by contacting:

iUniverse
1663 Liberty Drive
Bloomington, IN 47403
www.iuniverse.com
1-800-Authors (1-800-288-4677)

ISBN: 978-1-4759-8130-8 (sc)
ISBN: 978-1-4759-8133-9 (hc)
ISBN: 978-1-4759-8132-2 (ebk)

Library of Congress Control Number: 2013905084

Printed in the United States of America

iUniverse rev. date: 03/21/2013

For Vern and Mary C.

Table of Contents

Acknowledgements

There are several people I would like to thank for their support and help in preparing this book. Without their assistance it wouldn't have happened. My editor Abigail Goben; Adam Wilson for his help deciphering architecture; Helen Wilson for making me cups of tea and pushing me on; Arch. Giuseppe Morganti, Project Director, Ministry of Heritage and Cultural, Directorate-General for the Landscape, Fine Arts, Architecture and Contemporary Art, Rome, Italy; Werner Schmid, Director of Conservation of Mural Paintings, Santa Maria Antiqua, Rome, Italy; Ben Haley, Communications Manager, World Monuments Fund, New York, NY; Dr. Margaret MacCurtain; and my publishers for all their encouragement. Thank You!!

Acknowledgments

How to Use This Book

This book is intended as a companion guide. It is current through the spring of 2013. Addresses and phone numbers of the sites are included for your convenience. Because emails and websites are more ephemeral, they are usually not included. An updated list of emails and websites for the different locations can be found at the *Walking through Rome* webpage at http://www.BijouxPress.com. For a more detailed discussion on the practicalities of travelling in Rome (i.e., hotel recommendations, tourist information, day trips, etc.), I use Rick Steve's guides. He does a great job!

The maps included in the Appendices are not to scale but are intended to assist you with developing an itinerary. Free, up-to-date maps are available from the Italian Tourist Office. Their phone number in New York is 212.245.5618. Their website is http://www.italia.it. For information about Rome click on the *Discover Italy* tab, then the *Lazio* tab (Rome is a city in Lazio). Their offices can also be found throughout Rome. Look for the large "TI' signs.

All biblical references in this book utilize the *New Interpreter's Study Bible: New Revised Standard Version with the Apocrypha.* Dates in this book are of the *Common Era* (CE) unless otherwise noted. Pre-Christian dates are identified as *Before the Common Era* (BCE).

Introduction

September in Rome is a time of transition. The heat of summer still hangs in the air, yet most of the tourists have gone home. Almost collectively the city seems to sigh and settle in for a lazy afternoon nap before the crispness of fall and the flurry of the holiday season sets in. September is a chance to breathe. September is quiet.

It was on just such a day in 2010 that I was able to indulge in one of my greatest passions: wandering. A long meandering walk, exploring a new neighborhood, and stopping in at a local place if I get hungry is the perfect day for me. I found myself walking through Trastevere. One of the oldest and poorest parts of Rome, it is a working class neighborhood that has retained its medieval flavor.

By midmorning the streets are empty, save for housewives hanging laundry out of windows and the occasional delivery van. I entered the 12th century basilica of San Crisogono through a side door. It was dark and cool. A man was dusting the pews near the main altar and whistling softly. He stopped for just a moment, tipped his hat to me, and then went back to his work. It was a pretty church dedicated to a Roman soldier that had been martyred during the persecution of Diocletian. Didn't I read somewhere that this was probably the first parish church in Rome and that there was a crypt? I approached the man and asked him.

"Sì, signora, c'è una cripta."

"May I go in?" I asked.

"Oh Si, Si, this way, sorry, sorry."

I was surprised at the quickness of his step. He motioned for me to follow him. We walked to the left of the altar into an almost empty room that must have been part of the sacristy. He took a set of keys from a desk drawer, handed me a flashlight, and then said, in perfect English, "That will be 4 Euros please." He unlocked a door, flipped a light switch, and waved me through. I descended a metal staircase to an 8th century church, lower to a 2nd century church, and lower still to a Roman hall. He did not follow. He simply closed the door behind me and left me to explore. Around me were frescoes of saints with colors still vivid though they were 1200 years old. There was St. Pantaleon curing a blind man, and Pope Silvestro taming a dragon. I walked on the Roman tile floor that was probably 2000 years old and developed a particular affection for a solitary column which protruded from the ground at the lowest level. Surely, at one point in time it had had companions. What could it have held up by itself? I spent hours wandering around the different levels. When I emerged the man was refilling the leaflets near the door of the basilica. I handed him the flashlight and he reached into his pocket and tried to give me some of my Euros back. Apparently, I had been renting the flashlight.

The midafternoon sun was blazing outside and admittedly, I was a little dazed by what I had just seen. I next came upon a small courtyard with a dilapidated church and a small overgrown cloister. I had to remind myself that I was still in the heart of Rome. The roof had collapsed in on the church and the front door handles were tied together with a rope. I peeped into the cloister. Two men were sitting to the left playing chess and drinking wine from paper cups. A grape arbor ran across the center of the overgrown enclave and an ancient man was sitting about ¾ths of the way down on a bench. He waved to me and then asked me to bring him a drink of water. The chess players looked up, and nodded toward a table in the corner with a pitcher and stack of paper cups. I brought him some water. He introduced himself and invited me to sit down. Over the course of the next hour, he told me his life story. He had grown up on a farm in Umbria and didn't know much about Mussolini, still didn't. But whatever he was about, it had to be more exciting than being on the farm. So he joined up. It turned out not to be the grand adventure he thought it would be though. He never left Italy. He did fall in love. Lost his sweetheart and in time found another. I am not quite sure how that all happened. My Italian isn't that good. But, I don't think it mattered. As I stood to leave, he picked a small bunch of grapes from the arbor and handed them to me. The chess players had long since abandoned their game and were quietly smoking. They thanked me as I left for listening to his stories. They had heard them all before.

It was getting late; I headed back towards my hotel and stopped in at a small family restaurant that was one of my favorites. The menu that night was Pollo all' Arrabbiati (Angry Chicken). Marcella took a break from the kitchen and sat down at my table. We laughed and chatted. She asked me if I had met a man yet. I told her about my afternoon; it wasn't quite what she had had in mind. We laughed some more, and she gave me her grandmother's recipe for Angry Chicken. She swears by it.

It was a perfect day. I feel very privileged to have had the chance to wander around. That is what this book is about. It is a collection of some well-known and not so well-known secrets I have found while walking through Rome. And it is an invitation to you to have your own adventures.

Have fun.

Ancient Church of St. Mary at the Forum

Santa Maria Antiqua

St. Maria Antiqua is currently being renovated.
This site is scheduled to open in 2013.

The church of Santa Maria Antiqua is one of the most exciting entries in this book. On the south side of the Roman Forum, the church was built in the 6th century; however, an earthquake in 847 almost completely buried the structure. It was not rediscovered again until 1702. It is an excellent example of an early Christian church built into the remains of a pre-existing pagan building, and particularly interesting because it has not been renovated over the centuries.

The pagan building dates to the 1st century CE. The complex consisted of a central court with three doors that led into a square atrium on the north side; a covered ramp that led to the imperial palaces on the east side; a central chamber with smaller chambers on the south side; and to the west, a large brick building which was believed for many years to be a temple, though scholars are less sure now. The debate also continues as to the original purpose of the complex. Some scholars believe it belonged to the Emperor Domitian (81-96). Others think it was constructed by the Emperor Hadrian (117-138) as part of the Athenaeum (University). Still other scholars believe that the buildings resemble a library, and most lean to this latter interpretation.

The first records of the structure as a Christian church are in the *De locis sanctis martyrum* of 635, which called it Santa Maria Antiqua. When the building was transformed into a church, the east and west sides of the courtyard were closed in to form aisles and the central hall became the nave. The outer court to the north became the atrium. When the earthquake hit in 847, the building was severely damaged. Pope Leo IV ordered the building abandoned and had a new church built on the opposite side of the Forum. The new church can also be visited; it is now known as Santa Francesca Romana. Over the years, landslides and the crumbling structure buried the main body of the church. A chapel was built into the old atrium in the 14th century, though it was not widely used. Santa Maria Antiqua was rediscovered in 1702 by people looking for building material in the Roman Forum. The apse was excavated somewhat and became a popular tourist site. However, the owner of the property decided to rebury it after only 3 months. Major excavations did not take place until the 1900s when archaeologist Giacomo Boni decided to take on the project.

It has been a difficult church to visit, with appointments having to be made well in advance. However, in the spring of 2013, the fully excavated church will be open to the public for the first time in more than 12 centuries.

Visitors enter the structure through the atrium which has frescos that date to the time of Hadrian and some classical sculptures. Going through the glass door, one will be standing in the narthex of the original church. The herringbone pattern pavement is called opus spicatum and dates to the 1st century CE. Directly ahead is the nave which has frescos of biblical scenes. Beyond that is the Bema. This portion has seats along the walls and biblical frescos. Today, a Bema is more often associated with a Jewish synagogue, but in ancient Rome they were used by secular authorities as a place of judgment or courtroom. They had a raised seat for the judge, which could also be used as a lectern, and seats along the walls. Early Christians also incorporated them into early churches and it is believed they were used as teaching or lecture rooms. There are several references to Bemas in the New Testament, including: Matthew 27:19; John 19:13; Acts 25:10; and Romans 14:10.

Continuing on, the next small room is the presbytery which is paved with opus Alexandrinum. This is particularly exciting as some references state that this type of flooring, which is a highly geometric and somewhat Byzantine in design, had not been introduced to Italy until the 11th century. There are also numerous frescoes in the presbytery, all of which date to the 8th century. There are two 8th century chapels on either side of the presbytery filled with frescoes. The Chapel of Theodotus is on the left and the Chapel of the Holy Physicians is on the right. Scholars and archeologists have done an exceptional job documenting the 2690 square feet of frescoes found throughout and an onsite guide is planned for visitors when the church is opened to the public. The earliest painting they have dated so far is located on the wall to the right of the apse in the back of the presbytery. Known as a Maria Regina, it dates to the 6th century and shows the Virgin Mary enthroned, wearing a garment with pearls in the style of a Byzantine empress. It may be the earliest surviving depiction of Mary as Queen of Heaven. The Chapel of the Holy Physicians has several frescoes of medical saints which were painted during the early 8th century. Among those pictured are St. John of Edessa, St. Celsus, St. Abbacycus, St. Cosmas, St. Damian, and at least one unidentifiable female saint. Historians believe that people came to the chapel to pray and be healed by the saint's interventions. This is a tradition that is common in the Eastern Church and was gaining in popularity in Rome during the era of the Byzantine Papacy (537-752).

The most striking image of Christ is in the second level of the apse fresco. He is shown seated with his right hand raised in a blessing. There is a tetramorph of the four evangelists on either side of him. A symbolism of the tetramorph relates to the visions of the Old Testament Prophet Ezekiel (Ezekiel 1:10) as well as the Book of Revelation (Revelation 4:7) in the New Testament. It is a winged 4-headed creature that has the animal heads of the 4 evangelists. Specifically, St. Matthew is represented by a winged man, St. Luke by an Ox, St. Mark by a Lion, and John the Evangelist by an Eagle. The wings represent the divinity of the Evangelists. While this creature is a little creepy looking, it was a very popular symbol in early Christianity. It is commonly seen surrounding an image of Christ in Glory on the spherical ceiling inside the apse of churches. Similar, though, later frescoes of Christ flanked by the evangelists can be seen in the churches of Santa Pudenziana, San Clemente, and Santa Maria in Trastevere.

Pope Paul I is also shown in this apse fresco. He is depicted with a square nimbus, which tells us that he was still alive when the fresco was painted and dates it to between 757 and 767.

Address

Santa Maria Antiqua
1 Largo Romolo e Remo
(Forum Romanum archaeological site)
Opening in the Spring 2013

Basilica of the Holy Cross in Jerusalem

Basilica di Santa Croce in Gerusalemme

Built around 325 by St. Helena, the mother of Emperor Constantine, the *Basilica di Santa Croce in Gerusalemme*is one of the seven pilgrim churches of Rome. The church was built next to Helena's palace, the *Palazzo Sessoriano*. The story is told that Helena had soil from Jerusalem brought to Rome for its foundation, hence the dedication of the basilica to the city of Jerusalem. The church was built to house the Passion Relics and the basilica has a large collection of relics from the Holy Land supposedly brought back by St. Helena.

The basilica has been remodeled several times. There is an interesting story about a brick which was discovered by workmen on February 1, 1492 while restoring a mosaic. The brick was inscribed with the words *Titulus Crucis* (Title of the Cross). Behind it was a fragment of wood which had the word "Nazarene" inscribed in Hebrew, Latin, and Greek. Legend suggests that this was a relic of the cross on which Christ was crucified. St. Helena is said to have been given the relic while on a trip to Jerusalem. She divided the piece of wood into three parts, giving one to the Emperor Constantine to be kept in Constantinople, keeping one in Jerusalem, and sending the last to the basilica in Rome. The relic was supposedly hidden in the wall around 455 to protect it from the attacking Visigoths. Other relics kept in the church include two thorns from Christ's crown of thorns; an incomplete nail from the crucifixion; the bone from the finger of St. Thomas that he placed in the wounds of the Risen Christ; and small pieces of the Scourging Pillar to which Christ was tied as he was beaten. A larger piece of the pillar is kept in the Church of St. Prassade.

In 983, a monastery was added to the church by Pope Benedict VII. Inside the western door, there is a 17 verse epitaph for Pope Benedict VII (974-983) which tells of his founding of the monastery. The poem says he gathered monks who would both sing praises to God "night and day" and do charitable works for poor people.

Substantial renovations to the church were undertaken by Pope Lucius II in the 12th century, which included a basic floor plan of nave, aisles, a transept, and an apse. In addition to redesigning the interior of the church, Lucius II also had a portico and an 8-story Romanesque bell tower added in the 12th century. The front of the church has a baroque façade which was built under the direction of Pope Benedict XIV (1740-1758). The interior decoration is also baroque and dates from the 18th century. Benedict XIV also had new streets developed which connected this basilica with St. John in Lantern and St. Mary Major.

In the nave of the church there are 8 pink granite Corinthian columns from Aswan, Egypt. These are the only parts of the ancient church which are still visible since the baroque renovations. A painting of *Our Lady Presenting St. Helena and Constantine to the Trinity* by Corrado Giaquinto in 1744 decorates the ceiling of the nave. The wooden ceiling on which this was painted was added in the 18th century and covered 12th century frescoes. The frescoes seen today were rediscovered in 1913 by workmen surveying the roof. The main altar of the church is covered by a baldachin from the 18th century renovation. The 4 columns supporting it, however, are believed to come from the original basilica. Below the altar in the upper church is a basalt urn, containing the relics of St. Caesarius and St. Anastasius. The apse fresco shows scenes from the legend of the recovery of the True Cross at Jerusalem. There is some controversy as to the artist of this work. Some believe it to be Pinturicchio, others think it was painted by Antoniazzo Romano about 1492, and it has also been suggested that it is by an anonymous painter from the Umbrian school. All agree that it is from the 15th century and that it was commissioned by Cardinal Bernardino Carvajal.

Behind the apse, there are two chapels, the Chapel of St. Helena and the Chapel of the Pietà. The Chapel of St. Helena is down a flight of stairs to the right of the main altar. It is believed to have been her private chapel. When the church was consecrated, this was considered the holiest part of the complex. The statue in the chapel was an early Roman copy of a statue of Juno that was found in the Ostia. An unknown artist added arms, a head, and a cross to transform the figure into St. Helena. Although the Chapel of St. Helena was originally constructed to be at ground level, it is now almost 6.5 feet lower than the modern street. The original decorations including mosaics commissioned by Emperor Valentinian III (425-455) were replaced when the chapel was redecorated by Baldassare Peruzzi in the 16th century. There are rooms adjacent to the chapel, however, which were part of the original 4th century Sessorian Palace of St. Helena. The altar piece once held three painting by Rubens: *Christ Crowned with Thorns*, *The Crucifixion*, and *St. Helena*. They were removed in 1724 over concerns of water damage from the dampness of the surrounding chapel. They are now housed in the Notre Dame du Puy Cathedral in Grasse, France.

The Chapel of the Pietà, also known as the Gregorian Chapel, is of particular interest to pilgrims. The 1536 Decree on Purgatory, issued by the Council of Trent, linked the freeing of souls from Purgatory to the celebration of the Eucharist on specific altars. This is one of those designated altars. Dating from 1574, the altar is a famous reliquary, shaped as a triptych; it holds almost 200 relics and has a 13th or 14th century mosaic of the suffering Christ in the center. This chapel can be reached by descending a flight of stairs to the left of the main altar.

The most famous relics kept at the church can be found in the Chapel of Relics. These relics include fragments of the Holy Cross of Jesus, found by St. Helena on Calvarium in Jerusalem. This chapel is located down a flight of stairs on the left side of the church.

If one walks around the back of the Basilica of the Holy Cross in Jerusalem, some of the original Roman masonry and remnants of a medieval cloister that was once adjacent to the church can be seen in a few places.

Note: The monastery that was adjacent to this church was active from 938 until 2011. In May 2011, Pope Benedict XVI closed the monastery because of rumors of a lack of liturgical, financial, and moral discipline. The basilica's abbot, Simone Fioraso who was a former Milan fashion designer, was removed two years prior. In April 2009, the monastery received publicity for the performances of *The Holy Dance* by a nun at the monastery, Sister Anna Nobili, a former exotic dancer. Reportedly, she and the other nuns, known as the Jesus Dancers, performed a special dance with a wooden crucifix for the monks, which became a regular Tuesday evening event.

Fioraso and a group called the "Friends of Santa Croce" allegedly used other unusual strategies to raise money for renovation of the church and monastery. The tactics reportedly included the opening of a hotel, concerts, televised Bible-reading marathons, and hosting celebrity visitors. It was the monks' bookkeeping, however, that likely led to the closure. The official inquiry by the Vatican's Congregation for Institutes of Consecrated Life has not yet been made public, though the Vatican has released statements.

"An inquiry found evidence of liturgical and financial irregularities as well as lifestyles that were probably not in keeping with that of a monk," said Vatican Spokesman Father Ciro Benedettini. The monastery was closed and the 20 Cistercian monks were transferred to other monasteries in Italy.

Despite the controversy, the church itself is still open to visitors and Mass is said daily.

St. Helena

Helena was the consort of Emperor Constantius and the mother of Emperor Constantine. She traveled widely in the Holy Land and brought many relics back to Rome including the Santa Scala, or Holy

Steps. Constantine appointed her *Augusta Imperatrix* and gave her unlimited access to the imperial treasury to acquire relics and bring them back to Rome. She is usually depicted in art as holding a cross, as she is credited with finding the True Cross. She is considered a saint by the Eastern Orthodox, Oriental Orthodox, Eastern, and Roman Catholic churches, as well as the Anglican Communion and Lutheran Churches. Her feast day in the Roman Catholic Church is August 18.

Points of Interest

- The Chapel of the Holy Relics which has a large collection of relics from the Holy Land including the finger of St. Thomas which he used to touch the wounds of Christ.
- The Chapel of St. Helena in the Sessorian Palace. (down a flight of stairs to the right of the high altar) The two adjacent rooms are part of the 4th century Sessorian Palace.
- The brick inscribed *Titulus Crucis* can be seen in the outer relic chapel.

Address

Church of the Holy Cross in Jerusalem
Piazza di Santa Croce in Gerusalemme 12
00185 Rome, Italy
Telephone: 06 70 61 30 53

Castle of the Holy Angel

Castel Sant'Angelo

The Castel Sant'Angelo isn't technically a church. It is a mausoleum that was designed by the architect Demitriano for the Emperor Hadrian. Originally called the 'Hadrianium', the structure consists of three overlapping stone cylinders surrounded by a circular façade, with a spiral ramp on the inside. The walls are 11 feet thick and, when first built, there was a garden and bronze chariot featuring the Emperor Hadrian dressed as the sun god on top. Today there are 5 floors in all. The first floor is the base of the ramp; the second floor is comprised of prison cells; the third floor has a large courtyard and once served as the military headquarters; the fourth floor has lavishly decorated Papal apartments; and the fifth floor is a terrace overlooking the river.

Both Hadrian's and his wife Sabina's ashes were interred here. Succeeding Roman Emperors were also laid to rest in the mausoleum. The last recorded internment was Caracalla in 217. The building was included in the Aurelian Walls, a line of city walls built between 271 and 275 by Flavius Augustus Honorius. These walls enclosed all seven of the hills of Rome, the Campus Martius, and the Trastevere district. The Aurelian Walls remained in continuous use as Rome's primary fortification system until 1871.

In many ways, the utilization of the building as a fortress led to the destruction of the early site. The Visigoths looted the site in 410 and scattered the ashes of the emperors. Records show that many of the remaining bronze statues and decorations were thrown (literally) down upon the attacking Goths in 537. The name, *Castel Sant' Angelo*, dates to the time of the plague of 590. Pope Gregory the

Great led a solemn procession of the faithful to the fortress to pray for the end of a plague. He saw a vision of an angel standing atop the mausoleum sheathing his sword. He interpreted this to mean the plague was ending. A small chapel was built at the spot where the angel was supposed to have appeared and today a statue of an angel sheathing his sword keeps a watchful eye on the city of Rome. This statue was designed by Bernini as were 10 angels that adorn the bridge adjacent to the castle.

Several aristocratic families lived in the building during theMiddleAges. In1277, Pope Nicholas III had an enclosed passage constructed, *Passetto del Borgo*, which links the castle to the Vatican. The passage played a critical role in saving the lives of various Popes. The most famous papal escape was that of Clement VII who fled through this passage during the May 6, 1527 Sack of Rome by the Holy Roman Emperor, Charles V. During this battle, 147 of the Vatican's 189 Swiss Guards gave their liveson the steps of St. Peter's Basilica so that the Pope could escape. The date of May 6 is still a special one to the Swiss Guard and has been used as the date for induction of new recruits.

The Popes converted the fourth floor of the castle into apartmentswith frescoes by Giulio Romano, Perin del Vaga, and others painters of Raphael's school. They also used the Castel Sant'Angelo as a prison for political prisoners for many centuries. Executions were conducted in the interior courtyard on the third level. Today, the castle is a museum, *Museo Nazionale di Castel Sant'Angelo*.

Points of Interest

- *Passetto del Borgo*, also known as the Passetto, was the passage in the Dan Brown novel *Angels & Demons* through which the four abducted cardinals were removed from the Vatican. It also appeared in the Audrey Hepburn film *Roman Holiday*.
- Castel Sant'Angelo features prominently in Puccini's opera, Tosca. Cavadarossi is held prisoner, tortured, and executed

on the 2nd level and Tosca leaps to her death from its battlements, probably on the 5th level. Some falsely attribute Scarpia's quarters as being located here. They are actually in the Palazzo Farnese.

- The frescos in the papal apartments by Giulio Romano (1499-1546), Perin del Vaga (1501-1547), and others painters of Raphael's school.
- The papal bathroom of Pope Clement VII (1523 to 1534).
- The museum collection of armor and weapons.
- The statue of *Saint Michael Holding his Sword* on the 5th level.
- Be sure to walk across the Sant'Angelo Bridge and look back at the castle. It is one of the finest surviving ancient Roman bridges in the city. The bridge was completed in 135 and consists of seven stone arches. Pope Clement IV added the iron balustrade in the 13th century and Pope Clement VII added the angel statues by Bernini in the 16th century.

Address

Castel Sant'Angelo National Museum
Lungotevere Castello, 50
00186 Rome, Italy
Telephone: 06 681 91 11

Church of the Sacred Heart of Suffrage/Museum of the Souls in Purgatory

Chiesa del Sacro Cuore en Prati/ Picollo Museo Del Purgatoria

Also known as: Chiesa Sacro Cuore del Suffragio

The Chiesa del Sacro Cuore en Prati is a parish church in the Lungotevere Prati section of Rome. Located on the banks of the Tiber River and a short walk upstream from Castel Sant'Angelo, this neo-gothic church was constructed in 1890 by architect Joseph Gualandi. It is sometimes called the "small cathedral of Milan" (*Il Piccolo Duomo di Milano*) because its architecture mimics that of the larger cathedral. The church appears to be marble but is actually constructed of concrete. It was built by Father Victor Jouet, a French priest and founder of the *Association of the Sacred Heart of Jesus for the Suffrage of the Souls in Purgatory.*

Following a fire in the church on September 15, 1897, the image of a sad face was seen on the wall behind the altar in a chapel. Jouet determined that it was a soul from purgatory asking for help. He began collecting documentation, relics, and evidence of purgatory. His collection can be seen in a small museum next to the sacristy. Jouet believed that the signs he collected are proof that the souls in purgatory are asking for our prayers to shorten their stay and help them advance to heaven. He died in the museum room in 1912, surrounded by his collection.

The nave of the church has three aisles, each ending in a three-sided apse. There are three entrances to the church, one per aisle. Each entrance has a pointed arch enclosing a tympanum; the center is the largest of the three and is considered the main entrance. The feast of the Sacred Heart is celebrated on Friday after the second Sunday after Pentecost. To the right of the church is the residence of the Missionaries of the Sacred Heart.

Purgatory

Purgatory, in accordance with Catholic teaching, is a place or condition of temporal punishment. It is derived from the Latin word "*purgare*" which means: to make clean, to purify. The doctrine of purgatory was defined in the Decree of Union drawn up by the Council of Florence in 1031, and further explained in the decree of the Council of Trent in 1545. The Church declared:

"Whereas the Catholic Church, instructed by the Holy Ghost, has from the Sacred Scriptures and the ancient tradition of the Fathers taught in Councils and very recently in this Ecumenical synod that there is a purgatory, and that the souls therein are helped by the suffrages of the faithful, but principally by the acceptable Sacrifice of the Altar; the Holy Synod enjoins on the Bishops that they diligently endeavor to have the sound doctrine of the Fathers in Councils regarding purgatory everywhere taught and preached, held and believed by the faithful."

The Catechism of the Catholic Church states that purgatory was a place between Heaven and Hell whereby souls could "achieve the holiness necessary to enter the joy of heaven." The Roman Catholic Church recognizes two types of sins. A mortal sin is a "grave violation of God's law" that "turns man away from God." It can damn a soul to eternal hell and can only be redeemed through repentance and God's forgiveness. In contrast, a venial sin, or forgivable sin "does not set us in direct opposition to the will and friendship of God." However, it is still considered a "moral disorder". These sins can be redeemed through temporal punishment remitted by sufferings in this life, indulgences, or after death in Purgatory. The Roman Catholic Church teaches that the fate of souls in purgatory can be affected by the prayers and actions of the living. This teaching is based also on a passage from the Old Testament of the Bible in which Judas, the commander of the forces of Israel, sends a "collection of silver to Jerusalem for sacrifice to be offered for the sins of the dead" and declares "It is therefore a holy and wholesome thought to pray for the dead, that they may be loosed from sins." (2 Maccabees 12:42-4).

The most famous literary interpretation of purgatory is in Dante Alighieri's *Divine Comedy*. The poem, *Purgatorio,* written between 1308 and 1321, tells the story of Dante's climb up the Mount of Purgatory, guided by the Roman poet Virgil. In Dante's purgatory there is a lower level or entrance called Ante-Purgatory; seven levels of suffering and spiritual growth, each one associated with one of the seven deadly sins; and an Earthly Paradise at the top. Along the way, Dante examines the true the nature of sin, moral issues in politics, church corruption, and theological issues. The poem has been a source of inspiration for writers, composers, and painters since its publication.

Points of Interest

- This church is one of the few examples of neo-gothic construction in Rome
- Museum of the Souls in Purgatory
    - To find the museum: From inside the church, walk down the right aisle to a door on the right, before the end of the aisle.
    - A pillowcase with markings from a soul who asked for prayers to hasten the passage to heaven.
    - A robe and a shirt of a nun with the fingerprints of a dead person from purgatory.
    - A handprint burned into a prayer book in the museum.

Address

Church of the Sacred Heart of Suffrage
Museum of the Souls in Purgatory
Lungotevere Prati 12, Rome, Italy
Telephone: 06 68 80 65 17

Mamertine Prison/ St. Joseph of the Carpenters

Carcere Mamertino/ San Giuseppe dei Falegnami

The Mamertine Prison consists of two underground rooms, one above the other. The Church of St. Joseph is above that.

The Mamertine Prison, also known as San Pietro in Carcare, is located at the foot of the Capitoline Hill beneath the church of San Giuseppe dei Falegnami. The area was known as the Comitium, and served as the political center of ancient Rome. The Romans called the spot "carcer", which means prison. The name "Mamertine" has been use since the medieval ages. The fourth of the Kings of Rome, Ancus Marcius (640-616 BCE), built a prison on this site for condemned enemies of the State. It was probably the first maximum security prison in Rome and it is likely that this is the "the prison . . . in the middle of the city, overlooking the forum", discussed by the Roman historian, Livy (59 BCE-17 C.E.). It remained in use as a prison until the 4th century. Legend tells that Sts. Peter and

Paul were imprisoned here. Vercingetorix the Gaul and Simon bar Jiora, who defended Jerusalem against Titus, were other prisoners in the Mamertine. Because the saints were believed to have been incarcerated here, after the location ceased to be used as a prison, it became a pilgrimage site.

The prison consists of two underground rooms, one above the other. There were other cells dug into the hillside of the Capitoline which may have been part of the structure. They have since been lost. The remaining upper room has a plaque listing the prisoners that were executed on the site and a small altar with busts of Sts. Peter and Paul. To the left of the altar is another plaque which lists the saints and martyrs who were held there along with the names of their persecutors. The room is constructed of tufa stone from Montverde and is trapezoidal in shape. This room is at the original ground level of ancient Rome.

The lower room is called the Tullianum. Many guidebooks have mistakenly identified that the room was named after the sixth King of Rome, Servius Tullius (578-535 BCE). The shape of the room and presence of natural spring in the middle suggests that the chamber was a cistern and the name is likely derived from the archaic Latin word *Tullis* which means a jet of water. It is circular and made of blocks of peperino, a grey-flecked volcanic stone, which is held together without mortar. The room was originally accessed through an opening in the floor of the upper room that is now covered with a grate. Today, access is via a modern staircase on the left-hand side. There is a small altar and a circular opening in the floor through which a miraculous spring flowed. There is a column to the left where Sts. Peter and Paul were reportedly chained and a stone believed to have the imprint of St. Peter's head when he was thrown into the chamber. Historians believe that the upper room was used as a prison cell and that this lower room was the site of executions.

Above the prison is the baroque church, San Giuseppe dei Falegnami, St. Joseph the Carpenter, which was built in 1597 by the Congregation of the Carpenters. Until the 1930s, the church had two balustrade transverse staircases in front. These were demolished to facilitate excavation of the ancient road surface. The façade of the church is now raised above the floor, as a result of the 1930s construction. Though small, the church remains a vital part of Roman Catholic life. Pope Benedict XVI created Francesco Coccopalmerio a Cardinal-Deacon (the lowest ranks of cardinals) on February 18, 2012 and designated San Giuseppe dei Falegnami as his home church.

San Giuseppe dei Falegnami is decorated with angels throughout and frescos which were probably painted in the 1500s. Many of the angels are portrayed holding carpenters' instruments in honor of their patron saint, St. Joseph the Carpenter. The church has a gilt coffered ceiling, a rectangular nave, and a semi-circular apse. There are two chapels, one on each side of the nave. One of these chapels has a fresco, *The Nativity,* byCarlo Maratta. An accomplished painter in his own right, Maratta is remembered for his work restoring paintings and sculptures at the Vatican. He is best known for the cleaning the Raphael frescoes in the Vatican Stanze which is in the Vatican Museums.

Between the church and the Mamertine Prison is the Chapel of the Crucifix, which dates from the 16th century. It is not usually open to the public.

St. Joseph

St. Joseph is the husband of the Virgin Mary and the earthly father of Jesus Christ. He is mentioned in the Bible in the gospels of Matthew and Luke (Matthew 1:17, Luke 3:23-28), each of which contain a genealogy of Jesus tracing his ancestry back to King David. He does not appear in the gospel of Mark; and is only mentioned as Jesus' father in the gospel of John (John 6:41-42).

For centuries, theologians have tried to explain how Jesus could be simultaneously the "son of God" as well as the "son of Joseph" and if Mary remained a virgin throughout her life. The arguments are fueled by the discussion of "Jesus' brothers" in the Bible. (Matthew

13:55; Mark 6:3, Luke 8:19-21) The Bible also tells us that Jesus had sisters, but they are not named or numbered (Matthew 13:56). In the Eastern Orthodox Church, it is taught that Joseph's first wife was Salome, and that he was a widower. Therefore, any references to Jesus' "brothers and sisters" are to children of Joseph and Salome. They teach that Joseph was betrothed, but never married, to Mary. The Roman Catholic Church views Joseph as a husband to Mary. However, they teach that she remained a virgin and any references to Jesus' siblings should be understood to mean cousins or step-brothers/sisters. These views are based on the teachings of St. Jerome. Many Protestant churches follow the ideology of the Virgin Birth but not that of Mary's Perpetual Virginity.

St. Joseph is venerated as a saint in the Catholic, Eastern Orthodox, Oriental Orthodox, Anglican, and Lutheran Churches. In the Roman Catholic Church and most Protestant churches, his feast day is March 19. In the Eastern Orthodox Church, his feast day is the first Sunday after the Nativity of Christ.

Points of Interest

- San Giuseppe dei Falegnami is only open on Sundays for services and worth the visit. It is a good example of a non-tourist, Roman parish church.
- The Chapel of the Crucifix, which dates from the sixteenth century.
- The Mamertine Prison.
    - The stone believed to have the imprint of St. Peter's head when he was thrown into the prison.
    - The upside-down Cross of St. Peter on the altar.
    - The column to which both Sts. Peter and Paul were chained, and from which they converted their guards to Christianity.

Address

Located at the northwest corner of the forum, the church is only open on Sundays; the Mamertine Prison is usually open every day.

San Giuseppe dei Falegnami
Via di San Pietro in Carcere
Rome, Italy

Most Holy Name of Jesus

Santissima Nome di Gesù all'Argentina

Locally this church is often just called "Il Gesù"

The present day church of the Most Holy Name of Jesus is built on the site of a previous church, Santa Maria della Strada. Ignatius of Loyola and his followers had used this early church when he came to Rome in 1537 until it became too small and a larger one was needed. The baroque church seen today, built in 1568, is the mother church of the Society of Jesus, also known as the Jesuits. The church was designed in accordance with the requirements established by the Council of Trent. The Council recommended that churches not have a narthex; churchgoers should walk directly into the body of the church when they pass through the front door. They also recommended that newly constructed churches should not have aisles and should minimize their transepts. There should be a single center aisle and a single nave where the high altar is the main focus of attention. Chapels may be created in place of the side aisles; however, they should all be uniform in size and shape and should be behind arches, screens, or gates along the sides of the main body of the church. The intention is to maintain the high altar as the center of focus. This design, which was used in Santissima Nome di Gesù, established the layout for Jesuit churches that has continued to be used to this day.

The main altar of the church is decorated with a painting of the *Circumcision* by Girolamo Muziano (1587). Behind this painting is a niche with a statue of the sacred heart of Jesus. Sometimes the painting is removed and the statue is visible.

Santissima Nome di Gesù has several chapels and some very important works of art. The 15th century icon Madonna della Strada (Our Lady of the Way) is located in the chapel to the left of the main altar. This is in tribute to the previous church which stood on the site. The Virgin Mary is the patroness of the Society of Jesus. Legend says that Ignatius of Loyola, founder of the Jesuit order, was protected by the intercession of the Blessed Virgin Mary during the battle of Pamplona in 1521. He also had a vision of the Virgin Mary and the infant Jesus while at the shrine of Our Lady of Montserrat in March 1522. The Chapel of St. Ignatius of Loyola is next to the chapel of Our Lady Della Strada along the left side of the church. The saint is buried beneath the gilded bronze altar that was designed by Alessandro Algardi (1595-1654). Perhaps one of the most interesting statues in all of Rome is in this chapel. Created in 1702 by Pierre Le Gros, *Religion Overthrowing Heresy and Hatred* depicts a nun who represents the Catholic Church, whipping two Protestants into submission. The snake, Martin Luther, is being stepped on and a putto rips pages out of a book by the Swiss reformer Huldrych Zwingli. It leaves no room for doubt how the Church would like to have dealt with these reformers.

When the chapel to the right of the main altar was built, it was dedicated to St. Francis of Assisi. In 1760, this chapel was rededicated and renovated to the *Sacred Heart of Jesus*. The dome in the center of the church was painted by Giovanni Battista Gaulli Baciccia and is entitled "*The Triumph of the Name of Jesus*" (1676-1679). He used an overhead perspective that gives the painting the image of breaking through the vault. There is a small museum next to the sacristy. The first chapel on the right upon entering the church is the Cappella di Sant'Andrea. This chapel was built in honor of the original church of St. Andrew which was on the site and removed to build the present church.

The rooms in which St. Ignatius lived are part of the present day residence for Jesuit seminarians. Visitors can see the rooms on request. They contain memorabilia of the saint and information on the history of the Jesuit order. There are two altars in the rooms. One is decorated with a painting of the Holy Family, the other with a painting of St. Ignatius saying mass.

St. Ignatius of Loyola

Ignatius of Loyola was a Spanish knight from the Basque region born around 1491. He had a spiritual conversion while recovering from injuries received at the battle of Pamplona in 1521. While recuperating, he read the lives of the saints and Jesus. Inspired by the life of St. Francis of Assisi to lead a life of selfless labor and service to the poor, St. Ignatiusdecided to dedicate himself to becoming a soldier of the Catholic faith. He took his religious vows in 1534, and was selected to be the first Superior General of the newly formed Society of Jesus. This newly formed order sent missionaries to Europe, Asia, and the New World to create schools, colleges, and seminaries. He was known for his writings, principally his *Spiritual Exercises* published in 1548. He also wrote the Jesuit Constitutions which were adopted in 1540. St. Ignatiuswas questioned by the Inquisition, but was released. His feast day is July 31.

Points of Interest

- The 15th century icon *Madonna della Strada* (Our Lady of the Way), patroness of the Society of Jesus.
- *The Triumph of the Name of Jesus* (1676-1679), by Giovanni Battista Gaulli Baciccia, on the ceiling of the church.
- The Christmas Crib in this church is considered to be one of the finest in Rome.
- The rooms in which St. Ignatius lived are part of the present day residence for Jesuit seminarians.
- The statue by Pierre Le Gros, *Religion Overthrowing Heresy and Hatred.*

Address

Most Holy Name of Jesus
16 Via degli Astalli / Piazza del Gesù
00186 Rome, Italy
Telephone: 06 69 70 01

Most Holy Trinity at Monte Pincio

Santissima Trinità al Monte Pinco

This is the church that is at the top of the Spanish Steps. The first religious structure built on this site was a convent and church built in 1494 by Charles VIII of France in gratitude to St. Francis of Paola for aiding his father King Louis XI. Construction started in 1502 but was not completed until 1584.

The church was built for monks from the Order of Minims and there is a story that the monks were tortured by the Holy Roman Emperor Charles V's soldiers when they sacked Rome in 1527. They believed that the monks knew the location of buried treasure. The Italian monks found it very difficult to get along with their French landlords. In 1624, the monks moved out of the church to the nearby St. Andrea della Fratte. The church was little used and fell into disrepair. By the time Napoleon's forces occupied Rome (1798-1799), it had been abandoned completely. The French troops stripped the inside of the church of most of its decorations during this era. The church was renovated several years later by King Louis XVIII; and in 1828 the church and convent were transferred to St. Madeleine Sophie Barat, who founded the Sisters of the Sacred Heart, to be used as a school. In September 2006, the Sisters of the Sacred Heart withdrew from the church, and it was given to the Fraternités Monastiques de Jérusalem' (The Jerusalem Community), a group founded on All Saints' Day 1975, in the church of St. Gervais in Paris. They are dedicated to living a monastic life in the heart of the city.

The neo-classical façade of the church dates from 1570 and was constructed by Carlo Maderno. The double staircase was designed by Domenico Fontana. Inside, the church is Romanesque in style with a single nave and side chapels. Depending on how they are counted, there are 14-15 side chapels in this church. The painting over the altar in the second chapel on the left is *The Deposition* by Daniele da Volterra, a pupil of Michelangelo. When it was painted in 1545-1547, it was considered as important as the *Transfiguration* by Raphael, and it was called one of the three greatest paintings in the world at that time. Over time, however, it has since deteriorated and it is little known now. It was originally painted on wood, but was transferred to canvas in 1811.

The third chapel on the right has a fresco, the *Assumption,* which was painted by Daniele da Volterra. In this work, the last figure on the right and dressed in red is a portrait of none other than Michelangelo. He is boldly looking out at the viewer.

The sacristy anteroom to the left of the main altar houses the other major works of art left in the church, *The Coronation of the Virgin, The Annunciation,* and *A Visitation,* all by Frederico Zuccari. Some guidebooks attribute these paintings to Federico's brother Taddeo Zuccari. The paintings depicting *TheAssumption* and *The Death of the Virgin* in the fourth chapel on the left were probably done by Taddeo. It is known that Federico finished some of his brother's work in this church after Taddeo died in 1566. But no one seems to definitively know which brother actually did what.

On the upper floor of the convent adjacent to this church there are two anamorphic paintings that were created by the monks of the Order of Minims. These paintings are designed to create optical illusions of images that change depending on the viewer's vantage point. The first one, when viewed from down the corridor, shows St. Francis of Paola (Founder of the Order on Minims) kneeling in prayer beneath a tree. As one approaches the image dissolves and becomes a bay surrounded by hills. The other painting appears to be an image of St. John writing in the Book of Revelation, but as one approaches, the scene changes to the landscape of the island of Patmos. If able to view these painting, please also note the large sundial, the 12 signs of the zodiac, and the names of several cities from around the world that decorate the vault above. The local time in these cities is reflected by the sundial. It was created by Father Emmauel Maignan. This part of the convent is usually open to visitors on Tuesday and Saturday mornings. Please contact the church to arrange to visit this area.

Note: The main door of the church is usually locked. Visitors can enter through a side door in the convent building. If that door is locked during the day, ring the bell by the door and the sisters will usually allow entrance.

Mater Admirabilis—Mother Most Admirable

The fresco, Mater Admirabilis (Mother Most Admirable), is also in the convent adjacent to the church. It was painted by a young French novice of the order, Pauline Perdrau. Though she worked for hours on the painting, her Mother Superior did not feel the work was of a high quality. She hid the painting by covering it with a curtain. On October 20, 1846, Pope Pius IX visited the convent. On the tour, he drew back the curtain on the wall and exclaimed "Mater Admirabilis!" The painting soon became an object of veneration and has been associated with several miracles.

It is an unusual and pretty painting of the Blessed Mother. She is shown seated on a simple wooden chair between a distaff and a lily in a vase with a basket of books beside her. She is holding a spinning spindle on her lap and is looking downward. Twelve gold stars encircle her bowed head. The fresco has become a popular pilgrimage site for the Sisters of the Sacred Heart. Please ask one of the sisters in the church and they will usually escort visitors to see it.

Points of Interest

- The twisted columns in the sanctuary are from the 13th century.
- The fresco, Mater Admirabilis (Mother Most Admirable), located in the convent.
- The *Coronation of the Virgin, The Annunciation,* and *A Visitation,* by one if not both of the Zuccaris.

- *The Deposition* by Daniele da Volterra, called one of the three greatest paintings in the world at that time it was painted.
- The *Assumption,* also by da Volterra. In this work, the last figure on the right and dressed in red is a portrait of Michelangelo.

Address

Most Holy Trinity at Monte Pincio
Piazza Trinità dei Monti
Rome, Italy 00187
Telephone: 06 67 94 179

Our Lady above (over) Minerva

Basilica di Santa Maria sopra Minerva

Gian Lorenzo Bernini's elephant sculpture, *The Pulcino della Minerva*, in front of the church. The elephant is holding his tail to the left as if it were defecating. His rear end is pointing toward the office of Father Giuseppe Paglia, a Dominican friar, who was one of Bernini's main adversaries.

Built on the foundations of a temple dedicated to the Egyptian goddess Isis, Santa Maria sopra Minerva was the first gothic church built in Rome. In 50 BCE, Pompey the Great built 3 temples: the Minervium, to honor of the goddess Minerva; the Iseum dedicated to Isis; and the Serapeum dedicated to Serapis. These sites fell into ruin over the years. It is believed that Pope Zacharias (741-752) built the first Christian church on the site. The Dominican Friars took over the church in 1275 and built the structure seen today. The church has been renovated several times. The 3 doorways in the façade date to the 1453 renovation. The baroque front of the church dates from the 17th century. There are several plaques on the front of the church which indicate the levels that water reached during the various floods of the city over the centuries.

The inside of the church is constructed in a Latin cross design with a central nave, side aisles, transept, and apse. The ceiling is a brilliant blue and decorated with stars. The paintings on the main altar represent the cardinal virtues and are by Francesco Podesti. Beneath the main altar are the relics of St. Catherine of Siena (except her head, which is in the Basilica of San Domenico in Siena). She is one of the few women to be proclaimed a Doctor of the Roman Catholic Church.

To the left of the main altar is a marble sculpture by Michelangelo Buonarroti that was completed in 1521. This statue, the *Cristo della Minerva*, is also known as *Christ the Redeemer* or *Christ Carrying the Cross* and depicts Christ with his cross. This is actually the second version of the statue. Michelangelo abandoned the first one when he uncovered a black vein in the white marble that would have appeared on Christ's cheek. The first statue was given to Metello Vari in January of 1522 and displayed in the courtyard of his palazzetto near the present day church. It was then lost to history for many years and rediscovered again in 2000. The first statue is in the sacristy of the church of San Vincenzo Martire, at Bassano Romano in the province of Viterbo in the Lazio region of Italy.

Continuing toward the left wall is a small hallway which leads to the sacristy and the room where St. Catherine of Siena died in 1380. She actually died at a different location in Rome and her room was disassembled and reconstructed here by Antonio Barberini in 1637.

There are several chapels in Santa Maria sopra Minerva. The Carafa Chapel has late 15th century frescoes (1488-1493) created by Filippino Lippi. It is also known as the Chapel of St. Thomas Aquinas because his relics were kept here until 1511, when they were moved to Naples.

Santa Maria sopra Minerva is also famous for being the site on which Galileo Galilei pronounced his famous recantation on the June 22, 1633. After this abjuration Galileo allegedly said: "*E pur si move*" (And yet it moves!). It was in the adjacent Dominican Convent that Galileo was tried by the Inquisition.

Several cardinals and popes are buried in the church as is the Dominican painter Blessed John of Fiesole.

St. Catherine of Siena

Born in Siena on March 25, 1347, St. Catherine died in Rome on April 29, 1380. Catherine began having visions of Christ as a child. Her visions, which have come to be known as a "Mystical Marriage with Jesus," are frequently portrayed in art. She is well-known for her writings which include the 1377 manuscript: *The Dialogue of Divine Providence*, a discussion between a soul who "rises up" to God and God himself. Catherine served as an ambassador between Avignon, Florence, and Rome in an attempt to heal the schism in the church. She became a Dominican tertiary, and is often pictured in their habit carrying a peace lily. Along with Francis of Assisi, she is one of the two patron saints of Italy. She is also the patron saint of firefighters, women who experience miscarriages, and those who are ill. Her feast day is April 30.

St. Thomas Aquinas

A philosopher and theologian, St. Thomas Aquinas is best known for his writings the *Summa Theologica* and the *Summa Contra Gentiles*. He was born in Aquino in 1225, and was educated at Monte Cassino, though he would also study at the University of Naples, the University of Paris, and in Cologne, Germany. He studied under Albertus Magnus, the most renowned professor of the Dominican order. Though he is today considered one of the most influential theologians in history, Aquinas was nicknamed the "dumb ox" while in Cologne because of his silent ways and large size. Many of his writings address the doctrinal crisis that was facing the church at that time. These crises focused on how to reconcile science and theology. He died on March 7, 1274 while giving a commentary on the Song of Songs. He is the patron saint of Catholic schools and education. His feast day is January 28.

Some quotes from Thomas Aquinas:

- "Better to illuminate than merely to shine, to deliver to others contemplated truths than merely to contemplate."
- "Clearly the person who accepts the Church as an infallible guide will believe whatever the Church teaches."
- "Hence we must say that for the knowledge of any truth whatsoever man needs divine help, that the intellect may be moved by God to its act. But he does not need a new light added to his natural light, in order to know the truth in all things, but only in some that surpasses his natural knowledge" (*Summa Theologiae*, I-II, 109, 1).

Points of Interest

- Michelangelo's *Cristo della Minerva*, also known as *Christ the Redeemer* or *Christ Carrying the Cross*.
- Gian Lorenzo Bernini's elephant sculpture, *The Pulcino della Minerva*, in front of the church. The elephant is holding up a short obelisk that is nicknamed *Minerva's Chick*. It is probably called this because the obelisk is so short. The obelisk was likely taller at one time. It was found in the nearby ruins of the Roman Temple of Isis. (Please see the separate section on the elephant in this book for more information).
- In Dante's *The Divine Comedy*, the glorified spirit of Thomas Aquinas is in the Heaven of the Sun with the other great exemplars of religious wisdom. Dante believed that Aquinas was poisoned by order of the King of Sicily, Charles of Anjou.

Address

Our Lady above Minerva
35 Via del Beato Angelico / 42 Piazza della Minerv
Rome, Italy

Our Lady and the Martyrs /The Pantheon

Santa Maria ad Martyres

Also known informally as "Santa Maria Rotonda"

The Pantheon was built in 27 BCE and dedicated to the gods Mars and Venus and the murdered Julius Caesar. It was built by Marcus Vipsanius Agrippa, consul and son-in-law of Emperor Augustus. The word "Pantheon" actually means: "to every god". The structure was refurbished by the Emperor Hadrian in about 126 CE. He is said to have commented "My intentions had been that this sanctuary of all gods should reproduce the likeness of the terrestrial globe and of the stellar sphere." When the pagan religions were banned in 391, the Emperor Theodosius the Great closed the temple, leaving the building abandoned and unused for almost 200 years. In 609, the Emperor Phocis gave the Pantheon to Pope Boniface IV. This is when it was converted into a Christian church and consecrated to the Virgin Mary and the martyrs of the church. The Pope had 28 cartloads of martyrs' bones collected from across the city and reinterred in the Pantheon. Other notable tombs in the structure include the artist Raphael, fellow painter Annibale Carracci, composer Arcangelo Corelli, architect Baldassare Peruzzi, King Vittorio Emanuele II, King Umberto I, and Queen Margherita.

The exterior of the building has a portico with 16 granite columns. Thirteen of the columns are original, while the 3 at the far left were replaced during the 1600s. To identify the new columns, look for the Papal Coats of Arms for Urban VIII and Alexander VII on top of the column. The grey granite columns were quarried in Mons Claudianus in the eastern mountains of Egypt and were floated by barge down the Nile River on their way to Rome. Originally, there was a single medieval bell tower attached to the building. This was removed in 1626 and replaced with two smaller structures on either side in 1634. The two smaller towers were not popular with the locals and they were nicknamed "Bernini's Ass's Ears". They were removed in 1883. The two niches in the portico once held statues of Agrippa (on the left) and Augustus (on the right). Today they are empty. Look closely at the bronze doors at the entrance. They date from the 15th century and appear to be too small for the door frames and made to fit. These may be the original bronze doors that have been restored several times.

Inside, the building is circular with the high altar directly across from the main door. The 7 large niches around the walls originally housed statues of Roman gods. The height to the oculus and the diameter of the interior circle of the church are the same, 43.2 m (142 feet). The word "oculus" (plural oculi) is Latin for eye. The Pantheon's oculus is 27 feet in diameter, open to the air, and the only source of light in the church during the day. When it rains, the rain enters, falls to the floor, and is carried away through a series of drains beneath the floor. Throughout the day, the light from the oculus moves around the inside of the building like a giant sundial. Scholars have debated if this was intentional. In August 2011, Giulio Magli, a historian of ancient architecture from Milan Polytechnic, and Robert Hannah, a classics scholar from the University of Otago in New Zealand, published a paper which showed that at precisely midday during the March equinox, a circular shaft of light shines through the oculus and illuminates the Pantheon's entrance.

Five rows of 28 square coffers of diminishing size radiate from the oculus at the top of the dome. The dome and massive bronze doors are from the Emperor Hadrian's restoration. The dome was the largest one in the world until Brunelleschi's dome was constructed at the Basilica di Santa Maria del Fiore (Duomo) in Florence (1420-1436).

The high altar and the apse paintings were commissioned by Pope Clement XI in the 1700s and designed by the Italian architect and engraver Alessandro Specchi. The icon over the main altar may date from the 7th century. The painting was originally dated as being from the 13th century. However, the icon seen today was rediscovered in

1960 by workers doing restoration on the altar who noticed that the painting had several layers of paint on it. The 7th century icon was underneath it all. Immediately to the right of the main altar is a statue of St. Anastasius by Bernardo Cametti (1669-1736). The niche to the right of the apse has some 2nd century decoration from the pagan temple. To the right of the high altar and moving around the circle is the aedicula (small shrine) beneath which Raphael is buried. The inscription on his sarcophagus reads: *Ille Hic Est Raphael Timuit Quo Sospite Vinci / Rerum Magna Parens Et Moriente Mori* (Here lies Raphael, by whom the mother of all things (Nature) feared to be overcome while he was living, and while he was dying, herself to die). His fiancée, Maria Bibbiena, who died before the couple could marry, is buried to the right of his sarcophagus. There is also a bust of the artist in the adjacent niche.

It is interesting to note that Michelangelo studied the construction of the Pantheon's dome before he built the dome of the Vatican's St. Peter's Basilica. (St. Peter's dome is 2 feet smaller than that of the Pantheon.) Michelangelo described the design of the Pantheon as "angelic and not human design". In addition, during the reign of Pope Urban VIII, the bronze ceiling of the Pantheon's portico was melted down and used to fortify the Castel Sant'Angelo. The remaining bronze was used for a variety of projects. It has been written that the bronze was used by Bernini when creating the baldachin for the main altar of St. Peter's Basilica. However, Bernini's bronze likely came from Venice. Urban VIII was criticized for his actions and the saying: "*Quod non fecerunt barbari, fecerunt Barberini*" ("What the barbarians did not do, the Barberinis [Urban VIII] did") became popular around Rome.

Despite hundreds of daily visitors, the Pantheon is still an active church. Masses are said there on feast days and special occasions. Among the most famous services is the annual Easter Rose celebration on Pentecost Sunday. Thousands of red rose petals fall from the dome to the people below as a reminder of the gift of the Holy Spirit descending in tongues of fire upon the apostles. (A team of firemen actually scale the dome of the Pantheon and drop the rose petals at the end of the Mass.)

Points of Interest

- The Egyptian obelisk in the piazza in front of the pantheon was placed there by Pope Clement XI in 1711. It was originally one of a pair from the Temple of Ra in Heliopolis, Egypt.
- The 16 Corinthian columns in the portico that topped by a pediment with the inscription *M·Agrippa·L·F·Cos·Terti um·Fecit.* (Marcus Agrippa, son of Lucius, during his third consulate, built this)
- Raphael's tomb is to the right of the high altar.
- The memorial to Raphael's fiancée, Maria Bibbiena, is to the right of his tomb.
- The 7th century icon over the high altar of the Madonna and Child.
- The 2nd century decorations from the pagan temple in the niche just to the right of the apse.

Note: Near the Pantheon is the Sant'Eustachio Il Caffé. It is one of the most famous coffee houses in Rome and considered by "those who know" to be the best cup of coffee in Rome. (Whoever "they" are?) It is in the Piazza Sant'Eustachio, about 2 blocks from the Pantheon. Founded in 1938, it still does all its own roasting and has the original decorations. It is a fun place to visit. Their tins of coffee make great gifts. They also make a chocolate bonbon that is filled with coffee that is amazing.

Address

Our Lady and the Martyrs (Pantheon)
Piazza della Rotonda 12
00186 Rome, Italy
Telephone: 06 68 30 02 30

Our Lady of the People

Santa Maria del Popolo

There is an ancient legend that says the Emperor Nero haunts the city of Rome. His sprit was said to walk the slope of the Pincian Hill near his tomb. A large oak tree near the grave was home to a flock of ravens who were said to be his demonic servants. Pope Paschal II personally chopped the tree down in 1099 and scattered Nero's ashes in the Tiber. The Pope then built a small oratory over the remaining Roman tombs which belonged to the Domitii family. Dedicated to the Virgin Mary, there is some debate as to why the church was designated del Popolo (of the people). Some believe it is because the people of Rome financed the construction, while others think it is because the church was meant to serve as a parish church for the people of the area. Still others have said that Paschal exorcised the area for the benefit of the people of Rome in general, hence the name. Regardless of the reason, the oratory was widely used. The building was enlarged and consecrated as a church by Pope Gregory IX (1227-1241), was reconstructed in 1472-1477, and renovated again in the 1660s. The church was initially managed by the Franciscans, but in 1250 it was given to the Augustinian friars of the Tuscan congregation. They founded a monastery adjacent to the church. It is of particular interest to Protestants, because Martin Luther stayed in the neighboring Augustinian monastery when he visited Rome in 1511. The monastery was destroyed during the sack of Rome in 1527, but it is certain the Luther heard mass in this church.

The early renaissance façade of the church has recently been cleaned and has three doorways. The center door has a tympanum with an image of the Virgin above. Inside, the church is built in the shape of a Latin cross with a central nave and 2 side aisles. The decorations are baroque and were done by Gian Lorenzo Bernini. There are 3 domes in this church. The 2 external nave chapels have domes and there is a center dome for the church itself.

The church is an art lover's dream. There are several works by major artists. These include: the *Crucifixion of St. Peter* and the *Conversion of St. Paul* by Caravaggio; *The Assumption of the Virgin* by Annibale Carracci; the Chigi Chapel designed by Raphael; sculptures by Andrea Bregno; and sculptures of the prophet *Habakkuk and the Angel* and *Daniel and the Lion* as well as the organ case and the baroque façade, which were all designed in the late 1600s by Bernini.

There are several chapels of interest in this church. The Chigi Chapel is located to the left upon entering the church. This octagonal-shaped, domed chapel was commissioned by the Sienese banker Agostino Chigi (1465-1520). It was designed by Raphael. While he did much of the work himself, his death brought the work to a halt in 1520. The altarpiece of *The Nativity of the Virgin* was painted by Raphael's rival Sebastiano del Piombo. The bronze altar sculptures and the statues of Jonah and Elijah were created according to Raphael's design by Lorenzetto. The chapel was finally completed by Bernini for Cardinal Fabio Chigi (Pope Alexander VII) after 1652. He added the oval medallions on the pyramidal tombs and the sculptures of Habakkuk and the Angel and the prophet Daniel.

Directly opposite this chapel is the other domed chapel, the Cybo Chapel. It is considered one of the prettiest chapels in Rome. The Cybo chapel is in the shape of a Greek cross. It was originally built in the 15th century by Pinturicchio for Cardinal Innocenzo Cybo. Carlo Fontana renovated the chapel completely for Alderano Cybo between 1682 and 1687. There are 16 Sicilian jasper columns and a variety of colored marbles. The altarpiece is by Carlo Maratta and depicts *The Assumption and Four Doctors of the Church*. The saints shown in the painting are John the Evangelist, Gregory the Great, John Chrysostom, and Augustine.

The Cerasi Chapel is on the left-hand side of the main altar of the church. This chapel houses the *Crucifixion of St. Peter* and the *Conversion of St. Paul* which were painted by Caravaggio in 1601. The altarpiece, *The Assumption of the Virgin* by Annibale Carracci, was painted prior to Caravaggio's work.

The Icon of the Virgin Mary over the main altar was brought to the church from the Lateran Palace by Pope Gregory IX. The image dates to the 13th century. The main dome of the church is by Raffaele Vanni and depicts the *Virgin in Glory*. The pendentives are of 4 Old Testament women: Ruth, Esther, Judith, and Deborah. The vault above the choir has frescos by Pinturicchio which illustrate the *Coronation of the Virgin* in the center, the Four Evangelists, four Sibyls, and four Fathers of the Church (St. Gregory, Ambrose, Augustine, and Jerome). There is a light switch on the left side which illuminates the frescos.

Points of Interest

- Cerasi Chapel to the left of the choir in the north transept which has paintings by Caravaggio and Carracci.
- The Chigi Chapel was built and decorated by Raphaelfor the banker Agostino Chigi (1465-1520) who is buried there. The chapel was finished by Berniniafter 1652 (Raphael died in 1520 before it was finished).
- The organ case in the south transept was designed by Bernini.
- Piazza del Popoloinside the northern gate in the Aurelian Walls. This gate was called the Porta Flaminia. The Via Flaminia, the road to Ariminum (modern day Rimini) was the principle route from the north to Rome. For many pilgrims passing through the Porta Flaminia was their first view of the city upon arrival.
- The Egyptian obelisk of Sety I (erected by Ramses II) from Heliopolis is in the center of the piazza.

Address

Santa Maria del Popolo
Our Lady of the People
12 Piazza del Popolo
00187 Rome, Italy
Telephone: 06 36 10 836

Our Lady of Victory

Santa Maria della Vittoria

The modern day church of Our Lady of Victory is the only baroque structure designed and built by architect Carlo Maderno. The original structure dates to 1605 and was built as a chapel dedicated to St. Paul by the Discalced Carmelite Friars. The church was expanded and rededicated following the 1620 Catholic victory at the Battle of White Mountain near Prague. This battle reversed the Protestant Reformation in Bohemia. The Carmelite chaplain at the battle had carried a picture of the Nativity around his neck. After the battle, the image was taken to Prague, and then to Santa Maria Maggiore in Rome. The image was taken in procession from Santa Maria Maggiore to the chapel of St. Paul. The chapel was then expanded, renamed Our Lady of Victory, and dedicated to the Blessed Virgin in gratitude for the victory at White Mountain.

The façade of the church was designed by Italian-Swiss architect Carlo Maderno who also designed the Church of Santa Susanna and was appointed as the chief architect of St. Peter's Basilica (the Vatican) in 1603 after the death of Michelangelo. Santa Maria della Vittoria is the only church designed by Maderno and completed under his supervision. Today, this church is best known for Bernini's sculpture the *Ecstasy of St. Teresa* in the Cornaro Chapel.

Inside, the church is richly decorated in the Baroque style and has a central nave, a transept, apse, and dome. A painting of the Nativity was placed over the high altar, but it was destroyed in a fire in 1833. A copy of the painting hangs above the high altar today.

The theme of victory over heresy is continued throughout the church. Turkish battle standards captured at the 1683 siege of Vienna hang in the church. The frescoes in the vaults of the church are by Giovanni Domenico Cerrini (1609-1681) and are: *The Virgin Mary Triumphing over Heresy* and *Fall of the Rebel Angels.*

The Cornaro Chapel is to the left of the altar and houses Gian Lorenzo Bernini's sculpture the *Ecstasy of St. Teresa.* The statue depicts St. Teresa lying on a cloud with an angel standing over her. It is illuminated by natural light which filters through a hidden window in the dome above, and accentuated by gilded stucco rays which were designed to catch the light.

St. Teresa of Avila

St. Teresa of Avila (1515-1582) was a Spanish Carmelite nun, Counter Reformation writer, and an advocate of contemplative life through prayer. Her grandfather, Juande Toledo, was Jewish though he was forced to convert to Christianity. He was executed by the Spanish Inquisition for returning to the Jewish faith. Her father, Alonso Sánchez de Cepeda, bought a knighthood and assimilated into Christian society. He was very strict and Teresa was raised as a Christian. As a teenager, Teresa was sent for her education to the Augustinian nuns at Avila. She was sent home from their convent after eighteen months due to illness.

In 1535, Teresa joined a Carmelite convent where she struggled for many years with worldliness vs. the contemplative life. She experienced many illnesses, including malaria. It was during these illnesses that she had some of her visions. She is well-known for her writings (*The Way of Perfection, The Interior Castle,* and her autobiography: *The Life of Teresa of Avila*) on the meaning of prayer and founded her own convent which focused on a simple life of poverty devoted to prayer. The members of this order would come to be known as the Discalced Carmelites. She is considered to be, along with John of the Cross, a founder of this order. The statue in the church depicts the moment in one of her visions that an angel pierces St. Teresa's heart with a golden shaft, causing her both immense joy and pain. St. Teresa is the patron saint of headache sufferers. Her symbol is a heart, an arrow, and a book. Her feast day is October 15.

Points of Interest

- Bernini's sculpture the *Ecstasy of St. Teresa* in the Cornaro Chapel.
- The church and the sculpture are featured in Dan Brown's novel *Angels and Demons*. Brown moved its location to the Piazza Barberini. The church is actually located on the Via 20 Septembre.
- *The Virgin Mary Triumphing over Heresy* and *Fall of the Rebel Angels* by Cerrini.
- Domenico Fontana's *Fountain of Moses* (1585) is just across the road from the front of the church.

Address

Our lady of Victory
Via 20 Settembre, 17
00187 Rome, Italy
Telephone: 06 48 26 190

Sanctuary of Our Lady of Divine Love

Santuario della Madonna del Divino Amore

Locally known as "Saver of the City"

The Sanctuary of Our Lady of Divine Love is a Marian shrine site located on Via Ardeatina. Legend says that the entire area was once part the Benedictine monastery of San Paolo fuori le Mura. A castle was built here in the 13th century and called the Lion's Castle (*Castello del Leone*). Over time the name was changed into the *Castel di Levaa,* and the site is believed to have belonged to the Savelli-Orsini family. One of the towers of the castle had an image of the Virgin seated on a throne and holding the Christ child. Above her head was the image of a dove representing the Holy Spirit and Divine Love. In 1740, a traveler passing through the area was attacked by dogs. He appealed to the Virginwho intervened on his behalf, and the dogs went away. In gratitude, locals moved the image of the Virgin from the tower to a local church on the nearby estate, "La Falconiana", on September 5, 1740. Here they could give thanks and venerate the image. Meanwhile, Cardinal Carlo Rezzonico (who would later become Pope Clement XIII) began construction of a church on the original site of the tower. This church was completed in April 1745 and the image was moved back to this location. This newly constructed church and shrine became a popular site for pilgrimage.

During the Second World War, as Rome was being threatened with destruction, the image was removed again and brought in pilgrimage procession to various churches in the city for veneration. The Roman people were encouraged to pray and ask Mary to save their city. In return, they would rededicate their lives to her, erect a new Sanctuary, and carry out charitable work in her honor. Rome was saved. On

June 11, 1944, Pope Pius XII conferred the title of "Saver of the City" on Our Lady of Divine Love. The building contract for the construction of the new Sanctuary was signed on February 19, 1991 and was dedicated by Pope John Paul II on July 4, 1999. Please note that Pope John Paul II included the shrine in the pilgrim itinerary for the Holy Year 2000, replacing San Sebastiano fuori le Mura.

Visitors will notice that there are actually two churches on the site: the old church built in 1745 and the new church constructed in 1999 to honor the promise of a new sanctuary if the Blessed Mother saved Rome. The old church faces the central piazza and has a simple rectangular plan with an enclosed narthex. The Icon of Our Lady the Saver is enshrined above the main altar. The new church was designed by Luigi Leoni in the post-modern style and has been nicknamed by locals the "Blue Grotto". It is mostly blue glass throughout and seems to glow as the sunlight shines through it.

Plenary Indulgence

According to the Decree of the Apostolic Penitentiary of March 25, 1991, visitors can be granted a full plenary indulgence if they first fulfill three conditions:

- Sacramental confession
- Eucharistic communion
- Prayer for the intentions of the Supreme Pontiff

Visitors to the Sanctuary of the Madonna of Divine Love may be granted a plenary indulgence if they have fulfilled these three criteria and they have devoutly assisted at some of the sacred functions, or have prayed at least the Sunday Prayer (Our Father) and the Symbol of Faith (the Creed) on the solemnity of:

- Pentecost
- Immaculate Conception (December 8)
- Mother of God (January 1)
- The Annunciation of the Lord (March 25)

- Assumption of the Blessed Virgin Mary (August 15)
- While on pilgrimage
- Once a year, on a day freely chosen by each believer

Pilgrimage of Divine Love

The Pilgrimage of Divine Love takes place every Saturday night, from Easter until the end of October. Pilgrims leave from the Passeggiata Archeologica in the Piazza di Porta Capena in Rome at midnight. They walk along the Via Appia Antica (Old Appian Way) to the church Quo Vadis, then turn onto the Via Ardeatina and continue to the Catacombs of St. Callisto and past the Mausoleum of the Ardeatin Caves (Fosse Ardeatine). They arrive at the Sanctuary of Our Lady of Divine Love at 5 am in time for Mass, and place their burdens at the feet of the Madonna. The walks were traditionally for men only, though this has changed in recent years.

Points of Interest

- There are actually two churches on the site, the old 1745 church and the newer 1999 church.
- Behind the chapel is a staircase that leads to the site where the miracle occurred in 1740.
- The shrine/painting of the Virgin and Child is above the altar.

Address

Sanctuary of the Madonna of Divine Love
Via Ardeatina 1221-00134
Rome, Italy
Telephone: 06 71 35 51 21

St. Agnes Outside the Walls and St. Costanza

Basilica Sant'Agnese Fuori le Mura/Santa Costanza

According to legend, the daughter of the Emperor Constantine (306-337) suffered from a skin ailment. She visited the site of St. Agnes tomb on the Via Nometana. While there, she had a vision of St. Agnes. The emperor's daughter was not only converted to Christianity, her skin disease was cured. In gratitude, she had a church built on the site. This church is sometimes referred to as the Basilica Constantiniana as well as St. Agnes Outside the Walls. The building was renovated by Pope Symmachus (498-514), and again by Pope Honorius I in the 7th century. It was restored by Pope Pius IX in 1855.

Entrance to the church is through the courtyard of an adjacent monastery. Inside the courtyard, the building to the right is a hall which has frescoes from the 19th century. The paintings tell the story of Pope Pius IX along with several cardinals who were standing near the site when the floor suddenly gave way. The Pope and his entourage fell several feet but were unharmed. In gratitude, he restored the neighboring basilica of St. Agnes. This building is often closed; however, visitors are usually allowed to see it upon request.

The actual church is below ground level and reached by going down a flight of white marble stairs. Inscriptions and stones from the nearby catacombs are on the descending walls. The bas relief near the bottom of the stairs was originally the altarpiece over St. Agnes' tomb. Inside, the church is very similar to the way it was reconstructed by Pope Honorius I.

The basilica has a central nave with two aisles that are separated by marble columns. The galleries over the aisles are known as women's galleries. They are also sometimes called nuns' choirs and were reserved for use by women.

The apse mosaic is the most significant work of art in the basilica. It dates from the time of Honorius and is one of the oldest and best kept examples of Byzantine-Roman Mosaic work in the city. Unlike the work seen in other churches, it is very simple. St. Agnes stands in the center, dressed as a Byzantine empress and carrying a virgin's veil embroidered with flowers over her left arm. She is holding a scroll sealed by a cross. On the base of the cloth is a phoenix, symbolizing her immortality. Pope Symmachus is pictured to her left holding a book. Pope Honorius is to her right holding a model of the basilica which symbolizes that he was the builder of the structure. All three figures are dressed in similar clothing. Above their heads are a coronet of stars and the hand of God reaching through to place a crown on St. Agnes' head. The lengthy inscriptions beneath their feet read:

> *Golden painting comes out of the enamels, and daylight both embraces and itselfconfines.*
>
> *Dawn might think of plunging out of snow white springs into the clouds, watering the fields with her dews: Here is such a light as even the rainbow will produce between the stars or the purple peacock bright with color.*
>
> *God who might bring an end to night or light has banished chaos from here out of the tombs of the martyrs.*
>
> *What all can see in a single upward glance are the sacred offerings dedicated by Honorius.*
>
> *His portrait is identified by robes and by the building. Wearing a radiate heart, he radiates in appearance also.*

The Catacombs and the Mausoleum of St. Costanza

The entrance to the catacombs is in a room to the left at the front of the church. The catacombs are on three levels, dating from the 2nd-5th centuries. Many of the grave-cuts have never been disturbed and retain their original fill or blocking slabs. The 2nd century level can be visited with a guide, arranged in the church.

Santa Costanza is a 4th century mausoleum and funerary hall which was converted into a church. The building was once part of a larger imperial funerary complex which may have been originally intended for the Emperor Constantine. Legend tells that it was built between 351 and 357 as a mausoleum for Constantina, a daughter of the emperor and Fausta. What is definitely known is that she was the daughter who prayed at the site of St. Agnes and later built the basilica. The building was converted into a church in 1256 by Pope Alexander IV. The funerary hall was u-shaped. This layout is called a "circus basilica", because the layout is similar to that of an ancient Roman circus. Unfortunately, it is not possible to enter the funerary hall. It is, however, possible to see the buttressed outer wall of this structure while descending the hill from the nearby Piazza Annibaliano. Visitors can enter the mausoleum, a round structure with two concentric rings. It is likely that it was once surrounded by a columned loggia and also had a portico that led to the basilica. The outer circle ambulatory has a barrel vault and the original 4th century mosaics. As this structure was not originally built as a church, these frescos depict scenes of everyday pagan and Christian life from that era. There are eleven separate panels, which have geometric designs with dolphins and octopods; flowers; fruit; and birds. There are also a series of pictures which show cupids picking grapes, the grapes being trod upon in the winepress, and wagons bringing the wine to Rome. There are also eleven niches in the ambulatory. Historians are unsure of the date of the two surviving decorations of Christ in these niches. They may be 5th century or 7th century.

The inner circle has a domed vault with badly faded 18th century paintings. These paintings replaced an intricate series of two-tiered Biblical mosaics. The lower tier had scenes based on the Old Testament and a higher tier had New Testament scenes. Fortunately, drawings and paintings of this mosaic survive. Light enters the church from 12 large windows beneath the dome.

Points of Interest

- This church and the catacombs are rarely visited by tourists. They are an excellent change from the more touristy catacombs and bustle of downtown Rome. However, before visiting, please check their website. As an active church parish, their hours change seasonally.
- Please note the catacombs are closed in October and November each year.
- There is an urban legend that every lord mayor of Rome secretly comes to pray at this church, on the third night after his election; there is little evidence that they really do so.

Address

St. Agnes Outside the Walls and St. Costanza
Via Nomentana, 349,
00162 Rome, Italy
Telephone: 06 861 0840 or 06 86 20 54 56

St. Agnes at the Circus Agonalis

Sant'Agnese in Agone

This church is located on the site where St. Agnes was martyred in the Circus of Domitian, now the Piazza Navona. A Christian church on this site is mentioned in the 8th century pilgrimage route, the Itinerary of Einsiedeln. An inscription on the church also informs visitors that there was a church consecrated by Pope Callixtus II on January 28, 1123 here. The original name of the Piazza Navona was the "piazza in agone", hence the name of the church. The baroque church thatcan be seen today was commissioned by Pope Innocent X in 1652. The Pope took a particular interest in the church because he lived next door. The building to the left was his palace. Today it is the Brazilian Embassy.

The façade of St. Agnes' was originally designed by Girolamo and Carlo Rainaldi. However, the Pope did not like the design, so the commission was given to Francesco Borromini. The Pope died in 1655 and work on the structure was halted for a while. Finally, Gian Lorenzo Bernini and a group of other architects were brought in to finish the job. The two bell towers were constructed in the 1660s.

The church is built in a Greek cross plan. There are seven altars that are decorated with statues or relief. Most of the interior work was done by Bernini or his students. The interior dome is supported by red and white marble columns and has paintings by Ciro Ferri and Sebastiano Corbellini portraying the Martyrdom of St. Agnes (1670-1689). The addition of these columns is the principle change that Borromini made to Rainaldi's plan. The main altar has a sculpture of the *Miracle of Sant'Agnese,* commissioned from Alessandro Algardi, and completed by Ercole Ferrata and Domenico Guidi in 1688. There is a doorway to the left of the main altar that leads to the reliquary chapel where St. Agnes's head is kept. Her body is in a silver sarcophagus in the Basilica of St. Agnes Outside the Walls. Continuing to the left is the Chapel of St. Sebastian. This statue of this saint is actually a Roman statue that Paolo Campi replaced the head on and "transitioned" into St. Sebastian. Directly opposite this chapel, on the other side of the church, is the Statue of St. Agnes in Flames by Ercole Ferrata (1660).

To the right of this statue is the entrance to the crypt and rooms beneath the church. The tomb of Pope Innocent X and others of his family, the Pamphili, can be found here. The remains of a Roman house and the Stadium of Domitian have also been identified beneath the structure. The two rooms in the back of the crypt have exposed Roman pavement, though the frescoes in this area are likely from the 13th century.

The *Fountain of the Four Rivers* by Gian Lorenzo Bernini is in the piazza in front of the church. The four gods on the corners of the fountain represent the four major rivers of the world known at the time: the Nile of Africa, Danube of Europe, Ganges of Asia, and Platte of the Americas. Legend has it that the statue of the Nile covers his head so as not to see the church of Sant'Agnese in Agone. The statue of Sant'Agnese on the facade of the church is reassuring the world (represented by the 4 rivers) of the church's stability. It has been said that the fountain symbolizes the church's influence on four continents and asserts the triumph of church and papacy over the world. Both the fountain and the church were honored during Pope Innocent X's jubilee in 1650.

St. Agnes

Agnes of Rome (c. 291-304) was a member of a noble Roman family and was raised a Christian. The local Roman Prefect wanted the 12 or 13 year old Agnes to marry his son. She refused and was subsequently condemned to death. However, Roman law prohibited the execution of virgins. The authorities had Agnes stripped naked and dragged through the streets of Rome to a brothel. Agnes prayed for protection and long hair grew and covered her body. The man who attempted to rape her in the brothel was struck blind. She forgave him and healed him through prayer. Later attempts to burn her at the stake were equally unsuccessful. It is said that angels protected her from the flame. She was later killed by a Roman soldier who beheaded her. She is buried on the Via Nometana. The Church of St. Agnes fuori le Mura now stands on that spot. She is the patron saint of chastity, young girls, engaged couples, rape victims, and virgins. Her feast day is January 21. Each year, on the feast day of St. Agnes, two lambs are specially blessed by the pope after a pontifical high Mass. The lambs are then taken to the Benedictine Sisters of Santa Cecilia in Trastevere, who care for them, shear them when the time comes, and then spin and weave their wool into pallia, ceremonial neck-stoles, which are sent by the pope to new archbishops to symbolize their union with the papacy.

St. Emerentiana

St. Emerentiana was the milk sister of St. Agnes. This means that they shared the same wet nurse. Emerentiana is remembered as a virgin martyr in her own right, but is often pictured with St. Agnes. Legend says that after the death of St. Agnes, Emerentiana went to the grave to pray, and was suddenly attacked by pagans and killed with stones. She was buried alongside St. Agnes on the Via Nometana. Her feast day is January 23.

Points of Interest

- The Sacristy of St. Agnes in Agony was designed by Francesco Borromini and built between 1658 and 1666. The Cultural Association "The Association of the Borromini Sacristy" holds concerts on Friday nights in the sacristy. Call or check for details.
- The oratory steps lead down to a series of vaulted rooms that were a part of the Stadium of Domitian.

- The high altar in the Relic Chapel has the head of St. Agnes.
- The *Fountain of the Four Rivers* by Gian Lorenzo Bernini is in the piazza in front of the church.

Address

St. Agnes at the Circus Agonalis
30 Via di Santa Maria dell' Anima
(Piazza Navona)
00186 Rome, Italy
Telephone: 06 68 19 21 34

Church of St. Alphonsus Liguori/Shrine of Our Lady of Perpetual Help

Chiesa di Sant'Alfonso di Liguori all'Esquilino / Santa Maria di Perpetuo Soccorso

Built between 1855 and 1859 and designed by the Scottish architect George Wigley, the Church of St. Alphonsus Liguori is neo-gothic in design. The church is dedicated to St. Alphonsus Liguori, the founder of the Congregation of the Most Holy Redeemer(the Redemptorists). The church is best known for the 14th century Byzantine icon of *Our Lady of Perpetual Help* which was given to the Redemptorists by Pope Pius IX in 1866 and is positioned over the main altar.

The church is located on located on Via Merulana on the Esquiline Hill, just a few short blocks from St. Mary Major. The façade of the church has three doors, a rose window, a mosaic of Our Lady of Perpetual Help, and a statue of Jesus as Christ the King. The inside of the church has a central nave and two side aisles. It is decorated by Bavarian painter and Redemptorist Max Schmalzl (1850-1930). The apse mosaic shows Christ enthroned between the Blessed Virgin Mary and St. Joseph.

St. Alphonsus Liguori and the Redemptorists

Alphonsus Liguori was born into a wealthy family on September 27, 1696, in Marianella near Naples, Italy. He was well educated and earned a Doctor of Law degree, though he favored religious life. He studied under Matthew Ripa, the Apostle of China, who had founded a missionary college in Naples. This school became known colloquially as the "Chinese College". Liguori did not join Ripa's order. Instead, he founded the Congregation of the Most Holy Redeemer on November 9, 1732. The mission of the order is "to strive to imitate the virtues and examples of Jesus Christ, Our Redeemer, consecrating themselves especially to the preaching of the word of God to the poor." Members take vows of poverty, chastity, and obedience, and an oath of perseverance to live in the congregation until death. Today there are over 5,500 Redemptorists working in 77 countries on 5 continents. The motto of the order is taken from verse 7 of Psalm 130, in Latin: *Copiosaapudeum redemptio* (With him there is plentiful redemption). They use the letters "C.Ss.R." after their names, which stands for *Congregatio Sanctissimi Redemptoris*, Latin for *"Congregation of the Most Holy Redeemer"*. The feast day of St. Alphonsus Liguori is August 1.

Our Lady of Perpetual Help

Legend says that a merchant from the island of Crete stole the Byzantine icon of *Our Lady of Perpetual Help* from a church in Crete. While at sea his ship was caught in a terrible storm. The sailors prayed to the icon for help and were delivered. The merchant brought the picture to Rome, hung it in his house and soon after became seriously ill. On his death bed he confessed to stealing the painting and asked a friend, another merchant, to return it to a church. The friend's wife adored the picture and hung it in their home. The Virgin Mary appeared to the friend's daughter, grandmother, and neighbor, who implored that the picture be given to the Church of St. Matthew the Apostle, located between the basilicas of St. Mary Major and St. John Laterano. Finally, the merchant's friend's wife gave the picture to the Augustinian Friars and on March 27, 1499, it was placed in the church of St. Matthew where it remained for 300 years. In 1798, André Masséna, then governor of Rome, closed the church, along with several others in Rome. The icon was taken to the Church of St. Eusebius, then later to a side chapel in the Church of Santa Maria in Posterula.

In January of 1855, the Redemptorists purchased land on Via Merulana, where the ruins of the Church of St. Matthew had stood. They intended to build a headquarters for their missionary congregation. The Redemptorists were interested in the history of their new property. They found several references to the icon and to the Church of St. Matthew. The Superior General of the Redemptorists, Father Nicholas Mauron, petitioned Pope Pius IX to grant them the icon of Perpetual Help and that it be placed in the newly built Church of the Most Holy Redeemer and St. Alphonsus, which was located near the site where the old Church of St. Matthew had stood. The Pope gave them the icon in 1866.

Our Lady of Perpetual Help Icon

The icon is 17 inches by 21 inches (43 cm by 53 cm) and is painted on hard nut wood with a gold leaf background. The Greek letters above Mary's head proclaim her to be the Mother of God. She is dressed in dark blue robes with a green lining and red tunic against a gold background. Blue, green, and red were the colors of royalty. The eight-point star on her forehead was probably added by a later artist. The Archangels Gabriel and Michael are seen above her holding the instruments of the passion. Michael, on the left, holds an urn filled with the gall that the soldiers offered to Jesus on the cross, the lance that pierced his side, and the reed with the sponge from which Jesus drank water. Gabriel, on the right, carries the cross and four nails. Christ is depicted as an adult. It is believed that this icon depicts Christ as seeing his destiny and fleeing to the protective arms of his mother. In his haste, his sandal is falling off. Christ is also wearing the colors of royalty, specifically a green tunic, red sash, and gold brocade. The Greek initials to his right proclaim that he is "Jesus Christ". The icon was restored in 1990 and tests at that time date the image as being created between the years 1325-1480. According to tradition, novenas are conducted on Wednesday evening. This "Perpetual Novena" began in St. Louis, Missouri, in 1927 and continues around the world today. Each year, as part of the preparation of the feast of Our Lady of Perpetual Help on June 27, there is a Solemn Novena, which includes nine days of prayer and reflection on the Christian life.

Address

Shrine of Our Lady of Perpetual Help
Church of St. Alphonsus
Via Merulana
31-00185 Rome, Italy
Telephone: 06 49 49 0689

St. Andrew's at the Quirinal

Sant'Andrea al Quirinale

Designed by Gian Lorenzo Bernini and Giovanni de'Ross, this baroque church was completed in 1670. The church is considered to be one of the finest examples of Roman Baroque style architecture and decoration. Bernini is said to have preferred this church to all his other work and was frequently seen sitting in the church. He also attended mass here regularly. Among other worshippers known to frequent this church were St. Aloysius Gonzaga, St. Stanislaus Kostka, and St. Robert Bellarmine. An older church, Sant'Andrea a Montecavallo, previously occupied the site. Little is known about that structure.

The church is elliptical in shape with four chapels and four niches, a larger niche for the high altar, and a richly decorated golden dome. Bernini designed the main altar, though the work was executed by other artists. The oil painting of the *Martyrdom of Saint Andrew* (1668) by French painter Guillaume Courtois is located over the main altar. Above the painting are 3 angels, 9 putti, and several cherubs who are flying upwards into the dome. These sculptures are the work of Giovanni Rinaldi (1668-1669). The painting in the vault of the *Eternal Father* is also by Courtois.

There are several chapels including the Chapel of St. Francis Xavier with paintings by Baciccio depicting the baptism, preaching, and death of St. Francis Xavier (1705). There is also a chapel dedicated to St. Stanislaus Kostka. His relics are enshrined beneath the altar in an urn of bronze and lapis lazuli, by Pierre Legros, made in 1716. Carlo Maratta's painting of *The Madonna with Child and St. Stanislaus Kostka* is above the altar in this chapel. Visitors can also view the saint's rooms on the floor above the main church. He actually died in the building that stood on the corner to the right of the church (Via Ferrara). When he passed, the Jesuits had the room dismantled and reassembled above the church. There are 3 rooms on display which have paintings of the saint's life, copies of letters that St. Stanislaus brought with him to Rome in the 1500s, and a statue of the deceased saint lying on his bed by Pierre Legros. The entrance to the rooms is through the sacristy to the right of the main altar. Visitors have to ask the sacristan for permission to enter them and they usually charge a fee.

In the church, next to the chapel of St. Stanislaus, is a chapel and the tomb of King Carlo Emmanuele IV of Sardinia and Piedmont. He abdicated in June 1802 after the death of his wife and entered the Jesuit Novitiate in this church.

St. Andrew

St. Andrew, the Apostle, was the son of John. He was born in Bethsaida of Galilee. While preaching in Patrae in the region of Achaia, he was convicted and crucified by order of the Roman Governor, Aegeas or Aegeates. Andrew was bound, not nailed, to a decussate cross to prolong his sufferings. A decussate cross is in the shape of an "X". Today this is known as a St. Andrew's cross. St. Andrew's relics were moved from Patrae to Constantinople around 357. In 1204, when Constantinople was taken by the Crusaders, Cardinal Peter of Capua brought St. Andrew's relics to Italy and placed them in the cathedral of Amalfi, where most of them still remain. St. Andrew is the patron saint of Russia and Scotland. His feast day is November 30.

St. Stanislaus Kostka

Born in Rostkowo, Poland, on October 28, 1550, St. Stanislaus Kostka was a Jesuit priest. His principle claim to fame seems to be that he was beaten as a child by his brothers, bore it with dignity as long as he could, then escaped to travel some five hundred leagues to become a novitiate of St. Andrew in Rome. While he was "a model and mirror of religious perfection," he was also very frail, and died 10 months after his arrival in Rome on the evening of August 15, 1568. He was canonized on December 31, 1726. He is the patron saint and protector of novitiates and of those with heart illness. His feast day is August 15.

Note: St. Stanislaus Kostka is often confused with the more famous 11th century bishop and martyr, St. Stanislaus of Cracow who is the patron saint of Poland. His feast day is celebrated on April 8, May 7, and also on May 8 in Poland.

Points of Interest

- The rooms of St. Stanislaus Kostka (1702-03) in the Jesuit novitiate above the church.
- The Chapel of St. Francis Xavier.
- The dome of this church is spectacular.

Address

St. Andrew's at the Quirinal
29 Via del Quirinale
00187 Rome, Italy
Telephone: 06 47 44 801

St. Barbara of the Books

Santa Barbara dei Librai

Also known as: Santa Barbara Anglorum (The English church of St. Barbara); Santa Barbara alla Regola (St. Barbara of Regola); Santa Barbara in Satro (St. Barbara of the Satyrs)

Consecrated in 1306, this small parish church is known to have existed in the 11th century. It is built on the ruins of the Theater of Pompey (55 BCE); this is the place where the statue of Pompeius stood and Julius Caesar was assassinated. Pope Julius III (1550-1555) made Santa Barbara a titular church. However, Pope Sixtus V (1585-1590) revoked this status in 1587. In 1601, the church was granted to the Università dei Librai, an organization for bookbinders and printers and the name was changed to Santa Barbara dei Librai. They also adopted St. Thomas Aquinas as the patron saint of the church in 1601. St. John of God may also have been added as a patron saint at this time, though the records are less clear on this point. The façade of the church was designed by Giuseppe Passeri in 1680 and has a doorway flanked by columns with composite capitals. A Latin inscription below the window in the façade states that the Guild of Booksellers bought the piazza in front of the church for scudi 400 on February 22, 1683. Deconsecrated in the late 1800s, the building was used as a warehouse for many years. The building was restored in the 1980s and belongs to the Comunita di Santa Barbara, which is a community organization.

Prior to the Protestant Reformation in the 16th century, the English community in Rome used this church as their meeting place. Therefore it has been called St. Barbara of the English. The name St. Barbara of Regola is sometimes used, as the area is known as Regola. There are also some records which refer to this church as *Santa Barbara in Satro*, which is probably related to the discovery of two statues of satyrs nearby in the 14th century. The small piazza behind the church is still known as the Piazza dei Satiri. The statues, mirror images of each other, are known today as the Satyrs "della Valle" and are located in niches on either sides of the Marforio in the Capitoline Museums.

The two-level façade of the church was designed by Passeri in1680 and has a doorway flanked by two columns with composite capitals and an arched tympanum enclosing the head of a cherub on the lower level. The upper level has a niche enclosing the travertine statue of Saint Barbara by Ambrogio Parisi, and two windows with seashell designs. The floor plan of the current church is a Greek cross with 4 chapels, 1 at each arm. Over the main entrance is a choir loft, in which there is an organ from the 1600s.

The altars inside the church date from the 1600s and are made of Venetian stucco. The high altar is decorated with mother of pearl, ivory, and agate inlay. The fresco in the vault is *The Glory of Saint Barbara* which was originally painted by Luigi Garzi (1638-1721), and it was subsequently restored by Monacelli. To the right of the main altar is the Chapel of Our Lady, which houses a wooden triptych of the Madonna and Child, St. John the Baptist, and St. Michael, and is thought to date to 1543. The inscription in this chapel denotes that it belonged to the "*Society of the Most Holy Savior*" of the "Sancta Sanctorum". There are two other noteworthy inscriptions in the church: one celebrates the founding of the Guild of Book Sellers in 1699; the other is dedicated to Zenobio Masotti, a famous printer and bookseller in Rome who is buried in the church and who financed the 1680 reconstruction.

The cross-section of the vault is decorated with paintings by Luigi Garzi depicting St. Frances, St. Anthony, St. Theresa, and St. Filippo Neri. The ceiling fresco, painted by Monacelli, shows the Evangelists and Faith, Hope, Charity, and Love of God. The Chapel of the Crucifix is just off the right transept next to the Chapel of the Presbytery. This chapel has lunettes with paintings that depict scenes from St. Barbara's life by Moancelli and Garza.

On the right side of the transept, facing the door, are several more inscriptions. The uppermost acknowledges Paolino Arnolfi of Lucca who restored the church in 1601. An 11th century inscription identifies Giovani de Crescenzio and his wife Rogata as patrons of the church. The third inscription is a funeral notice of Antomnio Gherardino, a bookseller, who bequeathed his estate to the Guild of Booksellers in 1685.

Over the altar in the left transept is a painting by Francesco Ragusa of the Virgin Mary and Child, with St. Joseph, St. Peter, St. Paul, St. Thomas Aquinas, and St. John of God.

There is also a chapel donated by Specchi family, a noble family of Rome. In this chapel there is an inscription that was placed there by Francesco Orazio Specchi, son of Alessandro Specchi, and a painting by Brugi, of Saint Sabbas the Sanctified (439-532).

St. Barbara

St. Barbara was the daughter of a wealthy man, Dioscorus. Refusing offers of marriage, Barbara angered her father. He locked her in a tower to preserve her innocence from the world. When he ordered the construction of a bath house for her use, Barbara had three windows cut into the building to signify the trinity. She admitted to her father that she was a Christian; he brought her before the prefect of the province, who condemned her to death by beheading. Barbara was beheaded by her own father, but in punishment for this he was struck by lightning on the way home. Legend says she was beheaded on December 5 in the reign of emperor Maximianus and Prefect Marcien (286-305). St. Barbara is one of the Fourteen Holy Helpers. These are a group of saints venerated in Roman Catholicism because their intercession is believed to be helpful against various diseases. Prayers to St. Barbara are supposed to help with fevers and preventing sudden death. She is the patron saint of artillerymen, military engineers, firemen, miners, and the Italian navy. The feast of St. Barbara is celebrated on December 4.

St. Thomas Aquinas

Thomas Aquinas or Thomas of Aquino (1225-1274) was an Italian Dominican priest who is considered to be one of the Roman Catholic Church's greatest theologians and philosophers. One of the 33 Doctors of the Church he is also thought by many to be the model teacher for those studying for the priesthood. Aquinas is known for his writings: the *Summa Theologica* and the *Summa Contra Gentiles*. The *Summa Theologica* (Compendium of Theology) was written to explain the Christian faith to theology students and those studying to take their vows. The *Summa Contra Gentiles* (Of God and His Creatures) is more of a handbook for missionaries and those traveling in hostile lands. He also wrote several important commentaries on Aristotle, including *De Anima* (On the Soul), *Moribus ad Nicomachum* (Nicomachean Ethics), and treaties on Metaphysics. He is the patron saint of booksellers. His feast day is January 28.

St. John of God

Born at Montemoro Novo, Portugal, on May 8, 1495, St. John of God moved to Spain as a young man, where he served as a soldier under the Holy Roman Emperor Charles V, and fought in several battles. He left the army and began distributing Bibles, newly available because of Johannes Gutenberg's printing press. John of God settled in Granada, where he devoted his life to caring for the poor and sick of the city. St. John of God is the patron saint of booksellers, printers, heart patients, hospitals, nurses, the sick, and firefighters and is considered the founder of the Brothers Hospitallers. His feast day is March 8.

St. Sabbas the Sanctified (439-532)

St. Sabbas is venerated in the Eastern Orthodox Churches, Eastern Catholic Churches, and Roman Catholic Church. Born in Mutalaska, near Caesarea of Cappadocia in the 5th century, his parents left him with an uncle when he was 5 years old. At the age of 8, he entered a nearby monastery and studied the Holy Scriptures. When his parents returned 9 years later, they urged him to rejoin the world and marry. He refused and received monastic tonsure at the age of 17. He traveled to Jerusalem, then to the monastery of Saint Euthymius the Great who sent him on again to a local monastery, run by Theoctistus. After Theoctistus' death, St. Sabbas sought isolation and moved into a cave in the wilderness, only returning to the monastery on Saturdays for divine services and a meal with the other monks. In time he would abandon even these encounters and live is complete seclusion in his cave. Others followed his example and sought a monastic way of life. St. Sabbas is credited with founding several monasteries and the composition of the Jerusalem Typikon. His feast day is December 5.

Points of Interest

- The medieval triptych of the Madonna and Child between the Archangel Michael and St. John the Baptist.
- The multiple inscriptions throughout the church.
- The painting of St. Sabbas, which is rarely seen in a Roman Catholic Church.
- The Venetian stucco altars.

Address

St. Barbara of the Books
85 Largo dei Librai
00186 Rome, Italy
Telephone: 06 168 33 474

The Basilica of St. Bartholomew on the Island

San Bartolomeo all'Isola

A porphyry fountain dating to the Roman Empire can be seen in the center at the base of the altar.

Archeologists believe that the oldest human settlement in Rome may have been on Tiber Island (Isola Tiberina). Only 885 feet in length and 220 feet across at its widest point, the island is in the southern bend of the Tiber River as it makes its way through the city of Rome. It is connected to the main land by two bridges: the Ponte Fabricio, on the northeast end of the island; and the Ponte Cestio, which connects the island to the Trastevere district on the western side. The island was in fact once called Insula Inter-Duos-Pontes, which means the island between the two bridges. There are two legends as to how the island was formed. One says that when the tyrant Tarquinius Superbus (510 BCE) was deposed, the angry Romans threw his body into the river. His body sank to the bottom where dirt accumulated around it and formed Tiber Island. The other legend says that the Roman people threw wheat sheaves they had stolen from the king into the river, and those became the basis for the island. Today, the island is boat shaped and the addition of a travertine wall with points at either end of the island that mimic a prow and stern only enhances this image.

The Romans were among the first to isolate diseased persons to limit the spread of contagions. Tiber Island was used as their quarantine camp as well as a treatment center for those suffering from plague. The temple of Aesculapius, the god of medicine and healing, was constructed on the island around 291 BCE. Though not on the site of the original temple, St. John Calabita Hospital is still in operation today on the island across the piazza from the church of St. Bartholomew. The hospital is operated by the *Hospitaller Order of St. John of God* also known as the *Fatebenefratelli.*

The Basilica of St. Bartholomew on the Island, a titular minor basilica, sits on the site of the temple of Aesculapius. The church was built in 997 by the Holy Roman Emperor Otto III to honor the martyr St. Adalbert of Prague. Otto III also collected the relics of many saints, which he had buried in the church; among these were St. Bartholomew's. The structure was renovated by Pope Paschal II in 1113 and again in 1180. An inscription from 1113 over the entrance to the church indicates the presence of St. Bartholomew's and St. Paulinus of Nola's relics in the crypt below.

The high altar is made from a porphyry fountain basin dating back to the Roman Empire. In the center of the nave is an 11th century well-head constructed from a Roman column. It is unusual for a well-head to be located in the central portion of a Christian church. It may be a relic of the temple of Aesculapius and the belief in the healing properties of the waters which flowed through it. Inside the church there are also fourteen ancient Roman columns and two lion supports. The Basilica was badly damaged by a flood in 1557. The present baroque façade was completed in 1624.

In 2000, Pope John Paul II created a commission to the study the life and history of the New Christian Martyrs of the 20th Century. Based in the Basilica of St. Bartholomew, this commission worked for two years collecting roughly 12,000 dossiers on martyrs and witnesses of faith from dioceses all around the world. The culmination of this work was a solemn ecumenical ceremony, which included the Patriarch Teoctist of the Romanian Orthodox Church, which took place in October 2002. A large icon dedicated to the martyrs of the 20th Century was placed on the high altar, depicting the personal stories of the martyrs studied by the Commission. Personal belongings belonging to some of the martyrs are placed in the small side chapels in the Basilica.

The tower that is located behind the church is all that remains of a castle that was built on the island by the Pierleoni family in the 10th century. The castle was bought by the Caetani family who lived in the houses close to the tower until 1470. Two popes, Victor III and Urban II, lived in the castle while the anti-popes controlled the Vatican (1087 and 1089). As a home, the castle was abandoned due to frequent flooding. The tower became a monastery and later a hospice. Today, it is known as Caetani Tower (Torre dei Caetani) of Tiber Island and is a museum.

Legend of St. Bartholomew

St. Bartholomew was one of the 12 apostles. Little is known of him. He is mentioned in the lists of the apostles in the Gospels of Matthew, Mark, and Luke and as being a witness to the Ascension in the Book of Acts (Matthew 10:3; Mark 3:18; Luke 6:14, Acts 1:13). Some scholars believe that Nathaniel, mentioned in the Gospel of John, was in fact Bartholomew (John 1:43-51). Legend has it that Bartholomew preached in India, Mesopotamia, Persia, Egypt, Armenia, Lycaonia, Phrygia, and on the shores of the Black Sea. He is considered to be one of the patron saints of the Armenian Apostolic Church for bringing the gospel to that region. He was martyred in Albanopolis, Armenia. Some accounts say that he was beheaded; others say that he was flayed alive and crucified upside down. In the *Last Judgment*, a fresco on the altar wall of the Sistine Chapel in the

Vatican, Michelangelo depicts his own face in the empty skin that hangs from St. Bartholomew's hand. His feast day is August 24.

The Bartholomew Fair

The Bartholomew Fair was one of London's pre-eminent summer fairs. Held in Smithfield, London, the charter for the fair was granted by Henry I in 1133 to Rahere, a musician who had taken holy orders and founded the priory of St. Bartholomew. Though chartered to be a 3 day event, the celebrations at times lasted for up to 2 weeks. The Lord Mayor of London usually opened the fair on St. Bartholomew's Eve. Visitors could shop for goods, or marvel at sideshow acts, musicians, wire-walkers, acrobats, puppets, curiosities from around the world, and wild animals. The Fair is mentioned several times in the diaries of Samuel Pepys and is the setting for Ben Jonson's 1614 play, *Bartholomew Fayre: A Comedy*. The last Bartholomew Fair was held on September 3rd, 1855. London officials felt that the fair encouraged debauchery and public disorder.

Legend of St. Adalbert

A bishop of Prague, St. Adalbert was martyred in 997 while trying to convert the Baltic Prussians. In that era, many Christian missionaries would chop down sacred oak trees to demonstrate to the pagans that no supernatural powers protected the trees and that Christianity would triumph. Adalbert was warned by the locals on the Baltic Coast not to harm their sacred oak groves. He was martyred while trying to chop down one of their trees. Legend says that his body was ransomed for its weight in gold by Boleslaus the Brave. He is the patron saint of Bohemia, Poland, Hungary, and Prussia. His feast day is April 23.

Legend of St. Paulinus of Nola's

A Roman Senator who converted to Christianity, Paulinus was known for his poetic epistles to Ausonius, including the nuptial hymn to

Julianus, which extol the dignity and sanctity of Christian marriage and numerous letters to St. Augustine. He was first interred in the cathedral of Nola where he was Bishop; then moved by Otto III to St. Bartolomeo all'Isola, in Rome, and returned to the cathedral of Nola in 1908. His feast day is June 22.

Points of Interest

- "The Miracle"—A large cannonball lodged in the wall the chapel at St. Bartholomew's where it struck during the siege of Rome in 1849. The church was full at the time but no one was injured.
- The 11th century well-head created from a Roman column in the central nave of the church.
- The crypt with the remains of St. Bartholomew. It can be reached through the adjacent monastery.
- On Tiber Island: Below a stairway leading up to the police station are the remains of a Roman travertine decoration of the island as a warship. The ship's prow with an Aesculepius' snake climbing aboard can be seen.
- Look downstream from the island to the *Ponte Roto* or broken bridge. This is the only remaining arch of the ancient *Ponte Aemilius* built in 179 BCE by Marcus Aemilius Lepidus. It is the oldest stone bridge in Rome.
- During summer, the island hosts the *Isola del Cinema* film festival.

Address

St. Bartholomews on the Island
Piazza San Bartolomeo
Tiber Island
Rome, Italy
Telephone: 06 68 77 973

St. Bernard's at the Baths

San Bernardo alle Terme

Built in 1598, St. Bernard alle Terme is an abbey church for the Cistercians of Common Observance. The church is built in an ancient Roman spheristerium (game arena) that was part of the external perimeter of the Baths of Diocletian. Dedicated to the Roman god in 306 CE, the Baths of Diocletian were the largest of the imperial baths built in Rome. They were located on the northeast summit of the Viminal, the smallest of the Seven Hills of Rome. Water for the baths was supplied by a 2nd century aqueduct, Aqua Marcia.

St. Bernard de Terme is a circular church which was originally given to the Feuillants. The church has a central dome that is 72 feet in diameter, with octagonal coffers, and an oculus at the apex. This structure is similar to the Pantheon. There are niches around the walls of the church which house eight statues of saints carved by Camillo Mariani (1567-1611). Two side altars are dedicated to St. Bernard and St. Robert of Molesmes, founders of the Cistercian Order. There is also a painting by Andrea Sacchi of the Venerable Jean de la Barrière, founder of the Feuillants.

Legend of St. Bernard of Clairvaux (1090-1153)

St. Bernard, the founding abbot of the Clairvaux Abbey in Burgundy, France, was a noted author and declared a Doctor of the Church in 1830. Born into a noble family in Burgundy, Bernard was well educated as a child. He embraced the newly established and austere precepts of the Cistercian Monastic Order. In 1112, he entered the Abbey of Citeaux accompanied by thirty of his relatives including five of his brothers. Active in church affairs, St. Bernard served as a mediator to resolve the schism in 1130 which developed because of the election of Pope Innocent II and the antipope Anacletus II. The support of St. Bernard and other prominent church leaders helped Pope Innocent gain recognition from European rulers, leaving Anacletus with few patrons. St. Bernard also supported and sent armies to the Second Crusade. His feast day is August 20.

St. Robert of Molesmes

A native of Troyes, France, St. Robert was born to a noble family around 1028. At the age of fifteen, he entered the Benedictine Abbey of Moutier la Celle. He rose to the rank of prior and was appointed the abbot of Saint Michel-de-Tonnerre. Robert attempted to institute strict observances and reforms in this abbey but failed. He returned to MontierlaCelle. He was asked by some hermits living in the forest of Colan to form a new abbey and was granted permission to do so by Pope Gregory VII at Molesme in Burgundy in 1075. Molesme Abbey quickly became known for its piousness under his administration. In 1098, Robert and several monks from Molesme founded the Abbey of Cîteaux. After a year, Robert returned to Molesme. He was succeeded at the Abbey of Cîteaux by St. Alberic, and then by St. Stephen Harding, who wrote the *Carta Caritatis*, which outlines the organization of the Cistercian order. Robert died on April 17, 1111. His feast day was originally April 17, but today is celebrated on April 29. Molesme Abbey was destroyed during the French Revolution. The Abbey of Cîteaux was also seized during the French Revolution, and its contents sold by the government. In 1898, the remains of the abbey were bought back by monks of other abbeys. Today the Trappists, or Cistercians of the Strict Observance (OCSO), live and work at the Abbey.

Cistercians of the Strict Observance (OCSO)

The Cistercians of the Strict Observance (OCSO) are also known as Trappists. These monks follow the Rule of St. Benedict which is a book of precepts written by St. Benedict. The Rule outlines how to live a communal life in 73 chapters and provides both spiritual and administrative guidelines. Charlemagne was so impressed with the instructions in Benedict's Rule that he had it copied and distributed to encourage monks throughout Western Europe to adopt it as a standard. It is still the most widely used guide to monastic life in use today.

Jean de la Barrière and the Feuillants

Jean de la Barrière was appointed the abbot of Les Feuillants Abbey in southwestern France in 1562. He tried to implement a strict observance of the Cistercian Rule, but was met with resistance. In fact, the twelve monks at Les Feuillants disliked him so much, they tried to poison him. Barrière survived and offered them the choice of either accepting the reform or leaving the abbey. Most of the monks left, leaving only two professed clerics, two novices, and Barrière himself. The new group has come to be known as the Feuillants. The remaining monks ate only barley bread, herbs cooked in water, and oatmeal. They ate while kneeling; slept on the ground or on bare planks, with a stone for a pillow, and only for four hours. The order did grow and prosper. Pope Gregory XIII granted permission for the group to become a congregation separate from the Cistercian order in 1589. Pope Urban VIII then divided the congregation into two separate branches in 1630: one in France, under the title of the Congregation of Notre-Dame des Feuillants; and one in Italy, under the name of Bernardoni or Reformed Bernardines. By 1791, the French congregation had twenty-four abbeys in France. They were suppressed by the French Revolution, some of them fleeing to Rome and to other congregations. The Reformed Bernardines of Italy later rejoined the Cistercian order.

Points of Interest

- Tomb of German painter Johann Friedrich Overbeck, founder of the Nazarene art movement.
- Approximately 250 meters southeast, another tower from the Baths of Diocletian can be seen. It is now part of a hotel.

Address

St. Bernard at the Baths
Via Torino, 94
Rome, Italy
Opposite Santa Susanna on the Via XX Septembre

St. Cecilia in Trastevere

Santa Cecilia in Trastevere

This church dates from the 9th century, though the current façade was built in 1725 by Ferdinando Fuga.

The Church of St. Cecelia in Trastevere is believed to occupy the site of St. Cecelia's home. Legend says that after her death, Pope Urban II converted her home into a place of worship and veneration. This is likely to have happened around the year 230. By 499, St. Cecilia's was one of the more popular churches in Rome. Records also show that on November 20, 545, while celebrating the feast of St. Cecilia in the Church of St. Cecilia in Trastevere, and before the service was fully ended, Pope Vigilius was ordered to Constantinople by the Roman Emperor Justinian. The summons was because Vigilus had refused to support Justinian's edict condemning the *Three Chapters*, a series of (some say heretical) writings.

The current structure dates from the 9th century. The church has been restored several times, but the early structures are still visible in some areas. The current façade of this church was built in 1725 by Ferdinando Fuga. Visitors enter through a large courtyard with a garden and a fountain that incorporates a Roman cantharus urn. Fragments of tombstones, inscriptions, and architectural fragments are displayed in the portico. Upon entering the church there are two tombs directly ahead. These were originally in another section of the church but were relocated in 1891. In the main body of the church there is a wide central nave and two narrow side aisles. The pilasters dividing the nave and the aisles were originally columns; however, they were enclosed in 1823 to provide more support for the structure. Visitors should note that there is no transept in this church. This is known as the basilican style of design.

To the right of the entry, there is a hallway about midway up the aisle that leads to a chapel. This was the only chapel included in the original basilica's floor plan. It is constructed over the calidarium, a room where hot baths were taken in Roman bath complexes. Legend suggests that this is the room in which the Roman authorities tried to suffocate the saint.

The main altar is sheltered by a gothic marble baldachin that was created in 1283 by Arnolfo di Cambio. It is decorated with gilded angels, animals, and saints. Beneath the altar is a statue of St. Cecilia. Her body was found incorrupt on October 30, 1599. She was dressed in gold cloth that was stained with blood and also wrapped in a dark silk veil. St. Cecilia had deep axe cuts in her neck and was lying on her side. The artist Stefano Moderno was present at the time the sarcophagi were opened. He created the statue from his memory of the event. In front of the statue there is a round marble disk with Moderno's oath, that says:

> *Behold the body of the most holy virgin Cecilia, whom I myself saw lying incorrupt in the tomb.*
>
> *I have in this marble expressed for you the same saint in the very same posture.*

The mosaic of the Second Coming can be seen in the apse above the choir. Similar to the mosaic that is seen in the basilica of St. Clement, this byzantine style design was created in 820. The mosaic shows Christ delivering a blessing. He is wearing a broad stripe or band of purple on his tunic. Known as *lati clavi*, this was worn by Roman senators as an emblem of their office and is a sign of high rank. To Christ's right (the blessing side) are St. Paul, St. Cecilia, and Pope Paschal I. The Pope is shown with a picture of the church which identifies him as the builder of the structure. He also has a square halo signifying that he was still alive at the time the mosaic was constructed. The next level shows 12 lambs which represent the Apostles, and the cities of Jerusalem and Bethlehem are in the corners. The inscription beneath the apse mosaic reads:

Haec Domus Ampla Micat Variis Fabbricata Metallis
Olim Quae Fuerat Confracta Sub Tempore Prisco
Condidit In Melius Paschalis Praesul Opimus Hanc
Aulum Domini Formans Fundamine Claro Aurea Gemmatis
Resonant Haec Dindima Templi Laetus Amore
Dei Hic Coniunxit Corpora Sanctae Caeciliae Et Sociis
Rutilat Hic Flore Iuventus Quae Pridem In Cryptis
Pausabant Membra Beata Roma Resultat Ovans Semper
Ornata Per Aevum

This spacious house glitters built of varied enamels;
This hall, which once in ancient time had been demolished,
the generous prelate Paschal built to a better state,
shaping it on a famous foundation;
these golden mysteries resound with jeweled precincts;
serene in the love of God he joined the bodies of Saint Cecilia and her companions;
youth glows red in its bloom, limbs that rested before in crypts:
Rome is jubilant, triumphant always, adorned forever.

The crypt beneath the main altar of the church is phenomenal and is certainly worth seeing. It was decorated by Giovanni Battista Giovanale between 1899 and 1901 at the request of Cardinal

Rampolla. It is decorated in the byzantine style with inlaid geometric stonework, known as cosmatesque. There are 35 grey granite columns which support the highly decorated ceiling. The altar is located on the center of the back wall. The mosaic over the altar by Giuseppe Bravi depicts St. Cecelia being taken to heaven by angels. Looking through the small window in the altar visitors can see the sarcophagus of St. Cecilia and her husband St. Valerian along with the martyrs Tibertius and Maximus. The third sarcophagus has the remains of Pope Urban II and Pope Lucius I. There is a passage that leads behind the altar and allows viewing from a different angle.

Behind the main altar of the church to the right is a doorway which leads to the funerary monument of Cardinal Rampolla. A benefactor of the church, the cardinal is shown looking into the crypt which he had constructed below. The monument is by Enrico Quattrini and was created in 1929.

Moving back towards the front of the church, on the left side when facing the main altar, is the entrance to the excavations. Visitors can see the remains of two Roman houses and a bathhouse which are believed to have belonged to St. Cecelia. Additional excavations inside the crypt revealed eight cylindrical towers thought to be part of a tannery and a pagan household shrine with a relief of Minerva.

Visitors should also see the convent and the Nun's Choir in particular. In this gallery is the fresco *The Last Judgment* painted in 1293 by Pietro Cavallini. This fresco is painted on what was once the inside wall of the façade. It was covered for centuries and rediscovered in 1900. The fresco shows Christ in the center surrounded by angels and with the Virgin Mary, John the Baptist, and the 12 seated apostles. This fresco is considered one of the greatest hidden treasures of Rome by most historians and art experts.

St. Cecilia

Cecilia, a Christian woman from a noble Roman family, was given in marriage to a noble pagan youth, Valerianus. On their wedding night, Cecilia told Valerianus that she was betrothed to an angel who jealously guarded her body and that Valerianus must take care not to violate her virginity. Valerianus demanded to see this angel and was sent to the third milestone on the Via Appia where he met Bishop (Pope) Urbanus. Valerianus was baptized and converted to Christianity on the spot. The angel then appeared. Valerianus and his brother (who also converted to Christianity) were condemned to death by the prefect, Turcius Almachius, for their conversion. Cecelia was also condemned for her part in the matter. According to legend, she was sent to a brothel, but after a profession of faith, hair miraculously grew to cover her body. Brothel patrons left her untouched. The authorities had her removed and placed in a steam room in her own residence in an attempt to suffocate her. She survived this ordeal. The frustrated authorities then sent a soldier to behead her. She was struck three times, and left for dead. However, she survived an additional 3 days. During this time, she made provisions for the poor and asked that her home be made into a church. She was initially buried in the Catacomb of St. Callixtus and later her remains were moved to the church in Trastevere. She is the patron saint of virgins and music. Her feast day is November 22.

Points of Interest

- The sculpture: the *Martyrdom of Saint Cecilia*, by Stefano Maderno is a famous example of baroque sculpture. It is located under the altar of the church. Note the "ax marks" where Cecelia was beheaded. This is said to be a true likeness of the saint that was taken when her body was exhumed in 1599.
- A side chapel on the right side is part of the 9th century church and is constructed over the calidarium.
- *The Last Judgment* by Pietro Cavallini (c. 1293) is considered Cavallini's masterpiece and is a good example of Roman naturalism.
- The crypt and Roman ruins beneath the main church.

Note: Visitors may have to stop one of the priests or attendants and ask to see the excavations and choir. Still, they are worth it.

Address

St. Cecilia in Trastevere
22 Piazza di Santa Cecilia
Rome, Italy
Telephone: 06 71 88 626

St. Charles at the Four Fountains

San Carlo alle Quattro Fontane

San Carlo alle Quattro Fontane is a small baroque church which was built as part of a monastery on the Quirinal Hill. It is named this because of its close proximity to the four fountains on the adjacent street corner, though it should be noted that some guidebooks also call this church San Carlino or Little St. Charles. This church was the first independent commission completed by architect Francesco Borromini, who was a student of Michelangelo. Borromini also worked with Gian Lorenzo Bernini on the design of the baldachin over the high altar of St. Peter's Basilica in Vatican City. The two architects would become bitter rivals.

The monastic buildings of San Carlo alle Quattro Fontane and the cloister were completed first. The church itself was completed by 1641. The monastery complex was built for the Spanish Trinitarians. The exterior of the church has a flowing curved pattern. The serpentine design was added towards the end of Borromini's life and the upper portion was completed by his nephew after the architect's death. In a niche above the main entrance, there are cherubim surrounding a statue of St. Charles Borromeo by Antonio Raggi. In niches on either side, there are statues of St. John of Matha and St. Felix of Valois, the founders of the Trinitarian Order.

The inside of the church has an oval design with a main altar and two side altars. The walls were deliberately designed to weave in and out to suggest a flowing or water-like motion. The most important architectural feature is the elliptical domewith its intricate geometrical pattern. Crosses and hexagons can be seen in the dome as well as a lantern with the symbol of the Holy Spirit. The altarpiece is by Pierre

Mignard, and depicts Sts. Charles Borromeo, John of Matha and Felix of Valois. A room outside the sacristy was set aside for the artist Borromini's tomb, but it remains empty. Borromini committed suicide in the summer of 1667 following the completion of the Falconieri chapel in San Giovanni dei Fiorentini. He was intended to be buried in San Carlo alle Quattro Fontane, but instead he was buried in Maderno's tomb in S. Giovanni dei Fiorentini. At his request, no inscription was placed on the tomb. There is a portrait in the sacristy of San Carlo alle Quattro Fontane with the inscription: "*Knight Francesco Borromini of Como, illustrious architect of this church and convent of St. Charles at the Four Fountains, and outstanding benefactor, died in Rome 1667.*" A small chapel to the left of the main altar holds the remains of a martyred Roman soldier. The hallway to the right of the main altar leads to the cloister and the sacristy. The crypt beneath the church has a low pierced vault.

Legend of St. Carlo Borromeo (October 2, 1538-November 3, 1584)

Carlo Borromeo was the son of Gilberto II Borromeo, Count of Arona, and Margherita de' Medici (sister of Pope Pius IV). He served as the archbishop of Milan. He is one of only four people mentioned at the beginning of the Catechism of the Catholic Church, and was prominent at the Council of Trent. He was an advisor to Henry III of France, Philip II of Spain, and Mary, Queen of Scots. A leading figure in the Catholic Reformation, he is the patron saint of learning and the arts. Borromeo worked extensively to change the abuses by the clergy and the nobles of the times. He founded a Confraternity of Christian Doctrine for the religious instruction of children and the Oblates of St. Ambrose (now called the Oblates of St. Charles). His feast day is November 4.

Trinitarian Order

The Trinitarian Order was founded north of Paris on December 17, 1198 by St. John de Matha. St. Felix of Valois is considered a cofounder of the Order and companion of John of Matha. The mission of the new brotherhood was to ransom Christians held captive by non-Christians during the time of the Crusades. They also came to be known as the Order of the Holy Trinity for the Ransom of Captives. St. Louis created a house for the Order in his château of Fontainebleu. He also selected the Trinitarians as his chaplains, and to accompany him on his crusades. Their convent in Paris was established in 1228 and dedicated to St. Mathurin; therefore they are known in France as Mathurins. The Order was dedicated to the mystery of the Holy Trinity. With the suspension of the Crusades, the Order devoted itself to promoting devotion to the Holy Trinity, evangelizing to non-Christians, assisting immigrants, and educating the young.

In the late 1600s, the Trinitarians of Spain separated from the Trinitarians of France under Father Juan Bautista of the Immaculate Conception. He encouraged a fresh austerity to their order. The new Spanish Congregation was called the "Discalced Trinitarians of Spain". The Trinitarian Sisters were founded in Spain by Maria de Romero in 1612. Today, they work in parishes, hospitals, schools, and missions throughout the world. The other Trinitarian church in Rome is the Basilica of San Crisogono.

Points of Interest

- Note: this church is often closed to the public. You can, however, ring the bell and ask to see the church and admittance is usually granted.
- The elliptical dome.
- Portrait of Francesco Borromini with the inscription: "*Knight Francesco Borromini of Como, illustrious architect of this church and convent of St. Charles at the Four Fountains, and outstanding benefactor, died in Rome 1667.*" This is in the sacristy.
- The porcelain holy water stoop attributed to Borromini, which is kept in the sacristy.
- The four Renaissance fountains located at the intersection of Via delle Quattro Fontane and Via del Quirinale outside

the church. The figures of the four fountains are the River Tiber (the symbol of Rome); the River Arno (the symbol of Florence); the Goddess Diana (the symbol of Chastity); and the Goddess Juno (the symbol of Strength).

Address

St. Charles at the Four Fountains
23 Via del Quirinale
00187 Rome, Italy
Telephone: 06 48 83 261

Basilica of Saint Clement

Basilica di San Clemente al Laterano

This entrance to San Clemente leads to a courtyard and the original main entrance to the church. Most visitors, however, enter through the side street.

Perhaps one of the oldest churches in Rome, the Basilica of St. Clement is described in 392 CE by St. Jerome who noted that "a church in Rome preserves the memory of St. Clement." This multilayered basilica is one of the most interesting sites to visit in Rome. Historians believe that in the 1st century an apartment building and a mansion separated by a narrow Roman street were built on the site. These structures replaced earlier buildings that were destroyed in the great fire of Nero (64 CE). Christians are believed to have worshipped in the mansion since the 2nd century. A large hall was built over the inner courtyard and ground floor rooms of the mansion at some point. This is the lowest level of the church that is seen today. There is also a catacomb that was discovered in 1938 at this lower level but it is usually closed to the public. In the 4th century, the hall was converted into the lower church. An inscription near the entrance records the building's dedication as a Basilica by Pope Siricius (384-399).

The upper level of the church is the present day basilica, built by Pope Paschal II in 1108. The church still contains many of its rich 12th century decoration. The apse mosaic is a golden crucifix surrounded by vines that represent the Tree of Life and is supposed to represent a vision of paradise. Twelve doves are perched on the cross, symbolizing the apostles. The Tree of Life blossoms and extends its branches across the apse to symbolize the rebirth that comes from Christ's death upon the cross. The Virgin Mary and St. John are beside the cross and the hand of God the Father crowning Christ with a wreath of victory is above. Look carefully at the foliage of the Tree of Life and you will see many exotic animals and birds as well as Doctors of the Church. The four Doctors of the Church that are depicted are St. Augustine, St. Jerome, St. Gregory, and St. Ambrose. The four rivers of Eden flow from the base of the cross and move beneath the tree providing for the animals of the earth. Beneath the stream, 12 lambs are approaching from the cities of Bethlehem (on the left) and Jerusalem (on the right). The mosaic of the city of Bethlehem shows Christ and a boy running down a flight of stairs, symbolic of the flight of the first family. The prophet Isaiah is above the city and St. Lawrence and St. Paul are depicted at the highest level. In city of Jerusalem a cross and a cock are used as symbols of the Crucifixion and of Peter's denial of Christ. The prophet Jeremiah can be seen above this mosaic and St. Clement and St. Peter are shown above him.

The apse inscription along the band just above the sheep reads: *Ecclesiam Christi viti similabimus isti de ligno crucis Jacobi dens, Ignatiiq[ue] insupra scripti requiescunt corpore Christi quam lex arentem, sed crux facit esse virentem* (We have likened the Church of Christ to this vine; the Law made it wither but the Cross made it bloom.) The throne in the apse is part of a martyr's tomb. The high altar holds the relics of St. Clement of Rome and St. Ignatius of Antioch beneath a baldacchino. The entire church is dominated by the large box-like *schola cantorum* in front of the nave. Built in the 6th century by Pope John II, who had been a parish priest in this church, it was designed as a place for the teaching and practice of ecclesiastical chant. In the back of the church, near the entrance to a ground level cloister, is the Chapel of St. Catherine of Alexandria.

The entrance to the 4th century church is in the upper church sacristy. Descending the stairs from the narthex of the upper church, a visitor can see 4 aisles. The first aisle to the right is from the original basilica. There is a small niche about halfway down that houses a 16th century Madonna and also a pagan sarcophagus a little farther down. The second aisle was part of the 4th century basilica's nave. The third aisle was also part of the nave and has 6th, 8th, and 9th century frescoes. Among the most interesting of these is the *Anastasis* or the Descent of Christ into Limbo to Free Just Souls. This event does not appear in scriptures, but is a popular early Roman and Byzantine theme as it answers the question of what happened to the just souls who died before the time of Christ. On the left side of the painting, separated by a spiral column, there is a figure of an Eastern monk carrying a Book of the Gospels. Historians believe that this fresco is part of a funeral monument of this monk and that he may be St. Cyril, the Apostle of the Slavs. The altar in this aisle is modern. The fourth aisle, on the far left, leads to the burial place of St. Cyril and is also close to the door which leads to the 1st century structures on lowest level.

There is an interesting set of 11th century frescos in the lower church. The bottom right set of frescos show St. Clement celebrating mass and recount a curious story. The legend is that Sisinnius, a Roman prefect, suspected his wife Theodora of having an affair with Clement. In fact, she had converted to Christianity and was spending her time at the church in prayer and attending mass. The jealous Sisinnius confronted Clement but was struck blind and dumb by God. Theodora begged Clement to pray that her husband be healed. Clement prayed for his recovery and Sisinnius was restored. Despite this, Sisinnius was still jealous and he then ordered his servants to seize Clement and tie him to a column. The next fresco clearly shows Sisinnius, dressed in a toga and telling his men to bind Clement tighter with the inscription: "*Fili de le Pute traite*" (Pull harder, you sons of whores). The fresco even shows one servant turning to another and asking him for his help. The fresco caption says "*Falite dereto co lo paol Carvoncelle*" (Carvoncello, get behind him with a lever).

In the final fresco, however, Clement has escaped again and is standing in the distance watching the proceedings. He comments "*Duritiam cordis vestry saxa trahere meruisti.*" (You deserve to carry a great burden given the hardness of your hearts).

A 4th century staircase leads down to the 1st century buildings and the temple of Mithras on the lowest level. The Mithraeum, or Temple of Mithras, was built in the courtyard of the apartment building in the 3rd century. The temple has stars on the ceiling, long side benches, and a stone altar with a relief of Mithras slaying a bull in the center. When walking toward the mansion in the lower area, the sound of running water can usually be heard. This is probably water still passing through a 1st century aqueduct that runs towards the Tiber River via the Cloaca Maxima.

St. Clement

St. Clement is considered the first of the "Apostolic Fathers" of the Roman Catholic Church. He is often known as St. Clement of Rome to distinguish him from others named Clement. The ecclesiastical writer Tertullian in 199 said that Clement was ordained by St. Peter. According to St. Jerome, it was widely believed that Clement was the immediate successor of the Apostle Peter and the early Christian scholar and theologian Oregin identified Clement as one of the laborers with St. Paul that is mentioned in the biblical book of Philippians 4:3. Little is known of Clement's life. Many writings have been attributed to him. His epistle to the church in Corinth, called the First Epistle of Clement or 1 Clement, which asserts the apostolic authority of the bishops, is the only writing that has been verified as being his.

Legend says that while exiled in the ancient Greek colony of Chersonesus, Clement struck the ground and brought forth a spring for his fellow prisoners. He was martyred for this act by being tied to an anchor and thrown into the Black Sea. This is alleged to have occurred in the third year of Emperor Trajan's reign, around 101. The Inkerman Cave Monastery in the Crimea was said to be Clement's burial place. St. Cyril brought his relics back to Rome around 867. St. Clement's relics were reburied beneath the high altar of the Basilica around that time. In art, St. Clement usually has an anchor at his side or tied to his neck. A St. Clement's cross is a cross with an anchor base. His feast day is November 23.

St. Cyril, the Apostle of the Slavs

Saint Cyril and his brother Methodius were born in Thessaloniki in the 9th century. They were missionaries to the Middle East, Moravia, and Pannonia. They are credited with creating the Glagolitic alphabet which they used to translate the Bible to the Slavic language. Widely venerated in Bulgaria, the Czech Republic, Russia and the Republic of Macedonia, there are many shrines and churches dedicated to these brothers. The feast of Sts. Cyril and Methodius is July 7 in the Roman Catholic Church and either May 11 or May 24 in the Eastern Orthodox Church.

St. Catherine of Alexandria

St. Catherine of Alexandria, also known as Saint Catherine of the Wheel, was a 3rd century virgin who was martyred for her faith under the Emperor Maxentius. Catherine was the daughter of the pagan King Costus and Queen Sabinella of Alexandria. She was well educated and said to have been very beautiful. When she was 14, she had a vision of the Virgin Mary in which the Blessed Mother gave Catherine to Jesus in mystical marriage. She became a devout Christian and tried to convince the Roman Emperor Maxentius that it was morally wrong of him to persecute Christians. Catherine debated many of the Emperor's philosophers and won the debates.

Ultimately, she converted most of the Roman sages. Maxentius had her scourged and thrown into prison. He then executed the sages along with anyone who visited Catherine and subsequently converted to Christianity, including his wife, the Empress Valeria Maximilla. Maxentius offered to pardon Catherine and proposed marriage to her. She refused him and declared that her spouse was Jesus Christ, to whom she had consecrated her virginity. Maxentius ordered that she be killed on a spiked breaking wheel, however, the wheel broke. So, he had her beheaded. Veneration of St. Catherine was widespread in Europe after the Crusades. Along with St. Margaret, Catherine was one of Joan of Arc's divinely appointed advisers. St. Catherine's feast day in the Orthodox Church is November 25. In 1969, the Roman Catholic Church removed her feast day from the General Roman Calendar; however, as the faithful continued to celebrate the day, in 2002, her feast was restored as an optional memorial for November 25.

Tertullian

Quintus Septimius Florens Tertullianus, (160-225) has been called both the father of Latin Christianity and the founder of Western theology. Legend says he was the son of a Roman centurion, raised in Carthage and trained as a lawyer, only to be later ordained as a priest. He left a substantial body of theological writings which include his great apologetic works, the "Ad nationes" and the "Apologeticus". He is credited with being the first to use the Latin word "trinity" to describe the relationship between the Father, Son, and Holy Spirit, whom he taught were "one God in three persons." He also is remembered for the phrase "the blood of the martyrs is the seed of the Church."

Irish Dominicans

The Basilica of St. Clement was given to the Irish Dominicans in 1667, when England outlawed the Catholic Church in Ireland and expelled the clergy from the country. The Dominican Order was established in Dublin, Ireland in 1224. Today, the Irish Dominicans are a branch of the Dominican Order.

Mithras

Mithraism is a pagan religion which venerates the ancient Indo-Iranian sun god: Mithras. References to the god can be found in the religion and sacred books of both the Hindus and the Persians. He is considered a god of light, fidelity, manliness, and bravery. Legend has it he was born on December 25 and is the son of the sun.

In addition to the temple beneath the basilica, there are several other Mithraic sanctuaries in Rome. Perhaps the largest is located at the Sanctuary of the Baths of Carcalla near the Circo Massimo (Circus Maximas). Discovered in the 1930s, this mithraeum includes large barrel-vaulted chambers and its original white marble paving with a black tile rim. It is open to the public by appointment only via the cultural organization Roma Sotterranea.

The small parish church of Santa Prisca also has a 2nd century mithraeum. Guided tour appointments may be made via the parish superintendent. This mithraeum is also barrel-vaulted and includes a central temple that is oriented toward the rising sun in the east. There are three rooms on the left side of the temple which include an Apparatorium, where the clerics prepared for the mithraic ceremonies; a Caelus, which likely held an altar with a niche at the base; and a room which was believed to have held the bodies of believers sacrificed before the god Cronos and stored in large earthenware vases called dolium, which are still buried in the floor of this room.

Points of Interest

- 12th century apse mosaic in the upper church of a crucifix with vines that represent the Tree of Life.
- The frescoes in the lower church, particularlythe *Anastasis* or the Descent of Christ into Limbo to Free Just Souls.

- Look for the frescoes relating to the mass of St. Clement and his interactions with the jealous husband, Sisinnius.
- Tomb of St. Cyril at the end of the left aisle of the lower church.
- 3rd century cave like Mithraeum, or Temple of Mithras. (Listen for the water in the lower level.)

Address

Basilica of San Clemente
Three blocks from the Colosseum on the Via di S. Giovanni in Laterano
Via di San Giovanni in Laterano / Piazza San Clemente
00184 Rome, Italy
Telephone: 06 70 45 10 18

For tours of the Baths of Carcalla near the Circo Massimo (Circus Maximas): Roma Sotterranea: www.romasotterranea.it or send an email to visite@romasotterranea.it

Church of Santa Prisca
Via di Santa Prisca 11
00153 Rome, Italy
Telephone: 06 5743798

San Crisogono

Basilica of St. Chrysogonus in Trastevere

Main altar of San Crisogono which was dedicated in 1127 and encloses the relics of St. Chrysogonus and St. James the Lesser.

The first record of the Basilica of St. Chrysogonus in Trastevere dates from the Roman Synod of 499, during the reign of Pope Symmachus. Dedicated to the martyr St. Chrysogonus, the current church was built in the 12th century. Cardinal John of Crema had the new church built to celebrate his defeat of the antipope Gregory VIII. The cardinal was a close supporter of Pope Callistus II. It may also be that the 8th century structure was flooded by the Tiber. The new church was built on top of the old. The Romanesque bell tower was added in 1129. The church was remodeled in the baroque style in the 1620s by Giovanni Battista Soria. It was renovated again in 1847 at which time Pope Pius IX gave the church to the Order of the Most Holy Trinity for the Ransom of Captives (Trinitarians). Visitors enter the church through a large portico that was added in 1626. Above the portico there are vases alongside statues of winged dragons and eagles. The dragons and eagles are a theme that is repeated throughout the church and are from the coat of arms of Cardinal Scipione Borghese who financed the renovations done in the 1600s.

Inside, the church retains its 12th century layout. It is built in the basilican style with a wide nave and two side aisles. This church is interesting because it is built over a series of earlier structures including an 8th century church, the 4th century church mentioned above, and a collection of Roman buildings. In the upper 12th century church, the floor is made of green and red cosmatesque and believed to have been constructed with marble from the churches and houses below. To the right upon entering the church is the icon *Our Lady of Good Remedy.* This painting was created by Giovanni Battista Conti in 1944 in thanks for the liberation of Rome from the Nazis. The Christ child is holding the Trinitarian scapula and the Blessed Virgin Mary is holding purses of money symbolic of the ransoms that are paid for captives. The paintings in the left aisle are of St. Adalbert rescuing a Turk, the Holy family, the Trinitarian St. Michael of the Saints, and St. John of the Conception.

In a small chapel off the left aisle of the church are the remains of Blessed Anna Maria Taigi. A popular Christian mystic in the early 1800s, she was beatified in 1920 and is on her way to becoming a saint. The altarpiece above her relics is the Mother of God, Refuge of Sinners. The gold mosaic surrounding the painting has symbols of the evangelists. Above that is the painting by Aronne Del Vecchio of the *Trinitarian Saints in Glory.*

In the floor at the end of the left aisle (by the altar), there is a winged dragon motif repeated in the tiles. The eagles and dragons are also depicted in the window frames above the nave. The 22 red and grey Egyptian granite columns in the nave also predate the 12th century building and may have been part of the earlier structures. The painting in the center of the coffered ceiling is by Giovanni Francesco Barbieri (1591-1666) and depicts the *Glory of Saint Chrysogonus*. This painting may be a copy of the original. There is a story that during the French occupation of Rome in 1808 the painting was removed. Today, there is also a version of the painting in London which is claimed to be the original.

The high altar was dedicated in 1127, and encloses the relics of St. Chrysogonus and St. James the Lesser. The baldachin was created by Soria in 1626 and is supported by 4 golden alabaster columns. In the domes of the apse there are three reliefs on the trial and martyrdom of St. Chrysogonus. The mosaic beneath these reliefs depicts the Virgin Mary seated and holding the Christ child. St. Chrysogonus is to her left wearing a military uniform and St. James the Lesser is to her right.

To the right of the main altar, at the end of the right aisle, is a chapel that was designed by Gian Lorenzo Bernini. The fresco in this chapel is of the Holy Trinity and is by Giacinto Gemignani (1606-1681). The altarpiece is from the 1700s and depicts the founders of the Trinitarian order: St. John of Matha and St. Felix of Valois. The chapel to the left of the main altar has a statue of Christ as *Ecce Homo*. Christ is wearing the red robe and scapula of the Trinitarians. A relic of St. John of Matha is kept beneath the statue.

The entrance to the crypt is through a doorway in the sacristy of the 12th century church. Descending, the apse of the older church and the remains of a martyr's shrine in middle of the apse wall can be seen. The frescoes are believed to be from the 8th to the 11th century, and include *Pope Sylvester Capturing the Dragon*, *St. Benedict Healing the Leper*, and *The Rescue of St. Placid*. There are also the remains of a Roman house and several large basins that have been found in the crypt. Scholars believe that the basins may have been part of a *fullonica*, or laundry and dye-house.

Ecce Homo

Ecce Homo is the Latin phrase ascribed to Pontius Pilate in the Vulgate translation of the Book of John. Pilate utters the phrase which means "Here is the man." when he presents a scourged Christ, bound and crowned with thorns, to the crowd just before his Crucifixion (John 19:5). Today, the phrase is often used to describe artwork that shows a series of images that include the Flagellation of Christ, the Crowning with Thorns and the Mocking of Christ.

St. Chrysogonus

St. Chrysogonus was martyred and buried in the Adriatic port village of Aquileia (Italy), during the persecution of Diocletian. He is the patron saint of the Croatian city of Zadar. Chrysogonus was the Christian teacher of Anastasia, the daughter of the noble Roman Praetextatus. By order of Diocletian, Chrysogonus was condemned to death for his faith and beheaded. His corpse was thrown into the sea. It washed ashore and was buried by the priest Zoilus who is also a patron saint of Zadar. The feast of St. Chrysogonus is November 24.

St. James the Lesser

The identity of St. James the Lesser is obscure. There are several James in the New Testament including James the son of Zebedee, James the son of Alphaeus, James the brother of the Lord, and James the son of Mary of Clopas. James the Lesser appears in the New Testament Gospel of Mark. When Jesus dies on the cross the Bible says: "There were also women looking on from a distance, among them were Mary Magdalene, and Mary the mother of James the Less and Joseph (or Joses), and Salome." (Mark 15:40)

The Synoptic Gospels* list two apostles called James, who are differentiated there by their fathers: James, son of Zebedee, and James, son of Alphaeus. Tradition says that James the Lesser was James, the son of Alphaeus, and James the Great was son of Zebedee. James, the son of Zebedee is the one considered by the Roman Catholic Church to be one of the 12 Apostles and is therefore referred to as James the Great.

Blessed Anna Maria Taigi (1769-1837)

Blessed Anna Maria Taigi was born in Siena on May 29, 1769. She moved to Rome as a child with her family and later married Dominic Taigi. They lived in a house adjacent to the church of San Crisogono and had 7 children, three of whom died. She entered the Third Order of the Most Holy Trinity on December 26, 1808. She had several visions including an apparition of a luminous globe like a miniature sun which shone before her eyes and in which, she could see present and future events anywhere in the world as well as the state of grace of individuals, living or dead. She had these visions for 47 years. In her visions she saw the downfall and death of Napoleon Bonaparte. Anna Maria Taigi died June 9, 1837 and Pope Benedict XV beatified her on May 30, 1920.

Points of Interest

- The 8th to the 11th century frescoes in the lower church.
- The altars and sarcophagi also in the lower church.
- Giovanni Francesco Barbieri's *Glory of Saint Chrysogonus* in the upper church ceiling.

---

* The term "synoptic" is from the Greek *syn*, meaning "together", and *optic*, meaning "seen". Since the 1780s, the first three books of the New Testament, Matthew, Mark, and Luke, have been called the Synoptic Gospels because they tell the same stories. Historians believe that their parallel stories and sentence structure suggest a degree of interdependence among the 3 gospels. The Gospel of John has a different structure and tone and tells stories that do not appear in the first 3 Gospels.

- The icon of *Our Lady of Good Remedy*.
- The relics of Blessed Anna Maria Taigi.

Address

Basilica of San Crisogono
Piazza Sonnino, 44
(viale Trastevere)
00136 Rome, Italy
Telephone: 06 58 18 225

Church of St. Ignatius of Loyola at Campus Martius

Sant' Ignazio di Loyola a Campo Marzio

Also called the Church of the Most Holy Annunciation

Dedicated to Ignatius of Loyola, the founder of the Jesuit order, Sant' Ignazio di Loyola a Campo Marzio was built in the Baroque style between 1626 and 1650. The church occupies the site of the *Collegio Romano* which was founded by St. Ignatius on February 18, 1551 in a house at the base of the Capitoline Hill. The inscription over the door still reads: "*School of Grammar, Humanity, and Christian Doctrine. Free*". The site had been donated to the Society of Jesus by the Marchesa della Valle, in memory of her late husband the Marchese della Guardia Camillo Orsini. A small church was incorporated into the College. The school was successful and soon outgrew its original buildings. Following the canonization of St. Ignatius of Loyola in 1622, Pope Gregory XV, who had attended the he Collegio Romano and was strongly attached to the Church, encouraged his nephew, Cardinal Ludovico Ludovisi, to build a larger church dedicated to St. Ignatius at the College. That is the structure seen today. The new church was opened for public worship in the Jubilee year of 1650.

The church is constructed in a Latin cross pattern with multiple side chapels on each aisle. The painting in the center of the nave was painted by Andrea Pozzo in 1693. It depicts Sant' Ignazio di Loyola being welcomed into paradise by Christ and the Virgin Mary. His missionary activity throughout the world is the central theme of the work. In the painting, a ray of light proceeds from the Heavenly Father to the Heart of Jesus. St. Ignatius is pointing toward Jesus, from whose heart a ray of light shines upon Ignatius. The light in turn is transmitted from St. Ignatius to allegorical representations of the four continents of America, Asia, Africa, and Europe. At the time this painting was created these continents represented the reach of the Jesuit order.

The domed ceiling of this church is in fact an illusion. Construction of a cupola was included in the original plan, however, the Jesuits ran out of money. Using trompe l'oeil, Pozzo created the impression of a cupola that rises to heaven. There is in actuality no cupola; it is a painting on flat canvas. There is a marble disk on the floor which notes the best place to stand and see the effect. Some art historians have called this the most famous baroque fresco in Rome.

The frescoes over the high altar and in the apse are also by Pozzo. The apse painting depicts St. Ignatius receiving his divine calling in *The Vision of St. Ignatius at the Chapel of La Storta*. The exit to the sacristy is to the left of the main altar. To the right of the main altar is a small chapel with funeral monuments of Pope Gregory XV and his nephew, Cardinal Ludovisi. The pope's tomb is above the cardinal's. The inscription reads: "*One raised Ignatius to the altars; the other raised altars to Ignatius.*"

The relics of St. John Berchmans are kept in the chapel in the left transept. This chapel also has a marble altarpiece of the *Annunciation* by Filippo Della Valle, with allegorical figures and angels (1649) by Pietro Bracci. The relics of St. Aloysius Gonzaga are interred in an urn of lapis lazuli in the right transept chapel. The other side chapels present scenes in the life of St. Ignatius including the saint sending St. Francis Xavier to do missionary work in India. In the nave there is a famous group of sculptures showing*Magnificence* and *Religion* (1650) by Allessandro Algardi, who also designed the façade of the church.

In addition to the church, visitors can tour a suite of rooms that belonged to St. Aloysius and St. John Berchmans, who were students of the Collegio Romano. The site includes a scholastic's recreation room that was used by St. Aloysius, St. John Berchman's student room, a house chapel from the period, and the rooms where Blessed Anthony Baldinucci lived. Reservations are recommended and should be made by contacting the sacristans at the address below. To reach the rooms take the small staircase beside St. Aloysius' altar.

St. Ignatius

Ignatius of Loyola was a Spanish knight from Basque and founder of the Society of Jesus (Jesuits). He underwent a spiritual conversion after being seriously wounded at the Battle of Pamplona in 1521. He is the author of *Spiritual Exercises*, a series of meditations, prayers, and mental exercises intended to be completed over a period of 28-30 days. He also wrote the *Constitution of the Jesuit Order*. His feast day is July 31.

St. Francis Xavier

Francis Xavier was born in Navarre, Spain. He was a student of St. Ignatius, and is considered a co-founder of the Society of Jesus. He was a missionary to India, Japan, and China. His feast day is December 3 and the *Novena of Grace* is a popular devotion to Francis Xavier prayed on the nine days preceding his feast day.

St. Aloysius Gonzaga

Aloysius Gonzaga was born at his family's castle in Castiglione delle Stiviere, Italy. In 1585, he renounced his inheritance and moved to Rome to study for the priesthood. He attended the sick in the Jesuit Hospital during the plague of 1691 until he became ill himself and died. He is often depicted in art as wearing a black cassock and white rochet. He is holding a lily (for innocence); a cross (for piety); a skull (for death); and a rosary (for his devotion to the Virgin Mary). His feast day is June 21.

St. John Berchmans

John Berchmans was born at Diest, Belgium in 1599 and died in Rome in August of 1621. He was the son of a shoemaker, and one of five children, three of whom entered religious life. Renowned for his piety and service, he studied for the priesthood but died following a public debate defending the faith, and while clutching his rosary, crucifix, and rules of the Jesuit order. He was never ordained as a priest. He is the patron saint of altar boys and girls. His feast day is November 27.

Blessed Anthony Baldinucci

Born in Florence, Italy in 1665, Blessed Anthony Baldinucci was a Jesuit priest who worked primarily in the towns of Frascati and Viterbo, north of Rome. He was known for organizing processions to various parts of Italy. As part of these processions, the many participants wore crowns of thorns and scourged themselves as they went along. He himself often carried a cross, wore heavy chains, and scourged himself while preaching. He was also known for his devotion to the Blessed Virgin Mary. He died in 1717 at the age of 52. His feast day is November 7.

Points of Interest

- The trompe l'oeil cupola by Pozzo that is considered the most famous baroque fresco in Rome.
- The left transept chapel has a marble altarpiece of the *Annunciation* by Filippo Della Valle, with allegorical figures and angels (1649) by Pietro Bracci.
- The fresco of St. Ignatius being welcomed into paradise by Christ and the Virgin Mary across the nave ceiling.
- The apse painting depicts St. Ignatius receiving his divine calling in *The Vision of St. Ignatius at the Chapel of La Storta.*
- The west wall of the naves sculptures depicting *Magnificence* and *Religion* (1650) by Alessandro Algardi.

Address

Church of St. Ignatius of Loyola at Campus Martius
Via del Caravita, 8A
00186 Rome, Italy
Telephone: 06 67 94 406

Basilica of St. John Lateranin Laterano

Basilica di San Giovanni in Laterano

St. John in Laterano seen from the private papal garden next to the Santa Scala.

Founded on land that was donated by the Emperor Constantine, this basilica was started by Pope Melchiades and completed by Pope Sylvester in the 4th century. The inscription *Sacrascancta Laterensis Ecclesia Omnium Urbis et Orbis Ecclesiarum Mater et Caput* (All Holy Lateran, Mother and Head of all the Churches and all the World) can be seen above the front columns of the basilica. This was the first Christian basilica constructed in the city of Rome and is the cathedral of the city of Rome. The land that Constantine donated includes the remains of the *Castra Nova equitum singularium*, a fort built for the imperial cavalry bodyguard of Septimius Severus (193). Following his victory over Maxentius, Constantine leveled the fort and ordered the construction of the basilica. The new church was dedicated on November 9, 318, and served as the spiritual center of Rome for centuries. It was the Vatican of its day. San Giovanni in Laterano remained the headquarters of the church until the French Pope Clement V transferred the official seat of the Catholic Church to Avignon in 1309.

The structure itself has suffered many insults and reconstructions over the years. It was looted by Alaric in 408 and again by Genseric in 455. Pope Leo the Great (440-461) and Hadrian (772-795) restored the basilica. An earthquake in the 9th century and fires in 1308 and 1360 heavily damaged the building. The basilica was restored again in 1646 by Francesco Borromini under the direction of Pope Innocent X. The façade was reconstructed by Pope Clement XII in 1735. The adjacent Lateran Palace was the residence of the popes from the time of Constantine until 1375. Five ecumenical councils have been held in the basilica (1123, 1139, 1179, 1215, and 1512).

From a pilgrim's perspective, San Giovanni in Lateran is very special church. It was here that Pope Boniface VIII declared the first Jubilee year in 1300. This officially established the tradition of a spiritual trip or pilgrimage to Rome. There are seven oratories that have been incorporated in the basilica. Medieval tradition encouraged visiting each of these oratories for devotion. Today, many faithful still follow the practice of the *Devotion of the Seven Altars*. Depending on the day, the altars can represent the Seven Joys of Mary, Devotion of the Seven Sorrows, or other meanings.

The church was originally dedicated to Christ. It was renamed for John the Baptist following the earthquake, and the veneration of John the Evangelist was added in the 12th century. The bronze doors at the front of the church once adorned the Senate in the Roman Forum and date from 29 BCE. Inside the church, a 13th century fresco behind the pillar on the right in the nave shows Pope Boniface in a cone-shaped papal hat declaring the holy year and issuing a blessing which inaugurated the pilgrim tradition.

The gothic altar, constructed in 1357 at the direction of Pope Urban V, is reserved for use by the Pope. It is constructed of white marble and is said to contain a plank of wood that was used for Mass by St. Peter and the early Popes. Behind the grill work in the upper altar there are two gilded silver busts that were believed to contain the heads of Sts. Peter and Paul.

The altar in the left transept of the basilica has 4 fluted bronze columns that were believed to have been taken from the Temple of Jupiter Capitolinus. Above the altar is a bronze relief of the Last Supper. Known as the Altar of the Holy Sacrament, it is believed that the cedar plank in this altar was part of the table used at the Last Supper. Other relics of ancient Rome are also present in the basilica. The porphyry urn in the Corsini chapel, toward the front of the church on the left hand side, once held the ashes of the Roman Counsul Marcus Agrippa (63-12 BCE) as well as those of the Emperor Augusta (27 BCE-14 CE). The statue of Constantine, at the end of the narthex, once stood in the Baths of Diocletian.

There are several chapels in the basilica. The chapel of St. John the Baptist has doors of gold, silver, and bronze that vibrate when opened and are said to "sing". If asked, the attendants will sometimes demonstrate this for visitors.

The domed octagonal Baptistery stands apart from the Basilica. It was built by Pope Sixtus III, perhaps on an earlier structure. There is a legend that Constantine was baptized there. Visitors enter through carved columns dating from the 1st century. The ceiling fresco tells the story of the Battle of the Milvian Bridge.

Archeological excavations in 1934 and 1935 found pagan and early Christian relics including floor mosaics, household implements, and stretches of paved Roman streets beneath the central nave of the basilica. A 4th century statue of the Emperor Constantine which was originally in the Constantine Baths on the Quirinal is located in the atrium.

Adjacent to the basilica (on the left near the altar) is a 13th century cloister that also has many relics including a stone slab on which it is believed that Roman soldiers played dice for Christ's clothes.

The well in the center of the cloister dates from the 9th century. The baptistery was constructed by Constantine in the 4th century.

Visitors can exit the basilica using the door to the right near the main altar. In the piazza is the obelisk of Pharaoh Thutmos IV (1420-1411 BCE). It is the tallest obelisk in Rome. It was brought to Rome from Thebes by Constantius II and placed in the Circus Maximus. It was moved to its present location by order of Pope Sixtus V in 1588. In this piazza there once stood an equestrian statue of Marcus Aurilieus. It was mistakenly believed for many years to be a statue of Constantine and was moved to the piazza on Capitolione Hill.

The original Lateran Palace encompassed several city blocks and was demolished by Pope Sixtus V (1585-1590). He constructed a new palace compound on the location which housed the Pontifical Museum of Christian Antiquities for many years. These buildings are now used as the offices of the Diocese of Rome. A portion of the old palace can be seen across the street in the Scala Sancta.

Today the basilica is still a Vatican property and is designated as a Papal Archbasilica. St. John's is the oldest of the four Papal Basilicas and serves as the cathedral church of the Diocese of Rome. It is also the official ecclesiastical seat of the Bishop of Rome, the Pope. On Ascension Day (the 40th day after Easter) the current Pope traditionally says a blessing here each year.

Scala Sancta

Inside the Sancta Sanctorum, also known as the Holy of Holies, the private papal chapel at the top of the Scala Sancta.

Diagonally across the street from St. John's are the *Scala Sancta* or Holy Stairs. These 28 wooden steps, now encased in white marble, are believed to be the steps upon which Jesus walked while on his way to trial before Pontius Pilate. They were brought to Rome by Constantine's mother, St. Helena, around 326. Prior to the 16th century, the stairs led to a corridor of the Lateran Palace, near a chapel dedicated to St. Sylvester. When Pope Sixtus V in 1589 destroyed the old papal palace and built the new one, the stairs were moved to their present site. Today, the stairs lead to the *Sancta Sanctorum*, also known as the Holy of Holies.

Originally, this was the *privatissima* chapel used by the early Popes when they were in residence in the Lateran palace. Dedicated to St. Lawrence, the chapel is the only remaining part of the former Lateran Palace. Traditionally, only the Pope was allowed to enter this chapel. However, today the chapel is open on Saturdays to visitors who make an appointment. Inside the chapel is the image of Christ reportedly not made by human hands. This icon is used in processions through the streets of Rome. There are also several odd relics including the Holy Prepuce, a relic of Christ's foreskin from when he was circumcised. Legend says that this relic was a gift to the church by the Byzantine Empress Irene the Athenian. Visitors should note that other places in

Europe also claim to have this relic. A relic of Christ's umbilical cord is also housed in this chapel and another portion of the umbilical cord is housed in Santa Maria Del Popolo in Rome.

Modern pilgrims ascend the holy stairs on their knees for which they can be granted a plenary indulgence. Specifically, Pius VII on September 2, 1817, granted that those who ascend the stairs can shorten their time in Purgatory by nine years for each step. The stairs are also significant to Protestants. Martin Luther climbed these stairs on his 1510 trip to Rome. Replicas of these stairs have been created at Lourdes, France; St. Anne de Beaupre, Canada; Tytuvenia, Lithuania; Abruzzi, Italy; and Nasonville, Rhode Island.

John the Baptist

Mentioned in each of the 4 Canonical gospels, John the Baptist was an early spiritual leader who is said to have baptized Jesus in the River Jordan. John is recognized as a prophet in Christianity, Islam, and the Bahá'í Faith. His ministry predates that of Jesus, and he is well known for the story involving his beheading. John did not approve of Herod divorcing his wife (Phasaelis), and marrying his brother's wife (Herodias). On Herod's birthday, Herodias' daughter, Salome, danced for the king and his guests. In return for her performance Herod agreed to give her anything she desired. Under her mother's direction, Salome asked for the head of John the Baptist on a platter, which Herod delivered. The Jewish historian Flavius Josephus said that Herod killed John because of his continuing influence over the people of the region but the first story is more colorful. There are several feast days for John. His birth is celebrated on June 24. The Roman Catholic, Lutheran, Church of England, Eastern Orthodox, and Byzantine Catholic churches celebrate the feast of his beheading on August 29.

John the Evangelist

John the Evangelist is better known to modern readers as the apostle John. The younger son of Zebedee and Salome,* and the brother of James the Greater, he was a fisherman who was called by Jesus while fishing in the Lake of Genesareth (otherwise known as "the Sea of Galilee"). John held a prominent place in the apostolic order. The gospel of Luke says that John and Peter were sent into the city to make the preparations for the Last Supper (Luke 22:8). John is also believed by some to be the "disciple whom Jesus loved" who appears several times in the Gospel of John, though does not appear in the other Gospels. The unnamed disciple is seated next to Christ at the Last Supper and remained at the foot of the Cross on Calvary with Mary and the other pious women at the crucifixion. (John 13:23, 25; 19:25-27). According to the Gospel of John, after the crucifixion when Mary Magdalene discovers the empty tomb, she tells Simon Peter and the "other disciple, the one whom Jesus loved". The text says "Both of them were running together, but the other disciple outran Peter and reached the tomb first." (John 20:2-10) The Gospel of Luke, however, only mentions Peter running to see the empty tomb (Luke 24:12).

John was the only apostle thought to have lived into old age and not be martyred for his faith. He is believed to have died in Ephesus around 98. The 6th century Basilica of St. John in Ephesus was constructed by Justinian I over the burial site of the Apostle. Now in ruins, the basilica was modeled after the also lost Church of the Holy Apostles in Constantinople.

Tradition says that he wrote the Gospel, the three Epistles of John, and the Book of Revelation, all of which are referred to as Johannine literature. Modern scholars doubt that he actually did write all of these works. His feast day is December 27.

---

* The woman who requested John the Baptist head and John the Evangelist's mother were both named Salome, but they were two different people.

Points of Interest

- The bronze doors which once stood in the Curia (Senate House) of the Roman Forum.
- The nearby Scala Santa—the holy steps believed to have been a part of Pontius Pilots' house. It is said Jesus descended these stairs after he was convicted. St. Helena brought them to Rome. Pilgrims often climb the 28 steps on their knees.
- The fresco of Pope Boniface declaring the first Jubilee year and officially establishing Rome as a pilgrimage site.
- The two red granite columns that support the triumphal arch were part of the original 4th century church.
- The obelisk of Pharaoh Thutmos IV (1420-1411 BCE).
- The busts of Sts. Peter and Paul, now in the cloisters, are from the original church.

Address

St. John at the Laterano
Piazza San Giovanni in Laterano 4
00184 Rome, Italy
Telephone: 06 69 88 64 33

St. Lawrence Outside the Walls

Basilica Papale di San Lorenzo Fuori le Mura

Saint Lawrence Outside the Walls is one of the Seven Pilgrim Churches of Rome. The basilica is a mix of Byzantine construction from the 6th century and Romanesque construction from the 13th century. It is one of the few places in Rome to very clearly see this not so subtle intermingling of styles.

The present day church is built on the site of a small oratory that belonged to Emperor Constantine. The records show that Constantine built a funerary chapel over the grave of the martyr St. Lawrence sometime between the years 314 and 335. The site became a popular Christian cemetery and the opportunity to be buried near St. Lawrence is still considered an honor. An active municipal cemetery is located adjacent to the ancient catacombs. When Constantine's funerary chapel was excavated in 1957, archeologists found 3 successive levels of Christian burials dating to the 4th century.

By the early 6th century, the surrounding area had become a well-populated suburb of Rome. The area was a popular destination for pilgrims who came to venerate St. Lawrence whom legend says was also martyred on this land. The heavy traffic and procession of pilgrims climbing down into the catacombs had weakened the structure and the site was in danger of collapse. In 580, Pope Pelagius II built a Byzantine church incorporating the tomb of St. Lawrence into the nave of the new construction. Visitors could now look down into the tomb of St. Lawrence without having to climb through the old and crumbling catacombs. A 7th century pilgrim's guide tells us "There is also the new basilica of admirable beauty where he (sic St. Lawrence) now rests." The site continued to be a popular destination for pilgrims and a medieval route has been identified which may have originated near the Basilica of St. Clement but is confirmed to go from the Roman Forum, past Santa Maria Maggiore, through the city walls, and along the Via Tiburtina.

By 1200, the area was known as *Laurentiopolis*. Walls and fortifications were built around the basilica and Pope Honorius III enlarged the building and added the Romanesque bell tower. The church seen today is primarily this 13th century construction. The monastery beside the church also dates from this time.

As the basilica is entered, a bronze statue of St. Lawrence created in 1865 by Stefano Galletti stands in the piazza in front of the church. Visitors enter through a portico supported by six marble columns constructed in 1220 by Vassalletto and decorated with a frieze and red and green cosmatesque. The portico is filled with 13th century frescos and mosaics. This portion of the church was heavily damaged on July 19, 1943, when it was hit by a bomb during an allied air raid on the nearby railroad yards. It was extensively restored and reopened in 1949. The narthex was also heavily damaged. The reconstruction is decorated with frescoes of St. Lawrence and St. Stephen and houses early Christian sarcophagi from the nearby catacombs.

To enter the church, one descends four steps. The church has three naves that are divided by eleven columns on each side. The white marble (pavonazzetto) columns in the chancel are part of the original aisles and galleries of the Byzantine basilica. The chancel also contains an episcopal throne at the end of the choir and a marble cosmatesque screen that date from 1254.

There is a triumphal arch at the front of the nave which marks the connection of the 12th century building with the 6thcentury basilica. It is decorated with a gold mosaic of Christ seated on the globe, symbolic of his dominion over the earth. His right hand is raised in a blessing. Christ is surrounded by Sts. Peter and Paul, St. Stephen who is holding a book, and St. Hyppolitus who is holding a martyr's crown. The inscription on the high arch relates to the 6th century construction. It reads:

You once submitted, Deacon, to martyrdom by fire;
The sublime light duly returns to your sanctuary

Another poem which can be seen over the arch reads:

As the Lord removed the darkness and created light, so here there is splendor now in what was once a dim crypt.

Now where a more extensive hall encloses the people, the worshipped body was before approached from narrow galleries.

A plain was excavated and exposed beneath the mountain's hallowed core, and the ruin, menacing with its bulk, has been removed

Under Pelagius' prelateship it was once decided that this sanctuary, so precious, should be set up to him the martyr Lawrence.

A wonderful faith that the Pope by his merits would complete the church despite the weapons and the passions of his enemies.

Now, Lawrence, make the building that is dedicated to your name subject to the peace of heaven, since it is decreed that you will share in the communion of the saints.

The tomb of St. Lawrence lies underneath the main altar along with the relics of St. Stephen and St. Justin Martyr. Below the steps leading up to the chancel there is a room housing some 6th century ruins that were excavated in 1947-1949. Parts of an apse and the Shrine of the Unknown Martyr are also located here.

The cloister on the south side of the church was built during the reign of Pope Clement III (1187-1191). The entrance to the cloister is via a door in the south nave aisle of the basilica, which leads through the sacristy. There is also an entrance from the outside, near the bell tower. Inside the cloister is the entrance to the Catacombs of St. Cyriaca, which descend five levels. On display in the cloister are several sarcophagi, ancient tombstones, and inscriptions from the excavations of the catacombs, both pagan and Christian.

St. Lawrence

A native of Northern Spain, St. Lawrence was one of the seven deacons of ancient Rome who were martyred during the persecution of Valerian in 258. In August of that year, Valerian issued an edict commanding that all bishops, priests, and deacons should immediately be put to death. Lawrence was the last of the seven deacons to be apprehended and executed. Legend is that he was burned to death and he is therefore pictured in art holding the gridiron he was roasted upon. Legend further says he was buried in the Via Tiburtina in the Catacomb of Cyriaca by Hippolytus and Justinus, a presbyter. There are also stories that he was responsible for the distribution of alms to the poor. He is the patron saint of the poor, firemen, and cooks. The feast day of St. Lawrence is August 10.

St. Stephen

St. Stephen was one of seven men chosen to serve as a deacon of the early church at Jerusalem shortly after the crucifixion. Stephen spoke out publically of his faith and was stoned to death by a mob. He is considered the first martyr of the church. His story is told in the New Testament. (Acts of the Apostles, Chapters 6 and 7). For centuries the place of his burial was unknown. In 415, Christian pilgrims to Jerusalem followed the guidance of a priest named Lucian who had had a vision that the tomb was in *Caphar Gamala*. Stephen's relics were found and moved to a church in Jerusalem. They were later transferred to Constantinople during the reign of Emperor Theodosius the Younger (408-450). St. Stephen's remains were then brought from Constantinople to Rome by Pope Pelagius II. St. Stephen is venerated in the Roman Catholic, Anglican, Lutheran, Oriental Orthodox, and

Eastern Orthodox Churches. His feast day is December 26 in most churches. Westerners may be familiar with the "Feast of Stephen" mentioned in the English Christmas carol *Good King Wenceslas*. The Eastern Orthodox Church celebrates St. Stephen's Day on December 27. They also celebrate the discovery of the saint's relics on September 15 and the translation of his relics on August 2.

St. Justin Martyr

St. Justin Martyr was an early Christian apologist, and the foremost interpreter of the theory of the *Logos* in the early church. Born at Flavia Neapoli in Palestine, few of his written works survive. The writings that still exist explain the linkage between Old Testament prophesy about the coming of the Messiah and the life of Christ. He is venerated in the Roman Catholic, Anglican, and Eastern Orthodox Churches. His feast day is June 1.

Points of Interest

- The tomb of St. Lawrence beneath the altar in a crypt under the chancel.
- The Relics of St. Stephen and St. Justin Martyr.
- The 6th century Byzantine chancel.
- The stone on which Lawrence's body was laid after death.
- The Catacomb of Cyriaca (entrances are in the north aisle of the 6th-century basilica at the original floor level (under the chancel) and another is in the cloister).

Note: Some guidebooks mistakenly list the shrine that contains the gridiron that was used to grill St. Lawrence to death as being in this basilica. It is actually in the Church of St. Lawrence's at Lucina, which is a lovely 4th century church located just off the Via del Corso in Rome. It has a chapel designed by Bernini, an altar designed by Carlo Rainaldi, and is rich in history. In this small church Pope Marcellus I hid during Maxentius' persecution in 303 and Pope Damasus I was elected to the papacy in 366 CE. The church was flooded by the

Tiber River on several occasions and has been restored. The French painter, Nicolas Poussin is buried there along with composer Josef Mysliveček, and Charles Stewart. To get there: Take bus 62 from Acciaioli (in front of S. Giovanni dei Fiorentini) to the stop by Piazza del Colonna. Walk up the Via del Corso, turn left into the Piazza S. Lorenzo in Lucina. The church is to the left. (Address: Piazza San Lorenzo in Lucina, 16A). Don't ask a taxi driver to take you there, they won't know where it is and will take you back to the basilica of St. Lawrence Outside the Walls.

Address

St. Lawrence Outside the Walls
3 Piazzale del Verano
00185 Rome, Italy
Telephone: 06 49 15 11

St. Mary in Cosmedin

Basilica di Santa Maria in Cosmedin

Also known as *Santa Maria in Schola Graeca*
(Our Lady for the Greek Community)

Santa Maria in Cosmedin is a medieval church constructed by Pope Hadrian I (772-795). The church is built on the site of a 2nd century BCE Roman temple to Hercules Invictus. Later a temple dedicated to Ceres, the goddess of agriculture, was built in the area because the city's grain markets, the Forum Boarium, were located here. During the 4th century an office for the market inspector called a Statio annonae was constructed. It was a loggia open on 3 sides. In the 6th century this had been partially enclosed to create a diaconia which was used as a food distribution center by early Christians. This structure fell into disrepair by the 8th century and Hadrian had the structure demolished and the new church constructed. The church was named *Mariae in Cosmedi* (which means Saint Maria richly decorated) by Greek refugees who used the facility prior to the 9th century. This designation is due to the ornate decoration in the church constructed by Hadrian. The church for many years was serviced by Greek monks.

Santa Maria was refurbished by Pope Nicholas I in the 9th century. A sacristy and an oratory dedicated to St. Nicholas were added in at this time, but they were removed in 1085. The church was damaged heavily by the Norman invasion of 1084. The modern church was restored in 1869-1899 by Giovanni Battista Giovenale to its more medieval appearance. This restoration included revealing seven open arches and seven windows in the façade. On the portico is the *Bocca della Verità*, "Mouth of Truth." The actual history of this is unclear;

it is either a well-head or ancient Roman drain cover in the shape of a mask. The legend tells is that if a truthful person puts their hand in his mouth nothing will happen. If a liar or thief, however, places their hand in this mouth it will be bitten off. In the film *Roman Holiday,* Gregory Peck and Audrey Hepburn tested this legend.

The inside of the church resembles the way it would have looked in the 12th century. It has a central nave and 2 side aisles. Look closely at the columns separating the aisles. They are taken from various ancient Roman buildings in the area and are of a variety of styles and colors. Ten of the columns are known to have come from the Statio annonae. These are seen on either side of the entrance door, near the end of the left hand aisle, at the entrance of the sacristy and one is in the middle the sacristy. The remaining two are in the campanili. In the rear wall of the church are small niches with purple black marble stones. These stones were weight stones used in the Roman Market. There is a 12th century schola cantorum that stands in the central nave. Notice the intricate cosmatesque work in the floor. The entrance to the crypt is in the left corner of the schola. The crypt is a smaller version of the church with six columns, three on each side, and an altar that is reputed to have been the original altar of Hercules from the pagan temple.

In the main church, a gothic baldachin covers the main altar. It is signed by the artist, Deodato, and dated 1294. The high altar holds the skull of St. Valentine. On February 14, it is brought out and crowned with roses. The apse frescos are from the 19th century. One particularly interesting feature of Santa Maria in Cosmedin is the Winter Choir. Located through a doorway on the right aisle of the church, this chapel was used by the clergy to celebrate the liturgy in winter, when the main church was too cold. The 4 statues in the corners of this chapel represent the virtues and the altarpiece is Theotokos, a picture of Mary, the Mother of God.

The sacristy is next to the Winter Choir. Now serving as the gift shop, in addition to containing two of the ancient columns from the Statio annonae, there is also a mosaic fragment from the 8th century oratory in Old St. Peter's (the present day Vatican). Portions of the mosaics were sent to various churches around Rome in the 1600s, when the old St. Peter's was demolished and the new one constructed. This piece was used over the main altar in Santa Maria in Cosmedin for many years before being moved to the sacristy. It shows the Virgin holding the Christ child with St. Joseph sitting behind her and an angel. A hand is offering the child a gift and may have been attached at one time to a Magi.

The bell tower is perhaps the finest example of mediaeval Romanesque campaniles in Rome. At over 106 feet high and 9 stories tall, it is also one of the largest in Rome. Today the church is used by the Greek Melkite community in Rome. Mass is celebrated in both Arabic and Greek according to the Byzantine rite.

St. Valentine

Buried at the Via Flaminia north of Rome on February 14, little is actually known about St. Valentine. His name does not appear in the early list of Roman martyrs that was compiled in 354. The feast of St. Valentine, February 14, was established by Pope Gelasius I in 496. The first written record of St. Valentine is in the *Nuremberg Chronicle* (written circa 1493). It includes a woodcut portrait of Valentine and a story that he was a Roman priest martyred during the reign of Claudius II. The *Legenda Aurea of Jacobus de Voragine,* compiled in 1260 says that St. Valentine refused to deny Christ before the Emperor Claudius in the year 280. Before he was beheaded, he restored sight and hearing to the daughter of his jailer. In 1836, some relics were exhumed from the catacombs of St. Hippolytus on the Via Tiburtina that were identified as being those of St. Valentine. They were placed in a casket, and transported to the Whitefriar Street Carmelite Church in Dublin, Ireland, where they hold a place of honor today. On St. Valentine's Day, the casket is carried in solemn procession to the high altar for a special Mass dedicated to young people and all those in love. Because little is known of the saint, he was removed from the General Calendar for universal liturgical veneration of the Catholic Church, when this was revised in 1969. Millions still "unofficially" celebrate Valentine's Day on February 14.

Melkite Catholics

The word "Melkite" is derived from the Syriac word *melek*, which means king. The term refers to the followers of the Patriarchates of Alexandria, Antioch, and Jerusalem who accepted the Christological faith of the Byzantine Emperor Marcian after the Council of Chalcedon (451). They accepted the teachings of the Council that Jesus was both human and divine in nature. It is estimated that there are 1.2 to 3.5 million Melkite Catholics worldwide. They are primarily of Lebanese, Syrian, Jordanian, Palestinian, Iraqis, Sudanese, and other Middle Eastern descent. After the Maronites, the Melkite Catholic Church is the largest and most prosperous Catholic community in the Middle East. Their official leader is the Melkite Greek Catholic Patriarch of Antioch and All the East, of Alexandria, and of Jerusalem. He lives in Damascus, Syria.

Fourth Ecumenical Council at Chalcedon (451 CE)

By the 4th century there were 5 major centers of the Christian church: Alexandria (Egypt), Antioch (Turkey), Constantinople (Turkey), Jerusalem (Israel), and Rome (Italy). The leaders of these centers came together at the Fourth Ecumenical Council at Chalcedon in 451, which held from October 8 to November 1, 451. It was attended by some 520 bishops or their representatives and was the largest and best-documented of the early church councils. The main point of contention of this meeting was the divine nature of Christ. The monophysites believed that Jesus Christ's nature was altogether divine and not human even though he had taken on a human body. So Christ had only one (divine) nature. In contrast, the dyophysites believed that Christ had two natures, divine and human. The Council of Chalcedon (451) adopted the dyophysite position, as did the Church of Rome and the Eastern Orthodox Church, though these churches emphasized the complete and perfect unity of the two natures of Christ in one hypostasis.

The doctrine of monophysitism was accepted by the churches of Syria, Egypt, and the Levant. These churches are also known as the Oriental

Orthodox Churches, theOld Oriental Churches or Non-Chalcedonian Churches. The Oriental Orthodox communion comprises six churches: Coptic Orthodox, Ethiopian Orthodox, Eritrean Orthodox, Syriac Orthodox, Malankara Orthodox Syrian Church (India), and Armenian Apostolic churches. These six churches, while being in communion with one another, are hierarchically independent and are not in communion with the Eastern Orthodox Church.

Often called source of the "Great Schism", the Council of Chalcedon is considered the turning or breaking point between the Eastern and Western Christian traditions. It is also the last church council which many Anglicans and most Protestants religions consider to be ecumenical (convened to discuss and settle matters of Church doctrine and practice).

Readers should note that the filioque controversy also plays a role in perpetuating the schism. *Filioque* is the Latin word for "and of the son". It was added to the Nicene Creed at the Council of Nicaea suggesting that the Holy Spirit proceeded from the Father "and Son." As opposed to just from God the father. The word *Filioque* was first added to the Nicene Creed at the Third Council of Toledo (589). The Nicene Creed was added to the Roman Rite and is an ongoing source of conflict between the East and West, proving an obstacle to reunification of the two sides.

Points of Interest

- The Bocca della Verita "Mouth of Truth" placed on the portico in 1632.
- The inside of the church which was returned to its 8th and 12th century appearance.
- The mosaic on the back wall of the gift shop is from the 8th century mosaic and was commissioned by Pope John VII (705-07) for an Oratory of the Virgin inside the old St. Peter's Basilica.
- 8th century crypt, built by Pope Hadrian, below the altar which may contain the original altar of Hercules.

Address

St. Mary in Cosmedin
Piazza Bocca della Verità 18
00186 Rome, Italy
Telephone: 06 67 81 419

The Papal Basilica of St. Mary Major

Basilica Papale di Santa Maria Maggiore

Also known as Santa Maria della Neve (Our Lady of the Snow); Liberian Basilica in honor of its founder Pope Liberius; and Santa Maria Del Presepe (St. Mary of the Crib)

St. Mary Major is one of the seven pilgrim churches in Rome. It is also the largest of the 26 churches in Rome dedicated to the Blessed Virgin Mary. The church was constructed at the direction of Pope Sixtus III after the First Council of Ephesus in 431 which proclaimed the Virgin Mary *Theotokos*, Mother of God. It further declared that Jesus as her son is one person who is both God and man, both divine and human.

The basilica of St. Mary Major stands on the site of a temple to the goddess Cybele, the goddess of nature and fertility. This basilica has kept its original structure, despite an earthquake in 1348 which necessitated extensive renovations. The travertine façade was created by Ferdinand Fuga (1741). The rose window, created in 1995 by Giovanni Hajnal, confirms the declaration of the Second Vatican Council that Mary, the exalted daughter of Zion, is the link that unites the Old Testament and the church of Christ. Throughout this basilica, the image of Mary is used as a bridge to unite the Old Testament stories with the New Testaments teachings of Jesus. The seven-branched candlestick symbolizes the Old Testament, and the chalice of the Eucharist symbolizes the New Testament. The gilded angels on top of the loggia are by Pietro Bracci (1749).

The façade opens onto a portico of five arcades on the lower level and three arches in the upper loggia. When entering the portico, a statue of King Phillip IV of Spain, one of the Basilica's benefactors, is on the right. The clay model for this sculpture was created by Gian Lorenzo Bernini, though the actual statue was carved by Girolamo Lucenti. From the portico, there are five doors that open into the basilica. The Holy Door, which was blessed by John Paul II on December 8, 2001, is on the left. This door was commissioned by the Order of the Knights of the Holy Sepulchre in Jerusalem and was completed by the sculptor Luigi Mattei.

The church is constructed in the Basilican style which means it has a wide central nave and two lateral aisles that are separated by forty marble and granite columns. Visitors today can still see the 5th century mosaics in the central nave and the triumphal arch which date to the original century construction. The mosaics in the nave tell stories from the Old Testament and feature Abraham, Jacob, Moses, and Joshua. The triumphal arch at the head of the nave was originally called the apse arch, and is still listed as such in some guidebooks. The triumphal arch shows images of the Annunciation, the Adoration of the Magi, and the Massacre of the Innocents. The center of the arch includes a mosaic of an empty apocalyptic throne flanked by Sts. Peter and Paul.

The marble used in the cosmatesque floor was donated by the Roman nobleman Scotus Paparoni and his son Giovanni in the 13th century. The marble Athenian columns supporting the nave are some of the oldest visible parts of the church and are probably from the first basilica. The coffered ceiling is gilded with the first gold brought from the New World, which Isabella and Ferdinand of Spain offered to Pope Alexander VI. This ceiling was designed by Giuliano Sangallo and later completed by his brother Antonio.

Beneath the main altar is the 7th century Bethlehem Crypt, also known as the Crypt of the Nativity. It is believed that the wood from the Holy Crib of the Nativity of Jesus Christ is here. The relic can be seen through the crystal and silver urn which was designed by Giuseppe Valadier. The kneeling wooden statue in front of the urn is of Pope Pius IX, who commissioned the construction of the chapel.

St. Jerome, 4th century Doctor of the Church and translator of the Bible into Latin, is buried here.

There are several chapels of note in the basilica. To the right of the main altar is the Sistine Chapel. Created in 1585 by architect Domenico Fontana, this chapel is in the shape of a Greek cross with a cupola. The frescoes on the back wall of the chapel show Sts. Paul and John the Evangelist on the left and St. Paul as he enters Rome on the right. The marble used in the construction of the chapel is believed to have come from older Roman ruins. The altar has a ciborium which shows 4 gilded angels holding up the *tempietto* (a small temple-like Structure). Pope Sixtus V's tomb is to the right of the chapel and the tomb of Pope Pius V is to the left. Readers should note that there are several Sistine chapels in Rome. The designation "Sistine" means that it was built by Pope Sixtus. The Bernini family tomb is outside the chapel, close to the main altar of the basilica. The family was granted special permission to be buried here, because Gian Lorenzo Bernini's son, Pierfilippo, was a canon of this church. The inscription on the step reads: "*Gian Lorenzo Bernini, who brought honor to art and to the city, here humbly, lies.*"

To the left of the main altar is the Borghese Chapel (or Capella Paolina) which contains *The Assumption of Mary* that was painted inside the cupola by Ludovico Cardi. The papal monuments in honor of Clement VIII (1592-1605) and Paul V (1605-1621)in this chapel were designed by Silla di Viggiu. The caryatids (draped female figures used instead of columns) on the Clementine monument to the left were carved by Pietro Bernini (Gian Lorenzo's father).

The *Salus Populi Romani*, "Protectress of the Roman People," is an icon of the Virgin Mary that is also located in the Borghese Chapel. It is believed that the icon helped keep plague from the city. Its painting is attributed to St. Luke, though most scholars date it to the 13th century. This chapel is also called the Capella Paolina because it was the chapel used for prayer by Pope St. Pius V during the Battle of Lepanto on October 7, 1571.

The Sforza Chapel is on the left, next to the Borghese Chapel as one moves down the aisle towards the doors of the basilica. This chapel was designed by Michelangelo in 1564, begun by Tiberio Calcagno in 1566, and completed by Giacomo della Porta in 1573 for Cardinal Guido Ascanio Sforza di Santa Fiora. The altar painting, *The Assumption,* is by Girolamo Sicciolante Da Sermoneta (1521-1580). The fresco above this painting is *The Coronation of the Virgin* by Cesare Nebbia (1536-1614).

The next chapel closer to the doors is the Cesi Chapel, which is dedicated to St. Catherine of Alexandria. It was constructed in 1560 by Giacomo Della Porta at the direction of Cardinal Federico Cesi. Various scenes from the life of St. Catherine are depicted throughout the chapel. The painting over the altar of St. Catherine's beheading is by Girolamo Sicciolante Da Sermoneta (1521-1580) and was completed around 1567.

With the end of the Avignon papacy in 1378, St. Mary Major Basilica became the temporary Palace of the Popes. It remained so until the papal residence was moved to the Palace of the Vatican in what is now Vatican City. The Romanesque bell tower was built by Pope Gregory XI after his return from Avignon. It is the highest bell tower in Rome at 240 feet. St. Mary Major was renovated again in the 18th century for the Jubilee Year of 1750.

The Museum

John Paul II blessed the 8 room museum inside St. Mary Major Basilica on December 8, 2001. The museum includes exhibits on the history of the basilica, saints related to the basilica, objects from the last century's Jubilees, and several books and liturgical objects. Paintings in the museum include "*The Ascente on the Calvary*" by Giovanni Antonio Bazzi; "*The Madonna with the Child, St. Antony of Padua, and St. Catherine of Siena*" by Domenico Jacopo di Pace better known as Beccafumi; and three paintings of the history of the icon *Salus Populi Romani* (Protectress of the Roman People), the icon that can be seen in the Borghese Chapel.

Legend Our Lady of the Snows

Legend says that in August of 358, a childless couple dreamed that the Virgin Mary asked them to build a church in her honor. The couple told Pope Liberius of this dream and learned that he had had the same exact dream. In the dreams, the site for the structure was supposed to be ringed in snow. The next day, August 5, it snowed atop the Esquiline Hill and Pope Liberius built the basilica there. The feast, Our Lady of Snows, is still celebrated annually on August 5 and the official Latin title of the Basilica is *Our Lady of the Snow*. The church is equally known as the *Liberian Basilica* in honor of Pope Liberius and is sometimes referred to as *Santa Maria Del Presepe (St. Mary of the Crib),* since it houses a relic of the manger used at Christ's birth.

Points of Interest

- The Museum, which was opened by Pope John Paul II on December 8, 2001, has extensive information on the history of the basilica and some of the saints related to the basilica.
- The 5th century mosaics in the nave and the golden mosaics of the triumphal arch (explanatory guides are available in the church).
- The marble Athenian columns supporting the nave. These are the oldest visible parts of the church and are probably from the first basilica.
- The Bethlehem crypt or cave crypt and the burial site of St. Jerome.
- The Holy Crib, which was carried to Rome by Christian refugees during the Muslim conquest of the Holy Land in the 7th century.
- The tomb of Gian Lorenzo Bernini and his family.
- The *Salus Populi Romani*, "Protectress of the Roman People" icon of the Virgin Mary.
- The Sforza Chapel which was designed by Michelangelo in 1564.

Address

Basilica of St. Mary Major
42 Piazza di Santa Maria Maggiore
00185 Rome, Italy
Telephone: 06 44 65 836 / 06 48 14 287

Santa Maria in Trastevere

Basilica di Santa Maria in Trastevere

The Piazza Santa Maria in Trastevere in front of the church has an ancient Roman fountain and is a popular meeting spot for locals.

Located in one of the oldest parts of Rome, the Trastevere neighborhood, Santa Maria in Trastevere is believed to have been built around 350 under the direction of Pope Julius I (337-352). The church was partially destroyed by fire in 410, then restored and rededicated to the Virgin Mary by Pope Celestine (422-432). It was completely renovated by Pope Innocent II (1130-1143), using materials from the ancient Baths of Caracalla in the 12th century.

The mosaics on the façade of the church depict the parable of the wise and the unwise maidens. The Blessed Virgin is in the center of these mosaics, the maidens on the right side are not wearing crowns and they have let their lamps burn out. The maidens on the left have kept their lamps lit.

Upon entering the church, immediately to the left is a plaque that celebrates the *Olea Sancta*, or holy oil. There is also a cosmati column to the right of the altar with the inscription *Fons Olei* which marks the spot of an oil spring. Legend says that on the day Christ was born a spring of oil emerged from the ground on this very site. The oil was used to power lamps in the church for centuries. Both Eusebius of Caesarea in the 3rd century and St. Jerome in the 4th century wrote of the story. The magnificent ceiling overhead was painted by Domenichino in 1617. In the very center is his depiction of the *Assumption of the Blessed Virgin.*

The mosaics in the triumphal arch date from 1140 and represent the four Evangelists, along with the prophets Isaiah and Jeremiah. There are also caged birds representing sin, seven candlesticks, and a chi-rho. The mosaics in the apse are from this era and represent the coronation of the Virgin depicted with saints and Pope Innocent II holding a model of the church. There are six additional mosaics in the lower apse (between the windows) that were created by Pietro Cavallini in 1291. These mosaics depict scenes in the *Life of the Virgin.* Visitors can turn on a light to better see the mosaics by depositing a coin in the box at the side of the altar.

The oldest mosaics in the church date from the 1st century and are usually overlooked by visitors. Set into the wall to the right of the sacristy are 2 small scenes, one of birds and the other of the seaside with boats and dolphins. They are pagan works of art that are believed to have originated in Palestrina, an ancient city in Lazio, east of Rome.

Like Santa Maria in Cosmedin, this church has a Winter Choir which was used for services when it was too cold to heat the main church. Above the door is the British Royal Coat of Arms because this chapel was restored by Henry Stuart, Duke of York and the Jacobite of Britain in 1759, the same year he was named a cardinal. He is buried in the vaults underneath the Vatican.

Santa Maria in Trastevere was the first Rome church to be consecrated to the Madonna. There is a life-size icon, *La Madonna della Clemenza*, which is thought to be from as early as the 7th century in a side chapel. The granite columns in the church are from the 12th century restoration and may be from the Temple of Isis or the Baths of Caracalla.

Sts. Callixtus, Cornelius, Julius and Calepodius are buried beneath the high altar. The crypt holds relics of martyrs from the catacombs. They were moved here in the 9th century when Saracen raiders threatened to destroy them.

The Parable of the Wise and Unwise Maidens

The parable of the wise and unwise maidens is told in the Gospel of Matthew, Chapter 25. In this story Jesus described 10 maidens, all of whom have lamps. The wise maidens took oil for their lamps and prepared for the long night. The unwise did not and their lamps went out leaving them in darkness. There are two interpretations of the parable. The first is that Christians should be diligently preparing for the return of Christ (by taking oil). The second interpretation is that the light of Christ will sustain Christians through the darkness if they have prepared.

Fons olei

Fons olei means 'oil spring'. In 38 BCE, the site of the church was a hospice for wounded soldiers and veterans, called the *Taberna Meritoria*. One day an oil spring gushed from the ground. St. Jerome wrote of this natural oil spring in the 4th century. He said that the local Jewish community believed it was a sign that God's grace would soon flow into the world and a Messiah would be born. Because of the spring, this site became a meeting spot for the first Roman converts to Christianity. A column next to the altar in the church marks the spot where the oil is supposed to have flowed. In the six mosaic panels that depict the life of the Virgin, look for the little house just under the figure of Mary in the Nativity scene. The house has a stream of oil flowing from it.

Points of Interest

- The granite columns from the 12th century restoration and that may be from the Temple of Isis or the Baths of Caracalla. At the tops of the columns there are heads of female pagan deities.
- The golden 12th century mosaics on the façade, in the apse, and in the triumphal arch of church. There are light boxes to the left of the altar. Place a coin in them and the lights come on to light up the mosaics. The gold shimmers when illuminated.
- The Cosmati column to the right of the altar with the inscription *Fons Olei* marks the spot of the oil spring.
- At the end of the right aisle, there are purple black marble stones that were used as weights during the Roman era.
- The 1st century bird and marine mosaics to the right of the sacristy.
- On the north side of the piazza, a little street is named Via delle Fonte dell'Olio in honor of the oil spring.
- The Piazza Santa Maria in Trastevere in front of the church has an ancient Roman fountain and is a popular meeting spot for locals.
- During some Holy Years, when the plague or flooding prevented pilgrims from visiting the churches outside the walls, Santa Maria in Trastevere was substituted in the pilgrim's itinerary of the seven holy churches.

Address

Our Lady in Trastevere
Via della Paglia 14/C/ Piazza Santa Maria in Trastevere
00153 Rome, Italy
Telephone: 06 5819443

St. Patrick's at the Villa Ludovisi

San Patrizio a Villa Ludovisi

San Patrizio a Villa Ludovisi is one of the two national churches of Ireland in Rome. The other national church is Sant'Isidoro a Capo le Case. St. Patrick's is relatively new. Construction began on the church on February 1, 1888, and it was dedicated on St. Patrick's Day in 1911. The façade of the church is Florentine in the style of the 13th century. The sanctuary has mosaics of St. Patrick converting the High King Laoghaire at Tara and using the shamrock to explain the Trinity. There are also mosaics of St. Brigid and St. Colum Cille above the high altar. Shrines at the back of the church honor St. Brigid and St. Oliver Plunkett. The 14th century painting of *Our Lady of Grace* is to the right of the main altar. There is a Pieta on the left near the front door of the church. The artist is unknown.

The church is important because it is the home of the Irish Augustinians who have been in Rome since 1656. They came to Rome to educate as priests because such training was made illegal in Ireland by the English. The Augustinians have had several locations in Rome. Their first site was at the church and priory of San Matteo in Merulana. (Santa Maria di Perpetuo Soccorso now occupies this site.) Napoleon's troops demolished this church and the Augustinians moved to Sant'Eusebio in 1798; they moved again to Santa Maria in Posterula in 1819; and to San Carlo al Corso in 1888. In 1892, when St. Patrick's was completed, they moved to this location.

St. Brigid

Born in 451 or 452, St. Brigid of Kildare was baptized by St. Patrick. She was the daughter of Dubhthach, an Irish chieftain of Lienster. She founded a monastery at Cill-Dara (Kildare) as well as a school of art which became famous for its illuminated manuscripts. She is often known as *The Mary of the Gael* and is buried at Downpatrick with St. Columba and St. Patrick, with whom she is the patron of Ireland. She is also the patroness of students. Her feast day is February 1.

St. Colum Cille—also known as St. Columba

St. Colum Cille was born into the powerful O'Neill clan in Donegal in 521. He is referred to as the Dove of the Church and is sometimes called St. Columba, which is the Latin for Dove. He studied at both the monastery of Moville in County Down and the monastery of Clonard, both of which were founded by St. Finian. While at the Monastery of Moville, Colum Cille secretly made a copy of the psalms. He was brought before King Diarmait and accused of stealing the text. Diarmait decided: "To every cow its calf and to every book its copy". As penance for his theft, Colum Cille went into exile on the island of Iona in 563 and founded a monastery there. He died on Iona and is buried there. His feast day is June 9.

St. Oliver Plunkett

Oliver Plunkett was a Roman Catholic Archbishop of Armagh and Primate of All Ireland in the 17th century. He built schools both for the laity and clergy and founded a Jesuit College in Drogheda in 1670. Following the enactment of the Test Act in 1673, his College was destroyed by the English. Plunkett was arrested in Dublin in December 1679 for his faith, imprisoned in Dublin Castle, and later moved to Newgate Prison in London. He was tried twice and finally found guilty of high treason against the English crown in June 1681 "for promoting the Roman faith." He was the last Roman Catholic martyr to die in England. He was hanged, drawn, and quartered at

Tyburn on 1 July 1681. Plunkett was beatified in 1920 and canonized in 1975. He is the patron saint of Peace and Reconciliation in Ireland. His feast day is July 1.

Points of Interest

- An older church on the site, Santa Maria in Posterula, was demolished when San Patrizio was built.
- Mosaics of St. Brigid and St. Colum Cille above the high altar.

Address

St. Patrick's at the Villa Ludovisi
31 Via Boncompagni
00187 Rome, Italy
Telephone: 06 42 03 12 01

St. Paul Outside the Walls

San Paolo Fuori le Mura

The basilica of St. Paul Outside the Walls is believed to be built on gravesite of the Apostle Paul. When the apostle was martyred during the persecution of Nero (64-68), a Roman woman, Lucina, buried him in her family tomb near a vineyard on the road to Ostia. A small oratory was soon erected on the site. The Emperor Constantine replaced the oratory with a basilica around 324. He also had the apostle's body placed in a bronze sarcophagus. The site became a popular pilgrim destination, and by 386 the Emperor Valentitinian II had plans drawn up for a larger facility to accommodate the travelers. Emperor Theodosius started the new construction, and Emperor Honorius completed it. Because these three rulers demolished the church built by Constantine and built a large basilica to commemorate St. Paul, it is often called the Basilica of the Three Emperors. Excavations show that there is an extensive cemetery under and around the basilica which includes burial niches and underground graves that are believed to house the remains of poor people and free slaves.

The basilica has subsequently undergone extensive renovations and expansions over the centuries. The tower and walls encircling the church were completed in 833 to protect the church from the Lombard (772) and Saracen (847) invaders. Collectively, the enclosed area is referred to as "Johannipolis" (in Italian Giovannipoli), or "City of John" after Pope John VIII, who oversaw the fortifications. In the years 1083 and 1084, the walls held off several attacks by the Holy Roman Emperor Henry IV. The buildings have also borne several fires (in the years 1115 and 1823), earthquakes (1349), and floods (1700). The July 15, 1823, fire destroyed the basilica. It is believed a worker dropped a hot coal on the roof which smoldered for several hours and burst into flames around midnight. The news of the devastating blaze was kept from Pope Pius VII, who was on his deathbed. His successor, Pope Leo XII began renovations immediately. They were completed in 1854 and the new basilica was consecrated by Pope Pius IX. Tragedy struck again on April 23, 1891 when an explosion at the nearby Porta Portese gate shattered the stained glass windows. They were replaced with alabaster which can be seen today.

The basilica faces the Tiber River and the entrance is preceded by a large open court or atrium. Inside the atrium is a statue of St. Paul holding the sword with which he was beheaded. A Latin inscription on the plinth reads: *Predicatori veritatis, Doctori Gentium* (The preacher of the truth, the teacher of the Gentiles). The original mosaics that were on the façade were moved inside to the arch over the apse after the 1823 fire. The current façade mosaics were created between 1854 and1874 and depict Christ seated in the center giving a blessing upon all who enter. St. Peter is pictured on his left and St. Paul is on Christ's right. The Mountain of Paradise is directly below Christ on the next level along with four rivers flowing from it which symbolize the gospels. Twelve lambs drinking from the rivers represent the Apostles. The cities of Jerusalem and Bethlehem are on the far left and right. The lowest section shows the Old Testament Prophets Isaiah, Jeremiah, Ezekiel, and Daniel. There are three main doors. The green bronze entry doors in the center are by Antonio Maraini. The golden bronze Holy door on the right was created by the sculptor Enrico Manfrini and erected for the Jubilee of the year 2000.

The inside of the present day basilica is in the shape of an Egyptian cross or T. This layout was used in many early Christian basilicas and is still popular in the Coptic Church of Egypt. The basilica has a large central nave flanked by four lateral naves that are set within 80 granite columns. The interior portion of the apse with the triumphal arch is from the original 4th century building. The ceiling of the basilica is decorated with the coats of arms of the popes who oversaw the restorations and renovations. There are statues of ten apostles in niches along the walls. The statues of Sts. Peter and Paul are by the *confessio*. The *confessio* is below the high altar on the nave side and may be approached by a double staircase. It is considered to be the most sacred spot in the basilica as it is the point nearest the apostle's actual grave. The *confessio* originally included a canopy above the high altar and was made up of four alabaster columns that were given to the church by the Khedive of Egypt. The canopy of the *confessio* was removed several years ago. The baldachin that you see today is from 1285 and was created by Arnolfo di Cambio. It was his first commission in Rome. The inscriptions on the baldachin read: "Arnofolo did this work," and "With his assistant Pietro". The 4 figures on the corners are: St. Peter, St. Paul, St. Timothy, and the Bishop Bartholomew, who paid for the construction. The apse mosaic is from about 1220 and depicts Christ with the Apostles Peter, Paul, Andrew, and Luke.

The apostle's tomb was believed to be under the main altar. This was confirmed during excavations in 2002 which found a sarcophagus and a marble stone bearing the Latin inscription *Paulo Apostolo Mart* (Apostle Paul, martyr). It is believed the stone dates from the 4th century. Visitors can look through the grill covered window beneath the high altar and see the sarcophagus.

The Paschal (Easter) candlestick is 18 feet tall and located in the transept on the right. It was created by Nichola dell'Angelo and Pietro Vassalletto, around 1170. The candlestick shows seven scenes from Christ's Passion. They are: Christ before Caiaphas, the Mocking of Christ, and Christ before Pilate, Pilate washing his hands, the Crucifixion, the Resurrection, and the Ascension. Looking closely, one can also see acanthus leaves and various animals including sphinxes in the candlestick, and the artists signed their names along the base. Along the nave, there are mosaics of all the popes; from Peter to the present day. The series begins in the right transept. Pope Benedict XVI (2005-2013) is in the right aisle and has a light that shines on it. There is room for portraits of 27 more Popes.

Adjacent to the church is a lovely medieval cloister and a Benedictine Abbey. The cloister was constructed begun in 1193 and completed in 1208. It has a rose garden in the center and the walls are decorated with fragments of tomb stones from the cemetery. The columns in the cloister are interesting in that they are not all the same: some are round, some twisted, and some intertwined. At the back of the cloister is the Chapel of the Relics which holds the chains that were believed to have bound St. Paul while he was in prison. The Abbey was founded by Odon of Cluny in 936. It is still active today and not open to the public.

The bell tower, or campanile, behind the church was constructed in by Luigi Poletti between 1840 and 1860. The design uses multiple shapes according to the style of Leon Battista Alberti. Looking at the tower, the bottom level is a square, the middle level is an octagon and the top is a circle. The columns are graduated in the classical manner, which means the heavy Doric style is at the bottom, then the lighter Ionic style, and finally the elaborate Corinthian columns are on the top. Unfortunately, the structure resembles a light house and is laughingly called that by the Romans.

St. Paul

Called "the Apostle to the Gentiles", Paul was born in Tarsus (Eastern Turkey). His birth name was Saul and as a young man he was known for his persecution of the early Christians in and around Jerusalem. Legend says that while traveling from Jerusalem to Damascus the resurrected Jesus appeared to him in a great light. Saul was blinded for three days. His sight was restored by Ananias of Damascus, and Saul was converted and changed his name to Paul. He became an avid missionary, spreading the Christian word throughout the Middle East and Mediterranean. His writings to the various churches that he visited make up a substantial portion of the New Testament. Paul was imprisoned on several occasions for his beliefs. It is known that he was incarcerated in Philippi, Jerusalem, and Rome. He was also stoned in the city of Lystra and shipwrecked on Melite (Malta) while on the way to Rome. It is believed that he traveled to Rome around the year 60. The Bible does not say how or when Paul died. Legend says that he was beheaded in Rome during the reign of Nero at Tre Fontane Abbey. The feast of the Conversion of St. Paul is January 25.

In June 2009, a sarcophagus found at St. Paul Outside the Walls was examined and revealed pieces of incense, purple and blue linen, and small bone fragments. The bone fragments were radiocarbon dated to the 1st to 2nd century. Based on these findings, Pope Benedict XVI declared the tomb as being that of St. Paul's.

Points of Interest

- The 13th century tabernacle of the confession of Arnolfo di Cambio (1285).
- The cloister, possible built by Vassalletto, has double columns of different shapes.
- Since the Lateran Treaties of 1929, the *Giovannipoli* is considered to be the extra-territorial complex of the modern Papal Dominion (i.e. not under the jurisdiction of the Roman or Italian governments.)
- Approximately 4.5 feet below the present Papal Altar is a marble tombstone (2.12 m. x 1.27 m.), bearing the Latin inscription *Paulo Apostolo Mart* (Apostle Paul, martyr). It is believed the stone dates from the 4th century.
- The 5th century Triumphal Arch: Christ is in the center; to the sides are symbols of the Evangelists, the 24 Ancients of the Apocalypse and angels. Sts. Peter and Paul are below. St. Paul is pointing toward his own tomb.
- The Chapel of Relics which has a set of chains said to be the prison chains of St. Paul.
- There is an Art Gallery, located in the Sacristy and in two annexed rooms, which has paintings from the old Basilica.

Address

St. Paul's Outside the Walls
Via Ostiense
184 Rome, Italy
Telephone: 06 698 80 800 or 06 698 80 802

St. Paul's Within the Walls

Chiesa di San Paolo entro le Mura

The American Episcopal Church of Rome

St. Paul's Within the Walls is the American Episcopal Church of Rome. It was constructed in 1873 and was the first non-Roman Catholic Church to be built inside the walls of Rome during the period of *TheRoman Question*. The church was designed by the English architect George Edmund Street. The mosaics in the apse and arches are by Sir Edward Coley Burne-Jones, 1st Baronet (1833-1898). They depict the *Annunciation*, the *Tree of Forgiveness*, *Christ in Glory*, and the *Church on Earth*. The mosaics on the west wall are by George Breck, and depict the *Creation*, *Jerusalem and Bethlehem*, and the *Nativity*. The 17 stained glass windows by Clayton and Bell show scenes from the life of St. Paul. This church is well known for its 23 bell Carillion, which can be heard throughout the neighborhood.

During World War II, the church was closed and placed under the protection of the Swiss Legation in Rome. The city was spared from major damage during the War. On August 14, 1943, a day after the last allied bombing, the Germans declared Rome an "open city" and withdrew, leaving the city to the Allies. The church was reopened and used as a chaplaincy for American troops in 1943. The pews that are still used today were built by the US Army Quartermaster Corps from a stockpile of pine boards.

The Roman Question

The term *The Roman Question* (La Questione Romana) is used historically to identify a political dispute between the Italian Government and the Papacy which lasted from 1861 to 1929. The origins of the conflict lie in the *Risorgimento*, a 19th century movement for unification of the Italian peninsula into a single state. The Papal States comprised the middle of the Italian peninsula. The Pope also held the title of Sovereign Ruler of the Papal States. In 1861, Rome as part of the Papal States was under the protection of the French government.

The Kingdom of Italy was created in March 1861, when the first Italian Parliament met in Turin. The new Kingdom declared Rome its capital, but they could not move into the city because it was defended by French troops.

In July 1870, the Franco-Prussian War began. Napoleon III recalled his garrison from Rome because he needed the troops in France. The people of Rome petitioned the Italian government to take the city; doing so would have been construed as an Act of War against France. However, following the capture of Emperor Napoleon III and large numbers of his troops at the Battle of Sedan on September 1, 1870, the political situation changed. The Italians decided it was time to act. Italian nationalist soldiers under the command of General Raffaele Cadorna entered the city through a breach in the walls near Porta Pia. The Italian government offered the Pope the opportunity to retain control of the Leonine City on the west bank of the Tiber as a Papal State. But Pope Pius IX refused. So, the Italian soldiers took the rest of the city, with the exception of the Apostolic Palace. Pope Pius IX declared himself a prisoner in the Vatican on September 20, 1870. Meanwhile, the residents of the city voted to join Italy and Rome was designated the capital of the new nation. Rome was incorporated into the Kingdom of Italy and a new constitution was implemented. The new constitution allowed freedom of worship, and non-Roman Catholic churches were permitted to build within the walls of the city.

The refusal by Pope Pius IX to accept the Italian government's offer would have lasting effects. For the next 59 years, the Popes would refuse to leave the Vatican, to appear at St. Peter's Square, or to be seen at the balcony of the Vatican. Being seen was viewed by the papacy as an implied endorsement of the legitimacy of the Italian kingdom's rule over the former Papal States. The Pope also issued a papal decree known as *Non Expedit* which forbade Catholics, on pain of excommunication, to participate in elections in the new Italian state. Pope Pius IX declared on October 11, 1874, that the intention of this policy was based on the oath taken by Italian deputies which might be interpreted as an approval of the 'spoliation of the Holy See'. On June 11, 1905, Pope Pius X modified the *Non Expedit*, declaring that it should only be used when there was question of preventing the election of a "subversive" candidate. The Vatican did away with the policy altogether in 1918. The political stalemate between the Vatican and the Italian government would, however, continue. The issue would finally be resolved in 1929, when the Lateran Treaty created the modern state of Vatican City.

The Episcopal Church in Rome

In 1859, the Episcopal Bishop of Pennsylvania, Alonzo Potter, celebrated the Eucharist using the liturgy of the Protestant Episcopal Church in a private house on Trinità dei Monti. Later that year, the parish of Grace Church in the city of Rome was formed under the direction of the Reverend William Chauncey Langdon. At the time, non-Roman Catholic churches were not allowed to build inside the city walls. The Vatican granted the new parish permission to convert an old granary outside the Porta del Popolo as their church. The new Roman constitution of 1871 allowed freedom of worship to all faiths, and non-Roman Catholic churches were permitted to build within the walls of the city. In 1872, the land on which the church and rectory now stand was bought for the sum of $18,500. Construction was begun on the feast of St. Paul, January 25, 1873.

Points of Interest

- The mosaics by Sir Edward Burne-Jones and George Breck.
- The Carillion (bells). The pieces played are appropriate to the liturgical season. Standard playing times are: Weekdays: 09:00; 12:00 Angelus; and 18:00. Sundays: 08:30; 10:15; 13:00; 18:00; and at the end of each Eucharist service. A wonderful video of the carillon can be found at this site: http://www.stpaulsrome.it/english/music/carillon.html.

Address

St. Paul's Within the Walls
Via Napoli 58
00184 Rome, Italy
Telephone: 06 48 83 339

St. Peter in Chains

San Pietro in Vincoli

Also known as the Basilica Eudoxiana

Michelangelo's Moses was completed in 1515 as part of the Monument to Pope Julius II. The monument seen today was originally designed to be five times larger and placed in the center of St. Peter's Basilica in the Vatican.

This church is built on top of Roman ruins that are believed to date from the 3rd century BCE. A church dedicated to the apostles was originally constructed on the site. The basilica seen today was built in 432-440 CE to house the chains that bound St. Peter when he was imprisoned in Jerusalem. Legend says that the Empress Licinia Eudoxia, wife of Emperor Valentinian III, was given the chains while visiting Jerusalem. She sent half of the chains to Constantinople and the other half to her daughter, Eudoxia, the wife of Emperor Theodosius II, in Rome. Eudoxia gave the chain that her mother had sent her to Pope Sixtus III. When he laid the chain next to the chain that had bound St. Peter in the Mamertine Prison of Rome, they miraculously fused together. Sixtus III ordered the construction of a church to house the relics and it was consecrated on August 1, 438. The basilica was renovated in the 7th century, the 16th century, and the 19th century. Excavations in 1876 revealed the tombs of what were believed to be the seven Maccabean martyrs from the second book of Maccabees. (2 Maccabees 7-41)

The exterior of the church is dominated by an arched portico that was added in 1475 and a second story that was added between1570-1580. Unfortunately, the second story covers the original façade. There is a door on the far right side of the portico that leads to excavations conducted in the 1950s. The 3rd century BCE Roman ruins and the outline of the earlier church can be seen here.

The church has a central nave with two side aisles that are sectioned off by 20 fluted white marble columns. The capitals (tops) of these columns are Doric, while the bases are Ionic. Some historians speculate that these columns may have originated in a Greek temple, as they are not typically seen in Roman design. The coffered ceiling of the nave has a fresco in the center by Giovanni Battista Parodi, portraying the Miracle of the Chains (1706). The high altar is from the 5th century. The reliquary in this altar contains the chains of St. Peter. The story of St. Peter's arrest and imprisonment by Herod is told in the book of Acts. (Acts 12:1-11) To the right of the main altar is the monument to Pope Julius II, behind which is the ante sacristy and the sacristy. The fresco in the sacristy is of *St. Peter's Liberation from Prison* by Domenichino (1604). It shows an angel leading the saint to safety. In addition to the main panel, this painting has 4 other scenes from St. Peter's life. The sacristy is regularly closed to visitors; however, one can ask to be admitted in the gift shop and they will usually provide a brief tour. There is a copy of the main panel of the fresco by an unknown artist in the altarpiece further down on the right aisle.

The church is best known as the home of Michelangelo's *Moses* (horned Moses), which was completed in 1515 as part of the Monument to

Pope Julius II. Few are aware that the monument seen today was originally designed to be five times larger and placed in the center of a tribute in St. Peter's Basilica in the Vatican. The original design was three stories high, with carvings on 4 all sides, and had 40 statues. However, the Pope died, Michelangelo got another job (the Sistine Chapel), and the Pope's successor, Leo X, wasn't that interested in building it. The statue depicts Moses with horns on his head because of a description in the Vulgate, the Latin translation of the Bible by St. Jerome that was in use at that time. (Exodus 34:29-30) The original Hebrew phrase is *karan `ohr panav*. The word *karan* means "emitting rays of light" and *ohr panahv* translates to "the skin of his face". Scholars today interpret it as enlightened or radiant. St. Jerome interpreted it as horns coming from Moses' head.

There was originally a monastery that was associated with the church. The cloister designed by Giovanni da Sangallo (1493-1503) remains. The cloister has arches, supported by Ionic columns, and a well in the center with a cover that is attributed to Antonio da Sangallo the Younger (1517). Visitors can enquire at the Institute of Engineering (Università di Roma) to the right of the church to request admittance.

The Maccabean Martyrs

The biblical book of Maccabees tells the story of a mother and her seven sons, who were arrested. The authorities tried to force them to eat pork. When they refused, they were tortured and killed one by one. The mother was the last to be tortured and killed. She has been lauded in various stories for her steadfast devotion and bravery while watching her sons being killed. They are known as the Holy Maccabees or Holy Maccabean Martyrs in both the Roman Catholic and Orthodox churches. They were a popular subject in the mystery plays of the Middle Ages and may be the origin of the word "macabre." Their feast day is August 1.

Points of Interest

- Michelangelo's *Horned Moses* statue in the basilica.
- Reliquary containing the chains of St. Peter under the main altar.

Address

St. Peter in Chains
4/a Piazza San Pietro in Vincoli
00184 Rome, Italy
Telephone: 06 48 82 865

The Papal Basilica of Saint Peter
St. Peter's Square
Vatican City

Basilica Papale di San Pietro in Vaticano

Located in the Vatican Gardens, the Casina of Pius IV is an Italianate villa that was constructed in 1563 and was used by Cardinal Charles Borromeo to hold literary events.

The Papal Basilica of St. Peter in Vatican City could easily be a book in and of itself. Most visitors enter through St. Peter's Square. The square is ringed by a large colonnade that was designed by Gian Lorenzo Bernini and built between 1656 and 1667. The openness of the plaza was designed to symbolize the open arms of the Church welcoming the world. On top of the colonnade there are 140 statues of saints. In the center is an 84 foot-tall red granite obelisk, which was originally erected at Heliopolis by an unknown pharaoh of the 5th dynasty of Egypt (c. 2494 BCE-2345 BCE). The Emperor Augustus (c. 63 BCE-14 CE) moved the obelisk from Heliopolis to the Julian Forum of Alexandria, Egypt. In 37 CE, the Emperor Caligula demolished the Forum and moved the obelisk to Rome. He placed it in the spina which ran along the center of the Circus of Nero. Pope Sixtus V had the obelisk moved to its present location in 1586. A gilt ball that was believed to contain the ashes of Julius Caesar once sat on top of the obelisk. Today, there is a cross at the top. There are two fountains in the square. The fountain on the right when looking at the basilica was created by Carlo Maderno (1612-1614). The fountain on the left was created by Bernini.

St. Peter's Basilica (San Pietro in Vaticano) stands on the traditional site where the Apostle Peter, who is considered to be the first pope, was crucified and buried. During the first century the Circus of Nero and a cemetery were located on the site. St. Peter's grave was visited by pilgrims and it is believed Pope Anacletus (79-91) constructed an oratory over his grave. The first documented church was constructed by Constantine and consecrated by Pope Sylvester I on November 18, 328. Over the centuries the building fell into disrepair and by the 15th century was in danger of collapse. Renovations to this church were begun by Pope Nicholas V in 1452. This was abandoned, though, when Nicholas died in 1455. In the late 15th century, Pope Sixtus IV had the Sistine Chapel constructed. Later, Pope Julius II discarded any additional plans for the reconstruction of the Basilica. He decided to have a new building constructed and contracted Donato Bramante to design a new church. On April 18, 1506, Julius II laid the cornerstone for the present day basilica. Today, that stone is under the pier which holds St. Veronica's statue behind the baldachin, inside the basilica. The new building was completed in 1615 under the direction of Pope Paul V. The plan of the basilica is in the form of a Latin cross. Michelangelo di Lodovico Buonarroti Simoni was appointed architect for the basilica on January 1, 1547. The structure seen today is best known for the dome which he redesigned.

The modern day basilica houses many famous art works. As visitors enter through the central door of the basilica, they see a large round porphyry slab set into the floor. On this slab Charlemagne and subsequent Holy Roman Emperors knelt for their coronation in front of the high altar of the old basilica. Immediately to the right is Michelangelo's *Pieta* which depicts the Virgin Mary cradling the lifeless Jesus in her lap after the crucifixion. He sculpted it from a single block of white Carrera marble when he was 24 years old. His signature is on the band which crosses Mary's breast. Continuing up the right aisle is the monument of Queen Christina of Sweden, who abdicated in 1654 in order to convert to Catholicism. She is buried in the Vatican grottos. The *Monument of Pope Leo XII* (1823-1829) shows the Pope giving his blessingfor the Jubilee of 1825. It was created by G. de Fabris (1790-1860). Above the statue there are two reclining figures of *Religion* and *Justice*.

The two most prized treasures in the church are the tomb of St. Peter and his Chair. The tomb is under the papal altar in the center of the church and underneath the baldachin. Visitors will note that the altar is not centered under the dome, but instead is centered over the tomb of the apostle. The baldachin, which covers the main altar, is made of 927 tons of dark bronze which is rumored to have been removed from the roof of the Pantheon. This was constructed by Gian Lorenzo Bernini (1598-1680) at the direction of Pope Urban VIII. The design of the spiral columns is based on the designs from the original St. Peter's Basilica built by Constantine. Legend says that the Constantinian basilica was based on the design of Solomon's Temple in Jerusalem.

The Confessio is a 17th century chapel named in honor of the confession of faith by St. Peter which led to his martyrdom. It is located at the base of the baldachin. St. Peter's tomb is on the other side of the Niche of the Pallium at the back of the Confessio. This area is considered the "heart of the Basilica". Visitors can look down from the main floor of the basilica at the stairs which lead to the Confessio. The tomb itself can only be seen as part of the the Scavi/ necropolis tour (see below for details).

The Altar of the Chair is directly behind the baldachin. Also known as the Cathedra Petri or "throne of St. Peter", this chair was once used by the popes. Legend says that it was also used by St. Peter;

in actuality, it was a gift from Charles the Bald to the Pope in 875. The altar was designed by Bernini and most people recognize the golden rising dove in its center. The feast of the Chair of St. Peter is celebrated each year on February 22.

Directly overhead is Michelangelo's Dome which is supported by four great piers. Each pier has a large niche at its base, with an enclosed statue of a saint representing each of the basilica's four major relics (Reliquae Maggiori): These saints and their associated relics are:

- St. Helena who was Constantine's mother. She is holding a large cross which represents the True Cross that she found in Jerusalem.
- St. Longinus who was the Roman soldier at Jesus's crucifixion. He is holding the spear that he thrust into the side of Christ while he was on the cross.
- St. Andrew is shown with the diagonal cross upon which he was martyred. St. Andrew's head is the relic this was designed to commemorate. It is no longer housed at the Vatican; it was given to the Greek Orthodox Church in 1964.
- St. Veronica who is holding the veil she used to wipe Jesus' face on the road to Calvary.

The inscription around the Dome is from Matthew 16:18-19, and reads: *TV ES PETRVS ET SVPER HANC PETRAM AEDIFICABO ECCLESIAM MEAM. TIBI DABO CLAVES REGNI CAELORVM* (You are Peter, and on this rock I will build my church . . . I will give you the keys of the kingdom of heaven.)

The smaller inscription, further up reads: *S. PETRI GLORIAE SIXTVS PP. V. A. M. D. XC. PONTIF. V.* (To the glory of St. Peter; Sixtus V, Pope, in the year 1590 and the fifth year of his pontificate.)

Along the left aisle of the church is the Chapel of the Column which contains an image of the Virgin Mary that was painted on a marble column in the central nave of the original basilica. The column has been incorporated into the altar of this side chapel. Beneath the altar is a sarcophagus which dates to the 4th century and holds the remains of Popes Leo II (682-683), Leo III (795-816), and Leo IV (847-855). Moving down the left side of the basilica, visitors come to the monument to Pope Alexander VII which was created by Bernini when he was 80 years old. This is one of the most famous papal monuments in St. Peter's. The Pontiff is kneeling in prayer and does not notice Death who appears as a Skelton over a doorway lifting a fold of red marble drapery and holding an hourglass. The four statues surrounding the statue of the devil represent the virtues practiced by the Pontiff: Charity with a child in her arms; Truth, who rests her foot on a map of the world, and precisely on England where the Pope sought in vain to quell the growth of Anglicanism; Prudence; and Justice. The door under the monument actually leads to an exit from the basilica.

In the left aisle is the monument of Pius VIII. The Pope is shown kneeling beneath a statue of Christ enthroned. Statues of Sts. Peter and Paul are on either side of Christ. In front of the monument is where the current mass schedule for the basilica is posted. Under the monument is a door leading to the Sacristy and Treasury Museum. This hallway leading to the museum has a list of all the popes buried in St. Peter's. The museum is in fact a separate building that was constructed in 1776. The Sacristy in the center of the building is octagonal and decorated with eight columns from Hadrian's Villa in Tivoli. The 10 rooms of the Treasury Museum house several works of art. Of note is the 4th century twisted marble column, decorated with vine tendrils which served as the model for the baldachin. Numerous statues, chalices, and altarpieces can also be seen including the red cope and the tiara with precious stones that are put on the statue of St. Peter in the central nave for important occasions.

Further down the left aisle of the basilica is a monument by Antonio Canova which commemorates the Stuart Dynasty of Scotland, particularly James III, the 'Old Pretender' to the English throne, and his two sons, Bonnie Prince Charlie and Henry. They are buried in the Vatican grottos.

The Baptistery Chapel by Carlo Fontana is the last chapel in the left aisle and closest to the front doors of the Basilica. In the center is a baptismal font that is still used on Sundays to administer the sacrament of baptism. The altarpiece is a mosaic created in 1722 which shows the Baptism of Jesus by John the Baptist in the River Jordan. Other mosaics depict Jesus baptizing Peter; St. Peter baptizing the Centurion Cornelius; St. Philip baptizing the Eunuch of Queen Candace, and St. Silvester baptizing Constantine. Pope John Paul II's new coat of arms can be seen in the marble pavement in the center of the chapel.

The Vatican Grottoes and the Clementine Chapel

The Vatican grottos are located just below St. Peter's Basilica and above a 4th century basilica that was created by Constantine. Buried in these grottos are 91 popes, St. Ignatius of Antioch, the composer Giovanni Pierluigi da Palestrina, Queen Christina of Sweden, and the Scottish Prince James Francis Edward Stuart and his two sons, Charles Edward Stuart and Henry Benedict Stuart. The burial site of Pope John Paul II is located here and there is an eternal flame that marks the spot.

The Clementine Chapel holds the chest which is believed to hold St. Peter's bones. It is also the place where the pope's body lies in state. Below the grottoes there is an ancient Necropolis (City of the Dead) and St. Peter's Tomb. Tours of the grottos are available and tickets can be purchased on the day of the tour. The entrance is on the right of the Basilica porticos. However, in order to tour the necropolis, which is referred to as the Scavi, and St. Peter's Tomb, reservations must be made via the Vatican Excavation Office. The tour is roughly an hour in length and is limited to 15 people at a time. It is recommended that visitors book the tour at least 90 days in advance.

The Vatican Palace

The Apostolic Palace is the official residence of the Pope. It is built on the eastern side of Vatican Hill and can be reached by the road leading around St. Peter's and by the Scala Pia. There is also a covered walkway which leads from the Cortile di Belvedere to the Cortile della Sentinella, however, this is only used for official purposes. The

Scala Regia, or royal staircase, connects the Apostolic Palace to the Basilica. It was built by Antonio da Sangallo the Younger in the early 16th century and restored by Bernini from 1663-1666. At the base of these stairs is an equestrian statue of the Roman emperor Constantine the Great. It is meant as a reminder of the Battle of the Milvian Bridge when Constantine had a vision of the cross with the words *In Hoc Signo Vinces* (In this sign, you will conquer). The phrase appears in the glass on a ribbon unfurled with a passion cross to the left of the statue, beneath a window over the Scala Regia. Bernini considered the Scala Regia to be his most difficult artistic and architectural endeavor due to the irregularly shaped walls and asymmetrical widths at various places of the staircase. The doorway leading to this passage is usually guarded by the Swiss Guards and it is difficult to see, though you may be able to catch a glimpse of the stairs.

The Apostolic Palace incorporates a network of buildings which contain the Papal Apartments, various government offices of the Holy See, private and public chapels including the Sistine Chapel, Vatican Museums, and the Vatican Library. Visitors can see the structures associated with the palace from the cupola of St. Peter's Basilica. Construction of the current palace began on April 30, 1589.

The Borgia Apartments

The Borgia Apartments is a suite of rooms in the Vatican Palace that were adapted for personal use by Pope Alexander VI in the late 15th century. He hired Italian painter Bernardino di Betto (Pinturicchio) to decorate these 5 rooms with frescoes between 1492 and 1494. The paintings include the *Annunciation, the Nativity, the Magi, and the Resurrection*; scenes from the lives of St. Catherine, St. Antony and other saints; allegorical figures of music and arithmetic; plus representations of the planets. After the Pope's death, the work on the apartments stopped. There is also a sixth room which was repainted by Perin del Vaga. The apartments were opened to the public at the end of the 19th century and are now used to house the Collection of Modern Religious Art which includes works by Gaugin, Chagall, Klee, and Kandinskij.

Saint Martha's House

The Domus Sanctae Marthae (Saint Martha's House) was completed in 1996 at the direction of Pope John Paul II and is adjacent to Saint Peter's Basilica. It is, essentially, a hotel that is operated by the Daughters of Charity of St. Vincent de Paul. The five-story hotel has 106 suites, 22 single rooms, and one apartment. It is used by the College of Cardinals when they are taking part in the papal conclaves to elect new Pope. Visiting officials who have business with the Holy See also use the hotel. The 1995 building replaced the St. Martha Hospice which was built in 1891 during a cholera epidemic and later used during World War II by refugees and ambassadors from countries that had broken diplomatic relations with Italy. Prior to the construction of the new building, the College of Cardinals when participating in conclave reportedly slept in the Apostolic Palace on cots that were rented or borrowed from seminaries in Rome.

The Vatican Museums

The Vatican Museums were founded in 1506 by Pope Julius II. The Pope started the collection with a statue of Laocoon, a Trojan priest, which had been buried in the garden of the Roman Emperor Titus for more than 1000 years. Today, the collections include some of the finest Etruscan, Greek, Roman, Egyptian, Byzantine, and Medieval and Renaissance European treasures in the world which are subdivided into several smaller museum collections.

Classical antiquities are displayed over a variety of museums. The gallery of statues in the Pio-Clementine Museum is one of the largest collections and houses many examples of classical figures. Among the more famous artworks in this museum are the Torso of Heracles, the Belvedere Apollo, and the Laocoon.

The Galleria Chiaramonti is another fine collection of statues. This 492-foot long corridor holds more than 300 sculptures created by Greek artists living in Rome. The Daughters of Niobe, a relief in Bœotian limestone, and the head of Neptune are among the most famous pieces.

The Braccio Nuovo museum is considered to be an architectural masterpiece in and of itself. Constructed by Raphael Stern at the commission of Pius VII, it has a barrel-vault design decorated with richly gilt cassettes and 14 antique columns of giallo antico, cipollino, alabaster, and Egyptian granite. The museum houses numerous statues, busts, and mural consoles. Perhaps the most well-known art work in this collection is the enormous recumbent figure of the Nile, on whose body sixteen children are at play representing the 16 cubits in the annual rise of the river.

The Egyptian Museum includes statues, mummies, and numerous papyrus manuscripts, many of which are from a collection that was housed in the Villa Adriana (Tivoli). Antiquities of Mesopotamia including seals, cuneiform tablets, and funerary items from Syria-Palestina are also kept with this collection. The Museum occupies 9 rooms divided by a large hemicycle that opens towards the terrace of the "Niche of the Fir Cone".

The Etruscan Museum was founded in 1837 by Pope Gregory XVI and contains objects that originated in the excavations of the ancient cities of southern Etruria (today northern Latium), then part of the Pontifical State. The 22 rooms included in this museum house a large collection of Greek vases, which were found in the Etruscan necropolises, and of Italiot vases (produced in the Hellenized cities of southern Italy). Visitors can also see statuary and items from 9th through 1st century BCE Etruscan cities.

The Vatican Pinacotheca or picture gallery is among the most popular of the museums. It includes some 460 paintings arranged by chronology and school, from the Primitives (12th-13th centuries) to the 19th century. The works of Raphael, Caravaggio, Leonardo Da Vinci, and Bernini are among the most popular. The galleries cover some 28 rooms and can easily require a day to really see all of them.

The Gallery of Modern Paintings, Ceramics Museum, 18th-19th century; Miniature Mosaics Museum; and the Collection of Modern Religious Art are also open to the public. Another favorite is the

Gallery of Maps which includes a gallery of 40 maps which show the Italian and Papal states from the 16th century.

Portions of the Vatican Palace are also included in the tour of the Vatican Museums. Four rooms of the Pontifical Apartments known as the Stanze of Raphael are situated on the second floor of the Pontifical Palace and include paintings by Raffaello Sanzio da Urbino (Raphael).

The Sistine Chapel

Admission to the Sistine Chapel is included along with the tickets to the Vatican Museums. Michelangelo is the artist most often associated with the chapel, though many others also contributed to the frescos. The chapel is named for Pope Sixtus IV, who restored the Cappella Maggiore, (Major Chapel of the Popes) between 1477 and 1480. He hired Pietro Perugino, Sandro Botticelli, and Domenico Ghirlandaio to create a series of frescoes along the walls depicting the life of Moses and the life of Christ. Michelangelo was commissioned by Pope Julius II in 1508 to paint the ceiling of the Chapel. Prior to Michelangelo's work, the ceiling was painted with golden stars on a blue sky. When initially offered the commission, Michelangelo turned it down because he saw himself as a sculptor, not a painter. The Pope offered to allow him to paint biblical scenes of his own choice. Michelangelo subsequently painted a series of nine paintings showing images of *God's Creation of the World, God's Relationship with Mankind,* and *Mankind's Fall from God's Grace* with some 300 figures. He also painted the *Last Judgment* which is shown over the altar as part of a commission from Pope Paul III.

During special ceremonies the chapel uses tapestries designed by Raphael to cover the side walls. The tapestries depict events from the *Life of St. Peter* and the *Life of St. Paul.*

The Sistine Chapel is best known for being the location of Papal conclaves. Readers should note that there are other chapels throughout

Rome that are also called Sistine, the word merely means by or of Sixtus.

The Vatican Gardens

The Vatican Gardens were established in 1279 when Pope Nicholas III moved his residence back to the Vatican from the Lateran Palace. He planted an orchard, a lawn, and a garden. The gardens were redesigned in a Baroque style during the 16th Century. Today, there are more than 40 acres of gardens on the north and west side of the Vatican City enclosure. They include some 97 fountains which are fed by water from Lake Bracciano, which is 25 miles to the north. The aqueduct that supplied this water was originally built by the Emperor Trajan for the city of Rome in the 2nd century. In 1930, a reservoir was constructed under the gardens by a nephew of Pope Pius XI.

The Central Administration offices for the Vatican are located in the 4-story Palazzo del Governatorate. This building was constructed to be a seminary in 1922 to commemorate the Lateran Treaty. It is located inside the gardens directly behind the Basilica.

The church of St. Stephen of the Abyssinians (Santo Stefano degli Abissini) is located in the southwest section of the garden. It was built by Pope Leo I in the 5th century on the ruins of a pagan temple dedicated to Vesta. The original church was circular with 20 Corinthian columns. Pope Alexander III renovated the church in 1159 and also built a monastery for Ethiopian monks next to it. He copied the floor plan of the original St. Peter's Basilica built by Constantine. The church has a single nave that uses the original columns from the temple. Visitors today can see 7 of the 5th century columns set into the nave walls. The altar and canopy are probably from the 9th century. There is a 9th century crypt. The stairs descending into the crypt are from the Roman era. The 15th century fresco of the *Madonna with Child* is the most important art work in the church. St. Stephen's is the national church of Ethiopia and the services there are celebrated according to the Alexandrine rite of the Ethiopian Catholic Church. The Feast of St. Stephen is celebrated on December 26.

The Leonine Wall is easily seen in the gardens. These walls were erected in 847 by Pope Leo IV after the sack of St. Peter's Basilica by the Saracens in 846. The wall is 1.86 miles in length and completely encircles the Vatican Hill.

The Vatican Train Station (Stazione Vaticana) is located in the gardens behind St. Peter's Basilica. It is the only train station on this line and part of the shortest national railway system in the world. The Popes use the rail system for pilgrimages to Assisi.

The Vatican Gardens can be seen from the top of the dome of St. Peter's. It is possible to tour the gardens. Reservations must be made in advance via the Vatican website or via the Vatican Information Office in the Piazza San Pietro, on the left side as one faces the facade of St. Peter's Basilica.

St. John's Tower

St. John's Tower is a round medieval tower located along an ancient wall built by Pope Nicholas III, and overlooking the Vatican Gardens. It houses apartments that are used by popes when maintenance work is being done on the Apostolic Palace. It has also been used to house guests of the Pope.

The Vatican Library and Secret Archives

The Vatican Library is the Library of the Pope, established by Pope Nicholas V, on of April 30, 1451. It is open to all "qualified readers." Professors and researchers from universities and other institutions of higher education and other learned persons known for their writings and scholarly publications are considered "qualified". University students are not normally granted admission. Exceptions may be made for graduate students preparing a doctoral thesis, as well as for undergraduate students who have a need to consult the manuscripts or other materials preserved only in the Vatican Library. To gain access, a letter of introduction and written attestations of a reader's academic qualifications; valid identification; and a letter of surety are required. Readers are given passes which admit them to Vatican City and the library.

The Vatican Secret Archives (Archivum Secretum Vaticanum) is the central archives of the Holy See and contain the historical archives of different private and public institutions sent to the Holy See for safe keeping. They have been estimated to contain 52 miles of shelving, some of which is in the Bunker, a two-story underground vault below the Cortile della Pigna of the Vatican Museums. The oldest surviving document in the archive dates to the end of the eighth century.

In 1809, Napoleon wanted to consolidate the archives from the administrations of the countries occupied by French troops. Transfer of the Papal archives began in February 1810. A total of 3,239 chests of archival material were transported by wagon to Paris where they were stored in the Archives Nationales at the Palaise Soubise. Some of the documents were returned to Rome after Napoleon's fall in 1814. However, the Vatican could not afford the costs involved in transporting the documents. Between 1815 and 1817 only 2,200 chests of material were returned. Documents considered to be of lesser value were left behind or destroyed.

The archives were closed to anyone outside the Vatican until Pope Leo XIII opened them to scholars in 1881. To mark the 400th anniversary of the Vatican Archives, 100 original documents dating from the 8th to modern times were put on display at the Capitoline Museums, from February to September 2012. The display included letters between the Pope and Cardinal Thomas Wolsey negotiating England's King Henry VIII's request for a divorce from his first wife, Catherine of Aragon. The archives contain correspondence from the composer Wolfgang Amadeus Mozart, who was awarded the Golden Spur (or Militia Aurata), a chivalric order, by Pope Clement XIV. In a letter to his father dated October 1777, Mozart recounts that he had been mocked by some noblemen who had invited him to dinner in order to make him hold a concert, only to laugh at the Golden Spur cross he wore on his neck because it wasn't made of gold or silver. The humiliated Mozart removed the title "knight" from his signature and did not wear the order again. Other letters were from Marie Antoinette, Emperor Franz Joseph of Austria, Napoleon, Abraham Lincoln, and Confederate President Jefferson Davis.

Archive documents are usually made available to scholars after a period of 75 years from their original date. Entrance to the Archives is adjacent to the Vatican Library, through the Porta di S. Anna in via di Porta Angelica. The entry criteria are similar to those of the library.

Casina of Pius IV

The Casina of Pius IV is an Italianate villa that was constructed in 1563. The villa consists of 4 separate sections, with 2 pavilions and 2 arched gateways, connected by an oval inner court. It was used by Cardinal Charles Borromeo to hold literary events. A leading figure during the Counter-Reformation, he would later become St. Charles Borromeo. The Villa has been used since 1926 as the home of the Pontifical Academy of Science.

The Vatican Bank

The Vatican Bank is also known as the Institute for Works of Religion (Istituto per le Opere di Religione; Abbreviated as IOR) and is a privately held institution run by a Chief Executive Officer who reports to a committee of five cardinals appointed by the Pope and the Pope himself. It was founded on June 27, 1942 by Pope Pius XII. Its assets are not considered the property of the Holy See and it is not a department of the Roman Curia. Neither does it serve as the central bank responsible for the Vatican City's monetary policy or maintaining the stability of their currency and money supply. Vatican City uses the Euro and the fiscal policies are regulated by a Monetary Agreement between the European Union and the Vatican City State.

According to the Vatican: "The purpose of the IOR is to provide for the custody and administration of movable and immovable property transferred or entrusted the same to the Institute by individuals or legal entities and allocated to works of religion or charity." Article 3, Chapter 1 of the IOR statues also states that "For any disputes the jurisdiction is the State of Vatican City."

The bank is located in the 15th century Tower of Pope Nicolas V and is opposite the Vatican supermarket. The bank provides automatic teller machine (ATM) services with instructions in Latin, it pays out in Euros, and the bank's debit cards are not valid outside of Vatican City.

The Holy See

The term "Holy See" is often used interchangeably with the "Vatican", though they are not the same entity. The term Holy See is used to refer to the episcopal jurisdiction and supreme authority of the Church; and to the Pope as Bishop of Rome. The Holy See, according to the international laws and customs, has a juridical personality which permits it to sign treaties and to send and receive diplomatic representatives. The Roman Curia is the administrative apparatus of the Holy See and the central governing body of the Catholic Church.

The Vatican is technically a location with its own separate jurisdictions. This is similar to the way the United States (US) and other countries are organized. The Holy See is comparable to the U.S. government, (i.e. the President, Congress and the judicial system) and the Vatican is equivalent to the city of Washington, D.C. President Ronald Reagan and Pope John Paul II established official diplomatic relations between the U.S. government and the Holy See in 1984. The U.S. Embassy to the Holy See is located on the Aventine hill in the Villa Domiziana. The ambassador works in partnership with the Holy See on global issues including HIV/AIDS, world hunger, religious freedom, and human rights.

Vatican City

The Vatican City State emerged as an independent country as a result of the Lateran Pacts between the Holy See and Italy on February 11, 1929. Vatican City has an area of approximately 110 acres. Officially it is known as a sacerdotal-monarchical state that is ruled by the Bishop of Rome (The Pope). Citizenship of Vatican City is granted *jus officii* or by appointment to work in a certain capacity in the service of the Holy See. Official citizenship is also extended to the spouse, parents, and children of a citizen, provided they are living with the person who is a citizen. As of March 1, 2011, the Vatican had 572 official citizens, but only 220 of them were living in Vatican City. In total, approximately 800 people live in Vatican City. As a sovereign nation Vatican City mints its own coins and prints its own stamps. The coin they mint is a Euro with a picture of the Pope on it. This coin first entered circulation on January 1, 2002, and is highly sought after by collectors. It is easier for visitors to purchase a stamp at the Vatican Post Office and mail a letter or postcard to themselves to have it postmarked with the Vatican seal. In 2007, Vatican City installed solar panels and became the first carbonfree state in the world. The Vatican also has its own television station, radio, and newspaper called the "L'Osservatore Romano".

The Swiss Guard

The Swiss Guard celebrates their birthday on January 22 each year. On this day in 1506, a group of 150 Swiss soldiers commanded by Captain Kasparvon Silenen, of Canton Uri, entered the Vatican via the Porta del Popolo and were blessed by Pope Julius II. Until 1970, they shared their duties with the Palatine Guard and the Noble Guard; both of these groups, however, were disbanded by Pope Paul VI. Applicants to the guards must be Catholic; single males of Swiss citizenship who have completed basic training with the Swiss military and can obtain certificates of good conduct; have a professional degree or high school diploma; be between 19 and 30 years of age; and at least 5 feet, 8.5 inch (174 cm) tall. If admitted, their tour of duty can last from 2 to 25 years. If selected, they are sworn in on May 6, a day that commemorates the 1527 Sack of Rome by the Holy Roman Emperor, Charles V. During this battle, 147 of the Vatican's 189 Swiss Guards gave their lives on the steps of St. Peter's Basilica, so that the Pope could escape through the Passetto del Borgo to the Castel Sant'Angelo.

The oath that new Guards take states: *"I swear I will faithfully, loyally, and honorably serve the Supreme Pontiff________and his legitimate successors, and also dedicate myself to them with all my strength, sacrificing if necessary also my life to defend them. I assume this same commitment with regard to the Sacred College of Cardinals whenever the See is vacant. Furthermore I promise to the Commanding Captain and my other superiors, respect, fidelity, and obedience. This I swear! May God and our Holy Patrons assist me!"*

Guards who reach the rank of corporal are allowed to marry. The Swiss Guards are often seen as a ceremonial unit, carryinga long sword and a halberd which is a 14th century four-sided pole with an ax-like top. They also carry the SIG Sauer P220 handgun (P75) and the SIG SG 550 assault rifle as their standard issue weapons. The grand gala uniform of the Swiss Guard incorporates the Medici colors of blue, red, and yellow. The Commandant of the Guard, Jules Repond, created the current uniforms in 1914. They also wear a regular duty uniform which is a solid blue version of the more colorful uniform and is worn with a simple brown belt, a flat white collar, and a black beret.

Points of Interest

- The Vatican has its own post office, radio station, and bank. They also mint their own money. It is popular to mail a letter from the Vatican to have the Vatican stamp and postmark. The post office at the Vatican on St. Peter's Square is open year-round, Monday-Saturday from 08:30-18:30.
- Inside the basilica, watch for crepuscular rays (rays of sunlight that appear to radiate from a single point in the dome and

surround the high altar). These can be seen at different times each day and the times vary with the seasons.

- The tomb of Pope Alexander VII is located inside the basilica. The Pope is the kneeling figure. He is not wearing any symbols of his papal office. There are four allegoric figures, Charity, Prudence, Justice, and Truth. The foot of Truth rests upon a globe of the world; her toe is pierced symbolically by the thorn of Protestant England. Beneath the pope is a doorway which symbolizes the Gate of Death, from this doorway Death (a skeleton) holding an hour glass is raising the curtain.
- St. Veronica's statue underneath which Pope Julius II laid the first stone of the new basilica on April 18, 1506.
- The obelisk in St. Peter's square is called "The Witness". It is the second largest standing obelisk in Rome at a total of 130 feet high, and the only one to remain standing since its removal from Egypt and re-erection at the Circus of Nero in 37. Legend says that this obelisk was a "witness" to the crucifixion of St. Peter.
- The "Scavi" are the excavations of the underground necropolis under St. Peter's Basilica. Reservations are required. They can be made by fax: Excavation Office at 06.6987.3017, or e-mail to scavi@fsp.va, or by phone: 0669885318. Tickets are 12 euros per person and include a guided tour.

Address

Apostolic Palace
00120 Vatican City

Excavations Office/Scavi Tour

Fabbrica di San Pietro
00120 Città del Vaticano (Europa)
email to: scavi@fsp.va; uff.scavi@fabricsp.va
Telephone: 06 69 88 53 18

Please Note: Visitors will not be permitted inside the basilica unless they are dressed appropriately. There are monitors outside St. Peter's. The dress code allows no skirts above the knee, no shorts, no bare shoulders (i.e., tank tops or sleeveless blouses), and shoes must be worn. Bags will also be searched and visitors may be asked to go through a metal detector prior to entry. Vatican City is also a no smoking zone.

St. Prassede

Basilica di Santa Prassede all'Esquillino

(Prassede is the Italian for Praxedes)

Basilica di Santa Prassede all'Esquillino is a minor basilica located near the papal basilica of Santa Maria Maggiore. This church is tiny in comparison to other basilicas, measuring only 143 feet by 98 feet. It is, however, famous for its mosaics and for the Column of Flagellation, the pillar to which Christ was tied as he was whipped before the Crucifixion. The church was also the inspiration for Robert Browning's poem "*The Bishop Orders His Tomb at Saint Praxed's Church.*"

The basilica is dedicated to St. Praxedes and St. Pudentiana. They were the daughters of St. Pudens. Legend says the family members were St. Paul's first Christian converts in Rome. Praxedes, and Pudentiana sheltered Christians in their home during the persecution of Nero (54-68). Praxedes was also believed to have washed the blood of martyrs and placed the cloths containing the blood in the first church. Both girls became martyrs themselves and were originally buried in the catacombs of St. Priscilla.

The earliest records of a church on this site date from 489. It is believed, though, that an oratory dedicated to honor St. Praxedes was constructed here by Pope Pius I around 150. That building was replaced by a 5th century church to commemorate both St. Praxedes and St. Pudentiana. Pope Hadrian I, in 780, then constructed another church on top of the 5th century building. Most of the structure seen today was built in the 9th century by Pope Paschal I (817-824) to venerate the two saints. He moved their remains to this spot as well as the remains of other saints that were in the then abandoned catacombs. Pope Paschal I also had a funerary chapel constructed for his mother Theodora in the main church.

The 9th century façade can be seen when entering the church from the southern entrance on the Via di San Martino ai Monti. There is another smaller entrance on the eastern side of the church that is also frequently used. If entering through this smaller door, walk to the far end of the church near the main doors and turn to face the main altar. The church has a central nave and two side aisles that are sectioned off by granite columns. To the left is a marble slab that St. Praxedes is believed to have used as a bed. Directly in front of the 9th century door, there is a porphyry disk in the floor covering a well where St. Praxedes is said to have placed the bones of 1st century martyrs she rescued from desecration. There is a marble plaque which lists the names of the saints whose relics were taken from the abandoned catacombs in the 9th century on the right hand side, just past the porphyry disk, as one moves toward the altar. The frescoes to the left of the apse are also from the 9th century and depict the saints whose relics were transferred here by Pope Paschal. The inscription at the base of the apse reads:

> *This resting-place in honor of the noble Prassedes beloved of the Lord in heaven is resplendent with decoration of diverse precious stones thanks to the kindness of the Sovereign Pontif Paschal disciple of the Apostolic See. He it was who placed under these walls the bodies of numerous saints gathered from every part, confident that, by their own means, they have merited admittance to the resting-place in heaven.*

The crypt dates from Pope Paschal's reconstruction and is directly ahead, at the base of the altar. Inside are several sarcophagi which hold the relics of St. Praxedes and St. Pudentiana, as well as the remains of the saints moved from the catacombs. It is thought that there is a sponge in the sarcophagi that St. Praxedes used to soak up the blood of martyrs during the first century.

The main altarpiece depicts *St. Praxedes Gathering the Blood of the Martyrs*, and was painted by Domenico Muratori around 1730. On the ground level of the church to the right, when facing this altar, is the Chapel of St. Zeno. Along with St. Valentine, St. Zeno was among those martyrs whose relics were moved from the catacombs to this chapel. Paschal built this chapel as a mausoleum for Theodora, his mother, and decorated it with Byzantine mosaics. This chapel is the only chapel in Rome completely decorated by mosaics. They portray the Blessed Virgin Mary and saints on the inner arch and Christ and the Apostles on the outer arch. In the niche on the right-hand side is *The Harrowing of Hell (Anastasis)* which shows Jesus breaking down the gates of Hell to rescue Adam and Eve and other Old Testament figures. Theodora is pictured over the doorway with a square nimbus alongside St. Praxedes with a crown, St. Pudentiana, and the Virgin Mary. The square nimbus around Theodora's head signifies that she was still living when the mosaic was created. There is some controversy over one of the inscriptions in mosaic that depicts Theodora. The inscription reads: "*Episcopa Theodora*". Historically, the word Episcopa is a Latin feminization of the Greek episkopos, and the term that is used in the early church and biblically to denote an ordained bishop. This inscription suggests that Theodora was a bishop of the early church and is cited as evidence of the ordination of women in the 9th century Catholic Church. Scholars are divided on the matter.

Next to the chapel is the sanctuary of the *Pillar of the Scourging*. The black granite column was brought from the Holy Land in 1223 by Giovanni Cardinal Colonna the Younger. It is believed to be the pillar to which Christ was tied as he was whipped before the crucifixion. The Scourging at the Pillar is an event from the Passion of Christ. It is the fourth station of the modern alternate Stations of the Cross, and a Sorrowful Mystery of the Roman Catholic Rosary. The story is told in three of the four New Testament Gospels. (Mark 14:65; Luke 22:63-65; John 19:1) The story of Jesus being beaten is told in the Gospel of Matthew. However, while Jesus is struck, he is not tied to a pillar or "flogged". (Matthew 27:26)

The Legend of St. Praxedes (St. Prassede); St. Pudentiana; and St. Pudens

St. Praxedes was the daughter of the Roman Senator Pudente (also known as St. Pudens), and the sister of St. Pudentiana (also known as St. Potentiana). Their brothers were St. Novatus and St. Timothy. They were a wealthy family and used their position to aid persecuted Christians and bury those who could not afford a Christian burial. It is believed that the family gave refuge to St. Paul for seven years during Nero's persecution. Their father, Senator Pudente, was the son of Quintus Cornelius Pudens, a Roman Senator. St. Pudens is mentioned in the Bible in the Second Letter to Timothy (Chapter 4, Verse 21). St. Praxedes' feast day is July 21; St. Pudentiana is commemorated in the General Roman Calendar of 1962 on May 19; St. Pudens is commemorated on April 14 in the Eastern Orthodox Church calendar and May 19 according to the Dominican Martyrology.

Pilgrims should note that the 7th century itineraries to the graves of the Roman martyrs in the catacomb of St. Priscilla mention two female martyrs called Potentiana (Potenciana) andPraxedis (Praxidis). It is thought that these are in fact St. Praxedes and St. Pudentiana whom Pope Paschal moved to the current church.

The Legend of St. Zeno

St. Zeno was the eighth Bishop of Verona (362-380). Born in Africa, he was martyred under Gallienus. Zeno was active in missionary work, converted many faithful, and he fought against Arianism*.

* Arianism is a belief spread by Arius (250-336), a Christian presbyter from Alexandria, Egypt. He taught that Christ as the Son of God was created by God and is therefore subordinate to God the Father. This belief is based on the Gospel of John which says: "You heard me say, 'I am going away and I am coming back to you.' If you loved me, you would be glad that I am going to the Father, for the Father is greater than I." (John 14:28) Arius was declared a heretic by the First Council of Nicaea in 325, exonerated by the First Synod of Tyre in 335 and then, after his death, pronounced a heretic again at the First Council of Constantinople of 381.

He built a basilica at Verona, founded a convent, directed many charities, and wrote widely on ecclesiastical subjects including the virtues of suffering for the faith. The basilica, San Zenone, in Verona is dedicated to his honor. His feast day is April 12.

Points of Interest

- The main altarpiece, *St. Praxedes Gathering the Blood of the Martyrs,* painted by Domenico Muratori around 1730.
- The Column of the Flagellation—A portion of the pillar upon which Jesus was flogged and tortured before his crucifixion in Jerusalem.
- The crypt of St. Praxedes and St. Pudentiana.
- The St. Zeno chapel mosaics. In particular, the "Episcopa Theodora"; this fuels the debate on the ordination of women in the early church.

Address

St. Praxedes
9/a Via de Santa Prassede/ Via San Martino ai Monti
00184 Rome, Italy
Telephone: 06 48 82 456

St. Sebastian Outside the Walls

San Sebastiano Fuori le Mura

St. Sebastian was one of the original 7 pilgrim churches in Rome. It was replaced on the list of churches by Pope John Paul II for the Great Jubilee of 2000 with *Santuario della Madonna Del Divino Amore*, though some still prefer to visit the original 7 churches.

In 257, the Emperor Valerian issued a rescript which prohibited Christians from holding assemblies or entering subterranean places of burial inside the City of Rome. He also sent the Christian clergy into exile. Because they could not bury their dead within the city, Christians began burying their dead in a cemetery outside the city on a site that would become the modern day San Sebastiano. The 4th century cemetery was hidden amid a pagan cemetery and on top of an ancient Roman villa. Legend suggests that original relics of Sts. Peter and Paul were moved to this cemetery for safekeeping during this era. They were moved back to their original burial sites once the persecution ended. Graffiti in the San Sebastiano catacombs suggests this may be true, but not documented proof. The present church was built in 367 as a U shaped funerary hall by the Emperor Constantine. Because it was dedicated to Sts. Peter and Paul, it was known as a *Basilica Apostolorum* or Basilica of the Apostles.

A popular pilgrimage site, the hall was heavily used and required constant upkeep. Pope Hadrian I (772-795) restored the Hall. Tragedy would strike in 846. The Saracens invaded Italy through Ostia and marched on Rome. They were not a large enough force to take the city but they ransacked the Hall and anything else that was not protected by the city walls. The church was renovated again in the 9th century. At this time, it was renamed and rededicated to

St. Sebastian, who was buried in the cemetery in 288. In the 12th century, the U shape was closed in to form the church as seen today. A portico was added in the 15th century.

The church has a single center nave with no aisles, but arched recesses containing side chapels, instead. The carved wooden ceiling displays the Borghese arms and a depiction of the martyrdom of St. Sebastian by Anibale Durante. To the left of the entrance, there is a 4th century poem about St. Eutychius that was written by Pope Damasus I (366-384) and created by the calligrapher Furius Dionysius Philocalus. To the right is a bust of Christ that was created by Gian Lorenzo Bernini. This sculpture was the last work created by Bernini before he died. Over this statue is another inscription, also placed there by Pope Damasus. This inscription reads: "*You, who are looking for the names of Peter and Paul, should know that at one time their bodies were here.*"

The chapel on the left side of the church is above the tomb of St. Sebastian and was created under the direction of Cardinal Scipione Caffarelli-Borghese in the 17th century. The sculpture of St. Sebastian beneath the altar is by Antonio Giorgetti, a student of Bernini.

On the right side of the church is the Chapel of Relics that was decorated in 1625. This chapel houses one of the arrows that pierced St. Sebastian, the column to which the saint was tied, and a stone bearing the footprint of Christ called the *Domine Quo Vadis*. This stone is believed to be from the site southeast of Rome where the road crosses the Via Appia Ardeatina. It was here, while fleeing persecution, that St. Peter had a vision of Jesus. Peter asks Jesus "*Quo vadis, Domine?*" (Where are you going?), to which Jesus replies, "*Romam vado iterum crucifigi.*" ("I am going to Rome to be crucified again"). Peter returns to Rome to face his martyrdom.

The Catacombs of Saint Sebastian

The Catacombs of Saint Sebastian are small, but among the most popular of the catacombs visted in Rome. They contain mosaics, graffiti, pagan and Christian symbols, and the original tomb of St. Sebastian (now moved upstairs into the church). Visitors are escorted by a guide. The entrance to the catacombs is outside the church to the left of the portico.

St. Sebastian

Born at Narbonne, Gaul, St. Sebastian was a captain in the praetorian guards of Emperor Diocletian. He converted to Christianity and oversaw the conversion of other Roman guards. Diocletian sentenced him to death for this and ordered his fellow comrades to execute him. St. Sebastian was tied to a tree and shot several times with arrows. He was left for dead, but recovered thanks to the cures of a Christian woman, the widow of St. Castulus. St. Sebastian went to the Imperial Palace to testify his faith and was sentenced to death again by Diocletian. This time he was to be beaten to death in the Circus Maximus.

As a saint, his popularity grew in 680 and his relics were carried through Rome during a solemn procession. It was believed that this ended a pestilence that had been gripping the city. In art he is usually portrayed as being tied to a tree and shot with arrows. He is patron saint of archers, athletes, and soldiers, and as a protector of potential plague victims. His feast day in the Roman Catholic Church is January 2. In the Greek Orthodox Church his feast day is December 18.

St. Eutychius

Little is known about St. Eutychius. It is believed that he was a martyr of Thrace along with Heracleas and Plautus during the reign of the Emperor Diocletian. Another saint, by the same name, is said to have been martyred by pirates at Messina in the 6th century. As the inscription in Church of St. Sebastian was created in the 4th century, he could not be the latter. Yet, their legends are muddled. Still another St. Eutychius was the Archbishop of Constantinople.

There is a full biography of this saint and he is venerated in the Greek Orthodox Church. The feast day of the St. Eutychius that is found in St. Sebastian's is October 5.

St. Castulus

St. Castulus was the chamberlain (or valet) of the Emperor Diocletian and the husband of Irene of Rome. He was martyred for his faith in 286. He is popular in Bavaria after some of his relics were taken to Moosburg in 1171. In 1604, his relics were taken to the Church of St. Martin in Landshut, where they remain today. He is the patron saint of shepherds; invoked against skin infections (cellulitis), lightning, horse thieves, wildfires, and drowning. His feast day is March 26.

Points of Interest

- The catacombs which are entered to left of the portico.
- The *Martyrdom of St. Sebastian* by Anibale Durante.
- The statue of Jesus by Bernini.
- Note the floor decorations of the sun and bees, the heraldic symbols of Cardinal Francesco Barberini in the church.
- The sculpture of St. Sebastian at the altar in the first chapel on the left is by Antonio Giorgetti.
- The Relics Chapel with the footprint of Jesus (Quo vadis, Domine?).

Address

St. Sebastian Outside the Walls
Via Appia Antica, 136
00179 Rome, Italy
Telephone: 06 78 50 350

Church of St. Susanna at the Baths of Diocletian

Chiesa di Santa Susanna alle Terme di Diocleziano

The American Catholic Church in Rome

This church is situated on some of the highest ground along the eastern side of the city. This area was historically known as the collis Viminalis, one of the Seven Hills of Rome.

The Church of Saint Susanna is the American National Church in Rome. Cardinal William Henry O'Connell celebrated the first public Mass for the American community here on February 26, 1922. The church is constructed near the Baths of Diocletian. Beneath the nave of the church, archeologists have uncovered a mosaic floor which is believed to be from a 1st century Roman home. Originally a 4th century galleried hall, the site was designated a church during the reign of Constantine. The structure was remodeled by Pope Sergius in the late 7th century and again by Pope Leo III in 796. Further renovations were undertaken in the late 15th century and the 20th century.

The baroque façade seen today was created by Carlo Moderno and is considered his best work architecturally. The two statues in the niches on the lower level are St. Susanna and St. Felicitas. The statues in the niches on the upper levels are St. Caius and St. Gambinis. A large tympanum and finials cap the façade.

The inside of the church has a single nave with a shallow transept. The nave of the church has a semi-circular apse with 2 side chapels. The ceiling of the nave is made in polychromed gilt wood, carved to the design of Carlo Maderno. The statues are of the Old Testament prophets Ezekiel (back left), Daniel (front left), Jeremiah (back right), and Isaiah (front right). The frescoes are by Baldassare Croce and tell the story of Susanna and the Elders from the Old Testament Book of Daniel.

While many of the decorations harken to the Susanna found in the Old Testament, the church is, however, dedicated to a different Susanna, the daughter of Gabinius who lived on the site in the 3rd century. The relics of St. Felicity and 1 of her sons are beneath the main altar. To the left of the nave is the Chapel of St. Lawrence which has a shrine and tomb of St. Genesius. A series of frescos by Giovanni Battista Pozzo depicting Genesius' life can be seen in this chapel. The other chapel, the *Chapel of our Lady of Graces,* has frescoes of St. Benedict and St. Bernard.

Located on the Piazza Bernado, Santa Susanna is situated on some of the highest ground along the eastern side of the city. This area was known as the *collis Viminalis*, one of the Seven Hills of Rome. During the 1st century the Emperor Domitian decided to convert the house he was born in into the *Templum Gentis Flavia* as a memorial to the Flavian dynasty (his family). Archeologists believe that this memorial may be the 1st century remains that have been uncovered under Santa Susanna.

Susanna (Old Testament)

The story of Susanna is told in the Old Testament. Susanna is a virtuous wife of the wealthy Joakim. She is spied upon by two elders while she is bathing in her garden. They approach Susanna and proposition her and attempt to rape her. She refuses to have sexual relations with them and calls for help. The elders publically denounce her, and accuse her of adultery with another man. At Susanna's trial, Daniel asks each of the elders: "Under what tree did you see them (Susanna and the other man) being intimate with one another?" Each elder answers differently, exposing their story as a lie. Susanna is set free and the elders are put to death.

The story of Susanna is an addition to the book of Daniel (along with: Bel and the Dragon, The Prayer of Azariah, and the Song of the Three Jews). It is part of the Apocrypha/Deuterocanonical books of the Old Testament of Roman Catholic Bibles. It does not appear in most Protestant Bibles. Scholars believe that the story was written between 200-100 BCE.

St. Susanna

This Susanna, for whom the church was named, was a devout Christian who was martyred for her faith in the 3rd century. The daughter of Gabinus and niece of Pope Caius, she refused a marriage proposal from the Roman General Maxentius. Believing that the family might be Christian, Maxentius had Susanna brought to the Roman Forum where she was asked to prove her loyalty to the state by worshipping before the god Jupiter. She refused. She was beheaded at the command of the Emperor Diocletian, and buried in the catacombs. Her feast day is August 11.

St. Genesius

Genesius was an actor who was performing the role of a convert about to be baptized in a play satirizing the sacrament during the

3rd century. At the conclusion of the performance, he declared to the Emperor Diocletian that he had actually been converted by the ritual. The Emperor had him tortured and beheaded. Genesius is the patron saint of actors; his feast day is August 25.

St. Felicity (St. Felicitas of Rome)

St. Felicity was the widowed mother of 7 sons who was called to publically worship before the Roman gods. She refused and was martyred along with her sons during the reign of the Emperor Antonius Pius (138-161). She was buried in the catacomb of Maximus on the Via Salaria. Roman pilgrim itineraries and guides to the burial places of martyrs listed her burial place as being there. Today, some of her relics are in the Capuchin Church at Montefiascone in Tuscany, and some are in Santa Susanna in Rome. St. Felicity is first mentioned in the "Martyrologium Hieronymianum" in which her feast day is listed as January 25. For many years her feast was celebrated on November 23, and is now celebrated on July 10. She is the patron saint of parents who have lost a child.

Points of Interest

- The Shrine of St. Genesius.
- Five martyrs and saints are entombed in this church: Susanna, her father Gabinius, St. Felicitas of Rome, Pope St. Eleuterus, and Genesius of Rome.
- The ceiling of the nave and of the presbytery designed by Carlo Maderno.

Address

Saint Susanna at the Baths of Diocletian
Via XX (Venti) Settembre 15
00187, Rome, Italy
Telephone: 06 42 01 4554

St. Sylvester at the Head

San Silvestro in Capite

St. Sylvester was built between 757 and 767 as a monastery adjacent to the family home of Pope Paul I and his brother Pope Stephen II. The church was constructed on the ruins of a pagan temple, Aurelian's Temple of the Sun, which was dedicated to Apollo. The popes intended that the new church house the remains of early Christian saints/martyrs who were buried in the catacombs. Dedicated to St. Sylvester, it is called "in capite" because a portion of the head of St. John the Baptist is kept there as a relic.

Visitors today enter the church through an atrium and a large courtyard. The church itself has a central nave and two side aisles. The church has undergone several renovations. The Romanesque arcades and campinale (bell tower) were added in 1198. Extensive reconstruction by the architects Francesco da Volterra and Carlo Maderno took place from 1591-1601. Another restoration took place in 1681, and at this time the relics of Pope St. Sylvester, Pope Stephen I and Pope Dionysius were enshrined beneath the high altar. This altar is attributed to Michelangelo, though the evidence is limited. It is known that Piero Soderini, who was the patron of the church and friend of Michelangelo, commissioned the artist to create the altar in 1518. Historians have found letters between the two discussing the project, though there is no proof Michelangelo actually did the work himself. The altar does predate the 1681 renovations. The canopy above the altar is by Carlo Rainaldi and dates to 1667. The painting above the altar is the *Baptism of Constantine by Pope Sylvester*, and was painted by Ludovico Gimignani in 1688. The façade was created in 1703. The four statues across the top are: San Silvestro by Lorenzo Ouone, Saint Stephen by Michelangelo Borgognone, Saint Clare by Giuseppe Mazzoni, and Saint Francis by Vincenzo Felice. The confessio was added in 1906 to holds relics from the catacombs.

The church and cloister were given to the Order of St. Clare (better known as the Poor Clares) in the 13th century. They maintained the property until 1876.

In 1890, Pope Leo XIII designated St. Sylvester as the National Church of Great Britain in Rome. The church also serves the local Philippine community. It is served by the Irish Pallottine Fathers. The titular priest of the church is H.E. Desmond Cardinal Connell, Archbishop of Dublin, Ireland. Because this is the National Church of Great Britain, mass is said here in English.

St. Sylvester

Born in Rome, St. Sylvester served as Pope from January 31, 314 to December 31, 335. A friend of the Emperor Constantine, he oversaw the construction of several churches in Rome, including the Basilica of St. John Laterano, Santa Croce in Gerusalemme, and St. Peter's Basilica.

The 8th century document, *The Donation of Constantine*, discusses the Emperor's conversion, profession of faith, and instructions given to Sylvester for the church. The document alleges that Sylvester was offered the imperial crown, which he refused. Sylvester did not attend the First Council of Nicaea in 325, but he was represented. He was buried in the Catacomb of Priscilla on December 31.

Order of St. Clare

Originally referred to as the Order of Poor Ladies, the Poor Clares are a contemplative order founded by St. Clare of Assisi and St. Francis of Assisi on Palm Sunday in 1212. The sisters follow the *Rule of St. Clare* which was approved by Pope Innocent IV in 1253. There have been several spin-offs of the original order including the Colettine Poor Clares (P.C.C.), the Capuchin Poor Clares (O.S.C. Cap.) and the Alcantarines (O.F.M.). These branches follow different *Rules*. St. Clare is the patron saint of television. Her feast day is August 11. The American Cable television network, Eternal Word Television Network (EWTN), is operated by the Poor Clares.

Points of Interest

- The head of John the Baptist is in the first side chapel to the left upon entering the Church.
- The relics of Pope St. Sylvester, Pope St. Stephen I and St. Dionysius are beneath the high altar.
- *The Baptism of Constantine by Pope Sylvester*, painted by Ludovico Gimignani in 1688.

Address

St. Sylvester at the Head
Piazza San Silvestro
00187 Rome, Italy
Telephone: 06 67 97 775

Church of San Teodoro at the Bottom of the Palatino

Chiesa di San Teodoro

Greek Orthodox

San Teodoro is a tiny, round church that was built on top of the granaries of Agrippa by Pope Agatho (c. 678), and today is under the auspices of the Ecumenical Patriarchate of Constantinople (Greek Orthodox). The church is located along an ancient route between the Roman Forum and the Forum Boarium along the northwest foot of the Palatine Hill. Pope John Paul II granted use of the church to the Greek Orthodox Community of Rome in 2000.

The church is dedicated to the Roman soldier St. Theodore Tyro who was from Euchaita in Asia Minor. He was martyred at Amasea (Turkey) in 319 for refusing to worship in a pagan temple. It is believed that early Christians first occupied the site to make use of the abandoned granary and warehouses that were once located here. A Christian diaconia, called *ad scm theodorum*, was first documented on this site in the 8th century. The current round church was built in 1451 by Nicolas V and remodeled by Cardinal Francesco Barberini in 1674. The Capitoline Wolf statue, a 5th century bronze statue of a she-wolf suckling the twin infants Romulus and Remus, was kept in this church until the 16th century. Today, the statue is kept in the Musei Capitolini in Rome.

Behind the church there is a cemetery and crypt of Society of the Sacred Heart of Jesus (Paccanarists) that is decorated with human bones.

St. Theodore

Theodore was a "Tiro" or recently enlisted soldier or recruit serving in the Roman army at Amasea, which is the modern Amasya in northern Turkey. He was arrested when he refused to participate in pagan rites of worship. He was released with a warning. However, he then set fire to the temple of Cybele (the local mother-goddess) at Amasea for which he was condemned and thrown into a furnace. St. Theodore was widely venerated throughout the Eastern Church and was the first patron of Venice. The chapel of the Doge was dedicated to him until the relics of St. Mark were brought to the city in 828. St. Theodore of Amasea's feast day is February 8, or the 17, or the 1st Saturday in Lent.

Society of the Sacred Heart of Jesus (Paccanarists)

The Society of the Sacred Heart of Jesus was founded by Francois-Eleonor de Tournély and Prince Charles de Broglie on May 8, 1794. They were young seminarians from Saint-Sulpice who had emigrated to Belgium during the French Revolution. The group was forced to flee Belgium following the French victory at Fleurus (June 26, 1794). They settled in Germany and Austria and the order grew throughout Western Europe. They also became known as the Paccanarists as one of their more prominent leaders was Nicholas Paccanari, a native of Valsugnana, near Trent. He oversaw the adoption of the Original Jesuit Constitution by the new order which included the vows of religion and obedience to the sovereign pontiff. They also adopted the habit of the original Jesuits, a white tunic with the cowl. Paccanari was charged by Pope Pius VI with the care of the Paccanarist students who had been expelled from their seminary. He travelled to Rome to collect these young men three times; the third time he and his companions were arrested by the French military authorities and held in the Castel Sant'Angelo for four months. Upon his release he and the last group of young men were then expelled from the Roman Republic and discharged to Parma. The order continued to struggle, and in the early 1800s many became part of the Society of Jesus (Jesuits).

Points of Interest

- The pagan altar in the atrium in front of the church.
- The 6th century apse mosaic of Christ seated on a globe and wearing black clothing with a broad gold stripe. This garment was worn by Roman senators as an emblem of office. St. Paul is to his right and St. Peter is to his left.
- A portion of the Horrea Agrippiana brick arch can be seen on the south side of the church and from the western slope of the hill.

Address

Church of San Teodoro at the Bottom of the Palatino
Via di San Teodoro, 7
00186, Rome, Italy
Telephone: 06 67 86 624

The Basilica of Sts. Vitalis, Valeris, Gervase and Protase

Basilica di Santi Vitale e Compagni Martiri in Fovea

This church is below street level and easy to walk by without noticing.

The Basilica di San Vitale is a small church built in 400. This minor basilica was built using a financial endowment from a wealthy widow, Vestina. The church has a small columned entrance and covered portico, which is the oldest part of the church. This part of the structure dates back to the 5th century. The arms of Pope Sixtus IV are above the portico. The earliest records of the church date to the 499 synod of Pope Symmachus.

The church has been restored several times, most recently in 1956. It is likely that the original church was much larger than what is seen today. The current structure is believed to include only the nave and apse of the original edifice. The 17th century frescos are reason enough to visit San Vitale. The painting in the nave is of the *Martyrdom of St. Ignatius of Antioch*. The saint can be seen being attacked by 3 lions with a depiction of the ruined Coliseum in the background, above the saint's head. It is believed there may be 5th century paintings behind the wall of the apse. The paintings that are visible in the church were commissioned by the Society of Jesus, and were completed in 1603 by Commodi (apse), Ciampelli (the transept), Ligustri (the walls) and Fiammeri (the altars). They depict a variety of scenes in a style known as Tuscan mannerism. This style of art depicts twisting human poses, flattening of the pictorial space, and an emphasis on emotional content. The doors of the church are elaborately carved wood and depict the martyrdom of St. Vitale and his family.

Sts. Vitalis, Valeris, Gervase and Protase

The basilica is dedicated to St. Vitalis and his family. St. Vitalis is believed to be one of the seven sons of St. Felicity. St. Valeria was Vitalis' wife, and Sts. Gervasius and Protasius were their sons.

St. Vitale was a Roman officer and wealthy citizen of Ravenna. Vitale publically encouraged St. Ursicinus of Ravenna, a physician of Ravenna, to remain steadfast and true as he was being executed for being a Christian. Exposed as a Christian himself by this act, Vitale was arrested, tortured, and then buried alive by order of Paulinus. Vitale's wife, St. Valeria, was martyred in Milan. Their two sons, Gervase and Protasio, sold all their goods, and devoted their lives to prayer and meditation. Ten years later they were also martyred. The feast of St. Vitalis is April 28.

The most famous church that is dedicated to St. Vitalis is the octagonal San Vitale at Ravenna, Italy. This church is known for its mosaics and is one of eight buildings in Ravenna listed on the UNESCO World Heritage List.

Ignatius of Antioch

Ignatius of Antiochwas the third Bishop of Antioch in Syria and a student of John the Apostle. He was also called Theophorus, or *God Bearer*. Legend says that he was one of the children Jesus took in his arms and blessed. Ignatius was a patriarch of the church and is known as the author of 7 letters that had significant influence in the early church. His writings stressed the importance of unity in the early church, the loyalty to local bishops, and he was the first to use the term "catholic" to describe the universal Church. Ignatius was sentenced to death by the Emperor Trajan for refusing to renounce his Christianity. He was arrested and transported to Rome where he was thrown to the lions in the Coliseum on December 20, 107. He is venerated in the Eastern Orthodox Church (Feast day: December 20), the Coptic Orthodox Church of Alexandria (January 2), and the Roman Catholic Church (February 2).

Points of Interest

- The *Martyrdom of St. Ignatius of Antioch*, with a picture of the ruined Coliseum in the background.
- The paintings commissioned in 1603 by Commodi (apse), Ciampelli (the transept), Ligustri (the walls) and Fiammeri (pictures over the altars).
- The elaborately carved wooden doors that depict the martyrdom of Sts. Vitale, Valeria, Gervasio, and Protasio.
- Of note to pilgrims, the basilica still publishes instructions on how to acquire the Portiuncula Indulgence. This plenary indulgence can be earned by visiting the church and saying certain prayers on designated days. The prayers are: The Lord's Prayer and the Creed, and a prayer for the intentions of the Holy Father. The supplicant must also go to Confession and receive Communion. The designated days are:
    - The Friday of the second week of Lent
    - Feast of San Vitale (April 28)
    - Solemnity of the Sts. Peter and Paul (June 29)

- Recurrence of the indulgence of "portiuncola" (August 2)*
- Solemnity of the dedication of the basilica (October 25)
- Any day of the year chosen by the faithful

Address

The Basilica of St. Vitalis
Via Nazionale
194 B-00184 Rome, Italy
Telephone: 06 48 23 338

---

* Portiuncola is a town about three-quarters of a mile from Assisi where St. Francis of Assisi recognized his vocation on February 24, 1208. The small Portiuncola Chapel is where his conversion occurred and today is inside the Basilica of Santa Maria degli Angeli. The chapel is tiny; it is twenty-two feet by thirteen and a half feet. In 1216, Christ and the Virgin Mary appeared to St. Francis and asked what he desired most. St. Francis asked for a full pardon of all sins for all who entered a Church, repented, and confessed their sins. This indulgence was granted, if the faithful perform certain tasks. Initially these tasks, the Portiuncula Indulgence, could only be performed in the Portiuncula chapel between the afternoon of August 1st and sunset on August 2nd. Pope Sixtus IV later extended it to all churches of the first and second orders of St. Francis. (The Franciscans)

Other Sites of Interest

The Coliseum was used for gladiatorial contests and public spectacles such as mock sea battles, animal hunts, executions, re-enactments of famous battles, and dramas. The gladiatorial contests were always sponsored by private individuals not, as popularly depicted, by the state.

Archaeology and Art History Library

Biblioteca di Archeologia e Storia dell'Arte (BiASA)

The Museo del Palazzo di Venezia is located in the Palazzo Venezia which is a Renaissance palace built between 1455 and 1467 by the Venetian Cardinal Pietro Barbo, later Pope Paul II. The museum opened in 1920 under the direction of the art historian Federico Hermanin who had been selected to create a National Museum for Italy. He included many works which had been gathered in preparation for an International Art Exhibition in 1911. These included pieces from the collections of the Kircher Museum, the Galleria Nazionale d'Arte Antica di Palazzo Barberini, and the Castel Sant'Angelo and form the basis of the collection seen today. There are a wide variety of objects, including marble pieces from the thirteenth century, Coptic materials, more than 1200 pieces of weapons and firearms once owned by the prince Ladislao Odescalchi, porcelains, bronzes, furniture, ceramics, and pottery. (To say it is eclectic is an understatement. It is kind of like walking through someone's attic.) Among the masterpieces housed in the museum are Gian Lorenzo Bernini's terracotta *Angel with the Scroll* (1667-1668); Alessandro Algardi's bust of Pope Innocent X (1644-55); an ivory casket of Byzantine origin that is decorated in high relief with the stories of David (c. 9th century); and Donato Creti's painting of the Dance of Nymphs (1724-1725). The building was chosen by Mussolini as the Prime Minister's Office, so the museum was closed and the Palace became the Fascist headquarters from 1929-1943. Today it is open again as a museum on Tuesday-Sunday from 8:30 am-7:30 pm. One little secret to the museum: visitors can download an mp3 audio guide and .pdf from the website below rather than paying for one at the entrance.

The Archaeology and Art History Library of the National Library of Rome is a treasure in and of itself. Co-located with the museum, it is the largest artistic and archaeological library in Italy. Its holdings include books and manuscripts dating to the 16th century. There is also a branch library that is housed in the Palace of the Collegio Romano near the church of St. Ignatius Loyola. This palace was the headquarters of the Society of Jesus for centuries and was built between 1581 and 1584. Open to the public on Wednesdays from 9:30 am-5:00 pm, it includes a large cross-shaped hall with an adjacent reading room. The design was originally attributed to Ammannati, but was actually designed by the Jesuit Giuseppe Valeriani. It includes beautiful hand-carved double layer shelving that was built in the 1600s and is original to the Collegio Romano.

An interesting and little known collection is their cache of late 18th to early 20th century theatrical posters. It includes more than 2,500 posters purchased in 1926 from the collection of Rudolph Kanzler, who had taught Gregorian chant and the history of costume in the drama school of St. Cecilia for 20 years. They also have a very extensive collection of Italian classic theater and foreign manuscripts, especially French, from the 16th to the 19th century. The library is widely used by academics interested in Roman archeology and topography, but many of the other collections are rarely used. Their card catalog has been digitized, but some sections, like the theater and music, are separate from general catalog of the library. So researchers have to dig just to find the card catalog for the collection. Here is a hint: there is an old card catalog, both for authors and for subjects located in the Cruise Room of the Collegio Romano, and it is easier to navigate.

Address

Main Library/ National Museum of Venezia Palace
Via del Plebiscito, 118
00196 Rome, Italy
Telephone: 06 69 99 41

Museum audio guide: http://museopalazzovenezia.beniculturali.it/

Library Branch near St. Ignatius of Loyola Church
Via del Collegio Romano, 27
00186 Rome, Italy
Telephone: 06 6797877

Bernini's Elephant Obelisk

The Pulcino della Minerva

In front of the Basilica of Saint Mary above Minerva stands *The Pulcino della Minerva*, an elephant sculpture designed by Gian Lorenzo Bernini and carved by his student Ercole Ferrata in 1667. The statue was inspired by the *Hypnerotomachia Poliphili* ("Poliphilo's Dream of the Strife of Love"), a 15th century novel by Francesco Colonna. In the book, the main character meets an elephant made of stone carrying an obelisk. Because it is short and fat, locals nicknamed the statue "Porcino" ("Piggy"). It is officially called *Pulcino*, the Italian word for a small or little one. The elephant symbolizes the earth and the obelisk symbolizes the heavens. The elephant itself, on close inspection, is smiling. The Romans say that if visitors walkaround the back of the elephant they will notice that his tail is pulled to the left as if it were defecating. His rear end is pointing toward the office of Father Giuseppe Paglia, a Dominican friar, who was one of Bernini's main adversaries.

Address

Piazza della Minerva

Coliseum

One cannot write a book about Rome and not include the Coliseum. Also known as the Flavius amphitheater, it is the largest ever built in the Roman Empire. The name "Colosseum" is derived from the Colossus, a large statue of Nero that once stood nearby. Construction was started on the Coliseum in 72 by the emperor Vespasian and it was completed in the year 80 under Emperor Titus. The opening festival lasted 100 days, during which over 5,000 animals were killed in the arena.

The stadium is elliptical in shape and covers 6 acres. It is 615 feet long by 510 feet wide and can seat 50,000 spectators. It has 3 seating levels above the ground floor which were reserved based on social rank. The lowest level was reserved for nobles and senior military commanders; the middle level was reserved for wealthy citizens; and the top level was used by the general public.

The Coliseum was used for gladiatorial contests and public spectacles such as mock sea battles, animal hunts, executions, re-enactments of famous battles, and dramas. It is interesting to note that the gladiatorial contests, which were called *munera,* were always sponsored by private individuals not, as popularly depicted, held by the state. The uppermost portion of the structure had a retractable awning, known as the *velarium* that kept the sun and rain off spectators. To accommodate the large crowds of spectators, operators used numbered pottery shards, which served as tickets and directed attendees to specific rows and sections of the arena. Access to the sections was via vomitoria (singular vomitorium), passageways that opened into a levels of seats from either below or behind. The strategic placement of these vomitora allowed operators to rapidly fill and empty the arena when necessary. (The word is derived from the Latin for rapid release, and is the same root that the word *vomit*is derived from.)

Just outside the Coliseum is the *Arch of Constantine* which was built in 315 to mark the victory of Constantine over Maxentius at the Battle of Milvian Bridge. This is the battle that led the Emperor Constantine to convert to Christianity.

Address

Piazza del Colosseo

The Excubitorium of the Firemen

Excubitorium della VII Coorte dei Vigili

In the Trastevere district, the Excubitorium is a series of chambers 26 feet below street level and 65 feet to the south of San Crisogono, at the corner of the present Via Montefiore and Via della Settima Coorte. Originally part of a home during the time of Hadrian (76-138), the rooms were believed to have been used by firemen as a watch station against fires. There is a central room with a hexagonal fountain that has black-and-white mosaic tiles and a shrine which may have been built during the reign of Septimius Severus and Caracalla during the 2nd century. Several bits of graffiti that were created by the fireman were initially discovered, but are rapidly being lost. Visits to the site can be arranged through the group Roma Sotterranea: http://www.sotterraneidiroma.it/. Note: this site is in Italian and they do not have an English page. Please use an online translation page to make things easier and email them.

Address

Excubitorium della VII Coorte dei Vigili
Via della Settima Coorte 9,
Trastevere, Rome, Italy

The Forty Hour Device

The main altar in the Church of Santa Maria dell'Orto in Trastevere has a "40 hour device." Built in 1848 by Luigi Clementi, it holds 213 candles that are timed to burn for 40 hours. It is based on a medieval Easter tradition that evolved into 40 hours of prayer that starts on Good Friday and ends on Easter Sunday. The device is still used annually for the Mass of the Last Supper on Maundy Thursday, though the candles are extinguished at midnight.

Address

Church of St. Mary of the Garden
Via Anicia, 10
00153, Rome, Italy

Forum

Forum Magnum

The Forum was the heart of ancient Rome. The oldest part of Rome, it was used for triumphal processions, elections, public speeches, criminal trials, as a central market, and for gladiatorial matches. Today it is a piazza surrounded by the ruins of several important buildings in the center of the city. The Roman Forum is unique in that it was not designed on a grid pattern like other imperial city centers. Many important imperial buildings and shrines were located around the Forum based on the topography and available land. Interestingly, because the original site was on marshy ground, sediment from both the flooding of the Tiber River and the erosion of the surrounding hills has caused the land around the Forum to be rising for centuries. Roman residents simply paved over the debris as the ground around the buildings began to rise. This has created a boon for archeologists.

The main tourist sites today include the Tabularium, which was the official records office of ancient Rome, and the offices of many city officials. Inside the same building are the remains of the temple of Veiovis. Visitors can also see the Temple of Saturn, a temple dedicated to the god Saturn, which dates to 497 BCE; the Regia, or Royals residence, that dates to the 8th century BCE; the white marble Arch of Septimius Severus, a triumphal arch that dates to 203 CE and was erected to commemorate the Parthian victories of Emperor Septimius Severus; the Rostra, a speaker's platform that was originally built in the 4th century BCE; and the Curia Julia constructed in 283 CE by Diocletius and which served as the location where the Senate assembled. The Gemonian Stairs, a flight of steps that served as a place of execution are also a popular attraction. The condemned were strangled before their bodies were bound and thrown down the stairs. Called the Stairs of Mourning by locals, it was considered a disgrace to be executed on these steps. (Which begs the question: Was there an honorable or preferred place to be executed?) Yet, even the Emperor Vitellius was executed on the stairs in 69. There are also numerous temples, arches, and basilicas on the site. Visitors could easily spend several days exploring just the Forum. Many of the popular tourist sites are all linked by the Via Sacra, the main road through the Forum; this is a good way to start.

Italian Clocks/ Italian Time

It is easy to accuse Romans of being on Italian time. But in reality, there actually was such of thing. Until the Napoleonic Era, the Italian hour was not a uniform 60 minutes in length. It varied as the seasons changed. Italian *time* or Italian hours used a clock that had 6 rather than 12 numbers on it (the 6 is in the 12 position) and had only one clock hand which reached the 6 at sunset. The first hour of the day started at sunset with the ringing of the Angelus bell. So looking at the clock indicted the time left until sunset the next day. These clocks were reset every two weeks to adjust for the changes in the duration of daylight as the seasons changed. This manner of timekeeping dates to the medieval ages and is attributed to the monastic tradition of dividing the day according to prayer times. Monasteries and some churches still do this; it is called the Liturgy of the Hours (or *The Divine Office*). The architect Domenico Martinelli's treatise entitled *Horologi Elementari* published in 1669 provides a good explanation of how these clocks were used. He calls them "6 hour clocks in the manner of Rome". Examples of these clocks can still be seen. There is one in the courtyard of Palazzo del Commendatore which dates from 1743 (it is on the via Borgo di Santo Spirito near the Vatican).

Piazza of the Four Fountains

Piazza delle Quattro Fontane

At the narrow intersection of the Via delle Quattro Fontane and Via del Quirinale adjacent to the Church of San Carlo stand 4 fountains that were built during the pontificate of Pope Sixtus V between 1588 and 1593. The fountains represent the River Tiber as the symbol of Rome; the River Arno as the symbol of Florence; the Goddess Diana as the symbol of Chastity; and the Goddess Juno as the symbol of Strength.

Pope Joan

Via Vicus Papissa

Legend says that Pope Joan was a 9th century English woman who disguised herself as a monk. She used the name John Anglicus. In time, she was elected to the papacy. She maintained her guise until Easter 855. Following mass at St. Peter's, her papal procession was surrounded by excited crowds and well-wishers. Her frightened horse reared, throwing her to the ground, causing her to go into premature labor, and revealing her secret. After giving birth to a son, she was flogged, tied by her feet to her horse, and dragged through the streets of Rome. She was then killed on the banks of the Tiber and her body buried in a modern day shrine. Another version of her story is that she retired to an isolated convent, while her son grew up to become the Bishop of Ostia.

The main source for the life of Pope Joan can be traced to the writings of Martin von Trappau which date to 1265. Her story is also chronicled in the Dominican priest Jean de Mailly's 13th century *Chronica Universalis Mettensis* and Giovanni Boccaccio wrote about her in *De Mulieribus Claris* (1353).

The story of Pope Joan may also be connected to that of Guglielma of Bohemia, a very real woman who preached an alternative, feminized version of Christianity in the 1200s. Rumored to be the daughter of the King of Bohemia, she arrived in Milan in the mid-1200s and set up house living independently. She garnered a reputation for pious living and healing and soon had many followers. Though she denied it, many including Sister Maifreda da Pirovano, believed she was the Holy Spirit, incarnate in the form of a woman. When Guglielma died on August 24, 1281, she was buried in the Cistercian Abbey of

Chiaravalle della Colomba. After her death, her followers organized themselves into a church and elected their own Pope, Sister Maifreda, whom they called the "Papessa". Their activities were noticed by the Dominican tribunal charged with conducting inquisitions in Milan. In 1300, after a lengthy inquiry, the Dominicans labeled the deceased Guglielma and 30 of her living followers as heretics. Three were sentenced to death, including Sister Maifreda, who was burned at the stake. The Dominicans also set about expunging any record of the saint and her heresy. They dismantled her tomb, burned her bones, outlawed her feast day (the forth Sunday in April which is still celebrated locally in Lombardi), and destroyed the local shrines that had been constructed to her. But they missed a few things.

In the church of Church of San Andrea, Brunate, Italy, there remains today a painting of St. Guglielma. She is dressed in purple and wearing 3 golden rings which may be symbolic of the Holy Trinity. Her left hand is raised in a blessing. She appears to have been wearing a golden crown at one point in time, but it has faded. Though it is impossible to know, one of the figures kneeling in prayer may be Sister Maifreda. There is evidence that other frescos depicting the life of the Guglielma accompanied this one, but this is the only one that survives.

There is also documentation that a statue of the Female Pope was included among the busts of the popes that line the nave of the Cathedral in Siena, Italy. It was listed as *Johannes VIII, femina ex Anglia*. However, Pope Clement VIII (1592-1605), to prevent scandal, had the bust transformed into Pope Zacharias.

There is an even stranger continuation of the legend in esoteric circles. Sister Maifreda's family, the Viscontis of Milan, some 150 years later would commission a set of hand painted Tarot cards. Included in that deck there is a card called the *Papesse* which tarot historians say is a depiction of Sister Maifreda. On the card, she is wearing the three-tiered crown of the papacy, but her clothes are very plain, more like those of a nun. She holds a book in her right hand, a traditional symbol for this card. More modern tarots decks retain the card, but it is now called *The High Priestess* or the *Hierophant*.

The Church denied the legend of St. Joan in 1570 along with the idea that all popes since Joan are carried around in a chair with a hole in the bottom, to allow the cardinals to check for their manliness.

Whether one believes the story or not, there is an ancient portico in Rome which marks the spot where she allegedly gave birth. It is three blocks from the Coliseum, at the foot of the hill leading up to the medieval SS. Quattro Coronati abbey-fortress. Coming from the Basilica of San Clemente, it is one block south of the church on the corner of Via del Quattro and Via del Querceti, Rome 00184

Points of Interest

- Papal processions no longer travel along the street, *Via Vicus Papissa,* where she gave birth. Due to its narrowness, processions never actually used this street.
- In the Siena Cathedral there is evidence that there was a bust of *Johannes VIII, femina ex Anglia* among a line of papal busts.
- The shrine is a doorway with a gate jutting out from the wall at the corner.
    - It is traditional to leave a flower on the site.

Address

Corner of Via del Quattro and Via del Querceti
00184 Rome, Italy

The Protestant Cemetery

Cimitero Protestante

The Protestant Cemetery in Rome has often been known as the English cemetery, though now it is officially called the Cimitero Acattolico (The Non-Catholic Cemetery for Foreigners in Testaccio, Rome). It dates from 1732, when records show that papal land was dedicated to bury the remains of non-Catholic foreigners, mostly Protestants from northern Europe who, according to church law, could not be buried in consecrated ground in Rome. It is located near the Porta San Paolo alongside the Pyramid of Cestius. The cemetery is divided into two sections. The newer section is well landscaped and contains the graves of English poets John Keats (1795-1821) and Percy Bysshe Shelley (1792-1822). "It might make one in love with death, to think that one should be buried in so sweet a place," wrote Shelley, not long before he drowned near Viareggio and was buried here. His grave bears the Latin inscription, *Cor Cordium* (Heart of Hearts), and, a few lines of "Ariel's Song" from Shakespeare's The Tempest:

> *"Nothing of him that doth fade*
> *But doth suffer a sea-change*
> *Into something rich and strange."*

The cemetery became a popular tourist attraction during the 19th century. When Oscar Wilde visited he called it "the holiest place in Rome." Other notable graves include: Antonio Gramsci (1891-1937), the Italian political philosopher; Karl Brullov (1799-1852), the Russian painter; Hendrik Andersen (1872-1940), a sculptor, born in Norway but then an immigrant to the US; August von Goethe (1789-1830), the only child of Johann Wolfgang von Goethe; Richard

Wyatt (1795-1850), English sculptor; and William Wetmore Story (1819-1895), a prominent American sculptor and designer of the *Angel of Grief* statue.

Address

The Protestant Cemetery (Cimitero protestante)
Main Entrance
Via Caio Cestio, 6
00153 Roma
Telephone: 06 5741900
Monday-Saturday from 9:00 am-5:00 pm (last entrance: 4:30 pm)
Sundays and public holidays 9:00 am-1:00 pm (last entrance: 12:30 pm)

The Pyramid of Cestius

Piramide di Caio Cestio or Piramide Cestia

The Pyramid of Cestius was built around 12 BCE as a tomb for Gaius Cestius. He was a member of the Roman collegium, Septemviri Epulonum, and a prominent citizen of the city. It is made of brick-faced concrete that has been covered with white marble and stands on a travertine base. The pyramid is 100 Roman feet (97.1 feet) square at the base and 125 Roman feet (121 feet) high. The inside is a barrel vaulted chamber that was decorated with frescos, some of which can still be seen today. Look for the images of 4 winged victories in the vaulting. There is also graffiti from the 1700s and earlier visitors. The pyramid was incorporated into the Aurelian Walls between 271 and 275 and is close to the Porta San Paolo and the Protestant Cemetery. It was a frequent stop on the Grand Tour during the 18th and 19th centuries. When visiting the site in 1887, Thomas Hardy wrote the poem, *Rome: At the Pyramid of Cestius near the Graves of Shelley and Keats*, in which he questioned: "Who, then was Cestius, and what is he to me?" Today the pyramid is located on a busy thoroughfare. For a better view with less traffic, go inside the Protestant Cemetery to the northwest side.

Address

Pyramid of Cestius
Piazza di Porta San Paolo
Piazza Ostiense
I-00186 Rome, Italy

Spanish Steps

Scalinata della Trinità dei Monti

The widest staircase in Europe, the Spanish Steps are between the Piazza di Spagna at the base and Piazza Trinità dei Monti and Church of Trinità dei Monti at the top. The 138 steps were built with money donated by French Diplomat Étienne who wanted to link the Bourbon Spanish Embassy and the Trinità dei Monti church to the piazza below. At that time the French Bourbon government was in control of the Spanish Bourbon embassy. The stairway was designed by Francesco de Sanctis and Alessandro Specchi. The winding design of the steps, particularly on the upper level, makes them less steep and easier to climb. In the Spanish Piazza below there is an early Baroque fountain, Fontana della Barcaccia ("Fountain of the Old Boat"), built in 1627-1629 by Pietro Bernini, the father of Gian Lorenzo Bernini. The house on the corner to the right is where the English poet John Keats lived and died in 1821. It is open to the public as The Keats-Shelley Memorial House museum. Lord Byron lived across the square at #66. The Spanish Steps are a popular meeting place, but do not try to stop and eat there. It is illegal to 'picnic' in Rome and the police will ask those eating to leave.

Coffee and Tea near the Piazza di Spagna

If looking for a traditional English cup of tea, "Babington's Tea Rooms" are at No 23, Piazza di Spagna, at the foot of the Spanish steps. Established in 1893 by two English ladies, Anna Maria Babington and Isabel Cargill, this shop and café consistently is ranked as one of Rome's best. If coffee is preferred, Antico Caffè Greco is also nearby. Opened in 1760, it is perhaps the best known and oldest coffee bar in Rome. Stendhal, Goethe, Byron, Franz Liszt, Keats, Henrik Ibsen, Hans Christian Andersen, and Felix Mendelssohn all used to hang out here. It is located at 86, Via dei Condotti in Rome, right up the street from the Spanish steps.

Trevi Fountain

The largest baroque fountain in Rome, the Trevi Fountain is located on the site of the Aqua Virgo, one of the ancient aqueducts that supplied water to the city.

The Trevi Fountain is the largest baroque fountain in the city. Standing some 85 feet high and 65 feet wide, it is also one of the iconic symbols of Rome. Daily, some 2,824,800 cubic feet of water pour through the fountain. The fountain sits at the junction of three roads and the end of the Acqua Vergine, an aqueduct that provides fresh water to the city of Rome. Romans have a tradition of building large fountains at the end of aqueducts, from which locals could draw their water. The first aqueduct to provide water to this site was the Aqua Virgo, which was built by Marcus Agrippa in 19 BCE. It served Rome for more than four hundred years until the Ostrogoths, led by King Vitigis, sacked the city and destroyed the water system in 537.

In 1453, Pope Nicholas V repaired the aqueduct and renamed it the Acqua Vergine. He had a simple basin built in the Piazza de'Crociferi by architect Leon Battista Alberti for the people to use. The fountain was moved to its present location in 1570 by Pope Pius V, though it faced west. Pope Urbanus VIII decided that he wanted to be able to see the fountain from the Papal Palace on the Quirinal Hill, so he hired Gian Lorenzo Bernini in 1629 to redesign the fountain. This design was never realized, but eventually the fountain was turned. Unfortunately, the construction of Palazzo Castellani in 1868-1869 (the large white and pink building across from the fountain) hides the view.

In 1730, Pope Clemens XII held a contest to design a new fountain. Many important architects participated, and Nicola Salvi won. Much of what is seen today is his design. He, however, died in 1751 and Giuseppe Pannini finished the project.

The design has three elements: a façade; statues; and a reef. The statue in the center is *Ocean* carved by Pietro Bracci. To his left there is the statue of *Abundance* holding the horn of plenty. To his right there is a statue of *Health*, wearing a laurel wreath and holding a cup with a snake drinking from it. Salvi's design had statues of Agrippa and the Virgin where the statues of *Abundance* and *Health* are now. Pannini changed that. He included images of Agrippa and the Virgin in the reliefs just above the current statues. The symbolism for including these two characters is that the Virgin identified the source of the water to be used in the region and Agrippa commanded the construction the first aqueduct. Above the relief there are 4 allegorical statues that represent the good effects of water on the earth. The first statue on the left holds the horn of plenty which symbolizes abundance of fruits. The next statue is holding wheat and represents fertility of the land. The third statue is holding a cup and grapes which symbolizes autumn and the harvest. The fourth statue, on the far right is covered with flowers and symbolizes the joy of gardens. Throughout the fountain there are some 30 species of plants that are carved as if they were growing from the rock. The various inscriptions relate to the Popes and their different renovations over the centuries.

It is tradition to throw a coin in the fountain. In ancient times, Romans used to throw coins in fountains, rivers, or lakes and ask the gods of water to favor their journey and help them go back home safely. Another local legend says that those who drink from the fountain can be sure to come back to Rome. Today the water of the fountain is recycled and visitors can drink from the cast iron pipes located on the steps. There is also a tradition that water from the Trevi Fountain can solidify a relationship. The story goes that if a boy is leaving Rome, he should come to the fountain with his fiancé. They should drink the water with a brand new cup, after which they must break the cup to seal the permanence and strength of their love.

The church positioned diagonally to the fountain is the Church of Sts. Vincent and Anastasius. A small church dedicated to St. Anastasio was recorded at this location in the 10th century. The current church was built by architect Martino Longhi the Younger for Cardinal Giulio Mazzarino (Jules Mazarin) for the Holy Year 1650. It was intended to serve as the parish church for the area. In 2002, Pope John Paul II presented the church to the Bulgarian Orthodox Church, and it has been used as the Sts. Cyril and Methodius Bulgarian Orthodox Parish church in Rome. Still technically owned by the Roman Catholic Church, it is under the jurisdiction of Patriarch Maxim of Sofia. The carving of a woman above the entrance is said to be a portrait of Cardinal Mazarin's favorite niece, Maria Mancini. The church was renovated in the 19th century and the inside is decorated in the neoclassical style. To the left of the altar is a plaque listing the 22 popes from the time of Sixtus V (1585) to Leo XIII (1903) who bequeathed their hearts and viscera to the church. This practice was known as *Praecordia*. Due to the long interval between the death of the pope and his burial the inner organs (liver, heart, and lungs) were removed to avoid their deterioration. They are kept in marble urns.

Address

Trevi Fountain
Via di San Vincenzo
Rome, Italy

Closing Thoughts

Why did I write this book? As I stumbled across hidden little gems in my explorations of Rome, I needed something that reminded me where the lesser known churches were and what was inside. To be perfectly honest, I can't name the 7 hills of Rome off the top of my head and I have no idea when the Flavian Dynasty was; but, I have this great little notebook that I started that has all those sort of details.

That's really what this book is. It is a prettier version of my notes on the things I found. I am still finding things, and I'll put them on the website for the book at www.BijouxPress.com. I hope these notes are helpful to you. And I hope you'll join us to compare notes and share the treasures you find as you go *Walking through Rome*.

Appendix A

Timeline of Roman and Church History

Ancient Rome

753 (BCE)	The City of Rome is founded by Romulus and Remus
760	The Rape of the Sabine Women
715	The Roman King Numa Pompilius creates a 12-month calendar
700	The Etruscan civilization begins
616-579	The First Etruscan King of Rome, Tarquinius Priscus, establishes the Forum and Circus Maximum
565	The Servian Walls are built
510	Temple of Jupiter is completed and consecrated

The Republic

509	Lucius Brutus Junior founds the Republic and expels the Etruscans
451	Rome developed the first law code, the Twelve Tables
390	The Gauls attempt to invade Rome
312	The Via Appia and Aqua Appia are constructed. (First major road and aqueduct)
264-261	The First Punic War against Ancient Carthage (Rome is victorious)
218-202	The Second Punic War against Ancient Carthage. Hannibal crosses the Alps (Rome is victorious)

168	The Romans conquer Greece in the Macedonian War
149-146	The Third Punic War against Ancient Carthage (Rome is victorious)
73-71	Slave revolt led by the gladiator Spartacus. Spartacus is killed
51	Julius Caesar conquers Gaul

Imperial Rome

49	Julius Caesar crosses the Rubicon
47	Julius Caesar invades Egypt and proclaims Cleopatra queen
44	Julius Caesar assassinated on the Ides of March (15th)
30	Mark Antony (Roman triumvir) and Cleopatra committed suicide
0	**Traditional year in which Christ was born and the calendar changes from Before the Common Era (BCE) to the Common Era (CE).**
27	Augustus is made Rome's first emperor
30	Christ is crucified in Jerusalem
42	St. Peter the Apostle arrives in Rome
64	Rome burns, during the reign of Emperor Nero
65	Christians are first persecuted and killed by Nero
67	St. Peter is crucified in Rome and St. Paul is executed
72	Construction on the Flavian Amphitheatre (Colosseum) is begun
79	Vesuvius erupts, burying the towns of Pompeii and Herculaneum
79-91	Pope Anacletus constructs an oratory over the grave of St. Peter on Vatican Hill
96-138	The Roman Empire is considered to have reached its pinnacle under the Emperors Trajan (96-117) and Hadrian (117-138)

125	Emperor Hadrian has the Pantheon rebuilt in Rome and the wall built in England
270	The Aurelian wall is begun

Early Medieval Rome

285	Diocletian divides empire into four sections ruled by two co-emperors. This division will become the Western Roman Empire and the Byzantine Empire
303	Diocletian persecutes Christians
312	Constantine the Great converts to Christianity and wins the Battle of Milvian Bridge
325	First Council of Nicea establishes theNicene Creed
328	The first St. Peter's Basilica is constructed
380	Emperor Theodosius makes Christianity the official religion of Rome
382	St. Jerome is commissioned by Pope Damasus I to create the Vulgate, a translation of the Bible into Latin.
395	The empire is divided into East and Western Roman Empires
410	Rome is sacked by the Goths
452	Attila the Hun invades Italy, does not invade Rome
455	Rome is sacked by the Vandals
475	The fall of the Western Roman Empire
606	The Pantheon becomes a Christian church
778	Charlemagne conquers Italy and Rome
800	Charlemagne is crowned Holy Roman Emperor in St. Peter's Basilica by Pope Leo III on Christmas Day
846	Saracens sack St. Peter's Basilica
847	Pope Leo IV builds Leonine Walls enclosing the Vatican

961	King Otto the Great of Germany becomes the Holy Roman Emperor
1054	The Great Schism: Division of the church into the Western Roman Catholic Church and the Eastern Orthodox (Greek) branches

High Middle Ages

1084	The city of Rome is attacked by the Normans
1096-1099	First Crusade
1108	The church of San Clemente is in this year rebuilt
1140	The church of Santa Maria in Trastevere is rebuilt
1144-1155	Second Crusade
1187-1192	Third Crusade
1200	Rome becomes an independent commune
1202-1204	Fourth Crusade
1212	The Children's Crusade
1217-1221	Fifth Crusade
1228-1229	Sixth Crusade
1232	The cloisters in the Basilica of St. John Lateran are finished
1248-1254	Seventh Crusade
1270	Eighth Crusade
1271-1272	Ninth Crusade
1300	Pope Boniface VIII proclaims the First Jubilee Year establishing the practice of pilgrimages
1309	The Papacy is moved to Avignon
1348	The Black Death

Roman Renaissance

1377	The Papacy returns to Rome
1409	Papacy moves to Pisa
1452	First St. Peter's Basilica is demolished; construction on the present day Basilica is begun

1458	Eastern Empire defeated by the Ottoman Turks
1506	150 Swiss soldiers commanded by Captain Kasparvon Silenen, of Canton Uri, enter the Vatican and form the Swiss Guard
1508	Michelangelo paints the Sistine Chapel
1517	Martin Luther writes The Ninety-Five Theses on the Power and Efficacy of Indulgences and starts Protestant revolution
1521	Pope Leo X excommunicates Martin Luther
1527	Charles V's troops loot Rome
1538	England's King Henry VIII excommunicated by Pope Clement VII for divorcing his first wife, Catherine of Aragon
1547	Michelangelo is appointed by Pope Paul III as the main architect of St. Peter's Basilica

Baroque Period

1611	The King James Version of the Bible is completed in England
1626	New St. Peter's Basilica is completed
1633	Galileo is condemned for heresy
1656	Bernini creates colonnades in St. Peter's Square, Rome
1658	Borromini creates Sant' Agnese in Agone in Rome
1721	Bonnie Prince Charlie is born in Rome
1735	The Spanish Steps are built in Rome
1762	The Trevi Fountain is completed in Rome
1797	Napoleon Bonaparte captures Rome
1799	Napoleon Bonaparte forced out of Rome by the Russians and the Austrians

Risorgimento (The Resurgence)

1801	Napoleon Bonaparte retakes Italy and Rome

1809	Napoleon Bonaparte moves the Vatican archives to Paris
1815	Napoleon Bonaparte defeated at the Battle of Waterloo
1821	The English poet John Keats dies in Rome
1822	The English Poet Percy Bysshe Shelley drowns near Viareggio and is buried in Rome
1860	Garibaldi takes Naples and Sicily
1861	The Kingdom of Italy is founded with Turin as its capital
1870	Rome becomes part of the Italian kingdom

Modern Rome

1911	The Vittorio Emanuele monument is completed
1915	Italy enters World War I
1919	Woodrow Wilson, the first U.S. president to visit the Vatican, meets with Pope Benedict XV as part of his European tour after World War I
1922	Benito Mussolini marches on Rome and becomes the 27th Prime Minister of Italy
1929	Vatican City is created by the Lateran Treaty
1924-1939	Mussolini's public works programs
1940	World War II begins
1943 (September)	Germans occupy Rome
1944	Rome is liberated by the Allied troops
1957	Treaty of Rome signed which leads to the establishment of the European Economic Community (EEC) and the European Atomic Energy Community (Euratom)
1959	Dwight D. Eisenhower becomes the second U.S. President to visit the Vatican. He met with Pope John XXIII. Every U.S. president since has visited the Vatican
1960	Rome hosts the Olympic Games

1962	The Second Vatican Council reforms the Catholic Church
1981	Assassination attempt on Pope John Paul II in St. Peter's Square
1984	Formal diplomatic relations between the U.S. and the Holy See are established in by President Ronald Reagan and Pope John Paul II
1990	Rome hosts the football (soccer) World Cup
2004	The new European Union Constitution is signed in Rome

Appendix B

The Roman Emperors

Reign	Common Name	Full Name / Imperial Name
Julio-Claudian Dynasty		
27 BCE to 14 CE	Augustus	Gaius Julius Caesar Octavianus / Imperator Caesar Divi Filius Augustus
14 to 37	Tiberius	Tiberius Claudius Nero Caesar / Tiberius Caesar Augustus
37 to 41	Gaius	Gaius Caesar Germanicus / Gaius Caesar Augustus Germanicus
	More commonly known as Caligula which means "Little Boots"	
41 to 54	Claudius	Tiberius Claudius Nero Germanicus / Tiberius Claudius Caesar Augustus Germanicus
54 to 68	Nero	Claudius Nero Caesar (born Lucius Domitius Ahenobarbus) / Nero Claudius Caesar Augustus Germanicus
Year of the Four Emperors (Civil War)		
68 to 69	Galba	Servius Sulpicius Galba / Servius Galba Imperator Caesar Augustus
69	Otho	Marcus Salvius Otho / Imperator Marcus Otho Caesar Augustus
69	Vitellius	Aulus Vitellius / Aulus Vitellius Germanicus Imperator Augustus

Flavian Dynasty

69 to 79	Vespasian Took office as the final of the 4 Emperors in the Year of the 4 Emperors	Titus Flavius Vespasianus / Imperator Vespasian Caesar Augustus
79 to 81	Titus	Titus Flavius Vespasianus / Imperator Titus Caesar Vespasianus Augustus
81 to 96	Domitian	Titus Flavius Domitianus / Imperator Caesar Domitianus Augustus

Nervanto-Antonian Dynasty

96 to 98	Nerva	Marcus Cocceius Nerva / Imperator Nerva Caesar Augustus
98 to 117	Trajan	Marcus Ulpius Nerva Traianus / Imperator Caesar Divi Nervae Filius Nerva Traianus
117 to 138	Hadrian	Publius Aelius Traianus Hadrianus / Imperator Caesar Traianus Hadrianus Augustus
138 to 161	Antoninus Pius	Titus Aurelius Fulvius Boionius Arrius Antoninus Pius / Imperator Titus Aelius Caesar Hadrianus Antoninus Augustus Pius
161 to 180	Marcus Aurelius	Marcus Annius Aurelius Verus (also *Marcus Aurelius Antoninus*) / Imperator Caesar Marcus Aurelius Antoninus Augustus
161 to 169	Lucius Verus (co-emperor)	Lucius Ceionius Commodus / Imperator Caesar Lucius Aurelius Verus Augustus

180 to 192	Commodus	Marcus Aurelius Commodus Antoninus / Aurelius Commodus Antoninus Augustus

Year of the Five Emperors

193	Pertinax	Publius Helvius Pertinax / Imperator Caesar Publius Helvius Pertinax Augustus
193	Didius Julianus	Marcus Didius Severus Julianus / Imperator Caesar Marcus Didius Severus Julianus Augustus
193 to 195	Pescennius Niger Proclaimed emperor by Syrian troops, defeated in battle by Septimius Severus	Gaius Pescennius Niger
195 to 197	Clodius Albinus Proclaimed emperor by British troops, defeated in battle by Septimius Severus	Decimus Clodius Septimius Albinus

Severan Dynasty

193 to 211	Septimius Severus Last of the 5 Emperors from the Year of the 5 emperors and founder of the Severan Dynasty	Lucius Septimius Severus / Imperator Caesar Lucius Septimius Severus Pertinax Augustus
211 to 217	Caracalla	Born Lucius Septimius Bassianus later changed to Marcus Aurelius Antoninus / Imperator Caesar Marcus Aurelius Severus Antoninus Pius Augustus

211	Geta	Publius Septimius Geta / Imperator Caesar Publius Septimius Geta Augustus
217 to 218	Macrinus	Marcus Opellius Macrinus / Marcus Opellius Severus Macrinus Augustus
218 to 222	Elagabalus	Marcus Aurelius Antoninus / Imperator Marcus Aurelius Antoninus Pius Felix Augustus Proconsul
222 to 235	Severus Alexander	Marcus Aurelius Severus Alexander / Imperator Caesar Marcus Aurelius Severus Alexander Pius Felix Augustus

Crisis of the Third Century

235 to 238	Maximus I (or Maximus Thrax) Murdered by Praetorian Guard	Gaius Julius Verus Maximinus Thrax / Imperator Caesar Gaius Julius Verus Maximinus Pius Felix Invictus Augustus
238	Gordian I Committed suicide after the death of Gordian II	Marcus Antonius Gordianus Sempronianus Romanus Africanus / Imperator Caesar Marcus Antoninus Gordianus Sempronianus Romanus Africanus
238	Gordian II Proclaimed emperor with Gordian I, killed in battle	Marcus Antonius Gordianus Sempronianus / Imperator Caesar Marcus Antoninus Gordianus Sempronianus Romanus Africanus
238	Balbinus Murdered by Praetorian Guard	Decimus Caelius Calvinus Balbinus / Imperator Caesar Decius Caelius Calvinus Balbinus Pius Felix Augustus

238	Pupienus Murdered by Praetorian Guard	Marcus Clodius Pupienus Maximus / Imperator Caesar Marcus Clodius Pupienus Maximus Augustus
238 to 244	Gordian III Probably murdered by Praetorian Guard	Marcus Antonius Gordianus Pius / Imperator Caesar Marcus Antonius Gordianus Pius Felix Augustus
244 to 249	Philip I (the Arab) Killed in battle by Decius	Marcus Julius Philippus / Imperator Caesar Marcus Julius Phillipus Pius Felix Invictus Augustus
249 to 251	Traianus Decius	Gaius Messius Quintus Trajanus Decius / Imperator Caesar Gaius Messius Quintus Traianus Decius Pius Felix Invictus Augustus
251	Hostilian	Gaius Valens Hostilianus Messius Quintus Augustus
251 to 253	Trebonianus Gallus	Gaius Vibius Trebonianus Gallus / Imperator Caesar Gaius Vibius Trebonianus Gallus Pius Felix Invictus Augustus
253	Aemilian Murdered by his own troops	Marcus Aemilius Aemilianus / Imperator Caesar Marcus Aemilius Aemilianus Pius Felix Invictus Augustus
253 to 260	Valerian	Publius Licinius Valerianus / Imperator Caesar Publius Licinius Valerianus Pius Felix Invictus Augustus
253 to 268	Gallienus Unable to keep the empire together, he faced several revolts throughout his reign.	Publius Licinius Egnatius Gallienus / Imperator Caesar Publius Licinius Egnatius Gallienus Pius Felix Invictus Augustus

260	Regalianus A Dacian general who revolted against Gallienus. Held power for six months and minted coins of himself as emperor before being murdered by his own troops	

The Gallic Empire—a breakaway section of the Roman Empire that existed from 260 to 274

260 to 269	Postumus Usurped power from Gallienus in 260 and formed the Gallic Empire. He ruled Gaul, Germania, Britannia and Iberia until his murder in 269. Gallienus continued to rule the remainder of the Empire.	Marcus Cassianius Latinius Postumus / Imperator Caesar Marcus Cassianus Latinius Postumus Pius Felix Invictus Augustus
269	Laelianus A usurper against Postumus, the emperor of the Gallic Empire from late February to early June 269.	Ulpius Cornelius Laelianus / Imperator Caesar Gaius Ulpius Cornelius Laelianus Pius Felix Augustus

269	Marius Emperor of the Gallic Empire in 269. His reign probably lasted two or three months.	Marcus Aurelius Marius / Imperator Caesar Marcus Aurelius Marius Pius Felix Augustus
269 to 271	Victorinus Emperor of the Gallic Empire.	Marcus Piavonius Victorinus / Imperator Caesar Marcus Piavonius Victorinus Pius Felix Invictus Augustus
271 to 274	Tetricus Emperor of the Gallic Empire.	Caius Pius Esuvius Tetricus / Imperator Caesar Gaius Pius Esuvius Tetricus Felix Invictus Augustus

Roman Emperors (Cont'd)

268 to 270	Claudius II Gothicus Roman emperor during the Gallic Secession. So named because he defeated the Goths at the Battle of Naissus.	Marcus Aurelius Valerius Claudius / Imperator Caesar Marcus Aurelius Claudius Pius Felix Invictus Augustus
270	Quintillus	Marcus Aurelius Quintillus / Imperator Caesar Marcus Aurelius Claudius Quintillus Invictus Pius Felix Augustus
270 to 275	Aurelian Reunited the Provinces of the Gallic Empire with Rome following the Battle of Châlons in 274.	Lucius Domitius Aurelianus / Imperator Caesar Lucius Domitius Aurelianus Pius Felix Invictus Augustus

275 to 276	Tacitus	Marcus Claudius Tacitus / Imperator Caesar Marcus Claudius Tacitus Pius Felix Augustus
276	Florian	Marcus Annius Florianus Pius / Imperator Caesar Marcus Annius Florianus Pius Felix Augustus
276 to 282	Probus	Marcus Aurelius Equitius Probus / Imperator Caesar Marcus Aurelius Probus Pius Felix Invictus Augustus
282 to 283	Carus	Marcus Aurelius Numerius Carus / Imperator Caesar Marcus Aurelius Carus Pius Felix Invictus Augustus
283 to 285	Carinus	Marcus Aurelius Carinus / Imperator Caesar Marcus Aurelius Carinus Pius Felix Invictus Augustus
283 to 284	Numerianus	Marcus Aurelius Numerius Numerianus / Imperator Caesar Marcus Aurelius Numerianus Pius Felix Augustus

Tetrarchy and Constantinian Dynasty

284 to 305	Diocletian	Gaius Aurelius Valerius Diocletianus Jovius / Imperator Caesar Gaius Aurelius Valerius Diocletianus Pius Felix Invictus Augustus
307 to308	Maximianus	Marcus Aurelius Valerius Maximianus Herculius / Imperator Caesar Gaius Aurelius Valerius Maximianus Pius Felix Invictus Augustus
286 to 293	Carausius	Marcus Aurelius Mausaeus

307 to308	Maximianus The same emperor as preceded Carausius, he returned to office in 305	Marcus Aurelius Valerius Maximianus Herculius / Imperator Caesar Gaius Aurelius Valerius Maximianus Pius Felix Invictus Augustus
305 to 306	Constantius I Chlorus	Flavius Valerius Constantius / Imperator Caesar Gaius Flavius Valerius Constantius Augustus
305 to 311	Galerius	Caius Galerius Valerius Maximianus / Imperator Caesar Galerius Valerius Maximianus Pius Felix Invictus Augustus
306 to 307	Severus II	Flavius Valerius Severus / Imperator Severus Pius Felix Augustus
306 to 312	Maxentius	Marcus Aurelius Valerius Maxentius / Marcus Aurelius Valerius Maxentius Pius Felix Invictus Augustus
306 to 337	Constantine I The Great	Flavius Valerius Constantinus / Imperator Caesar Flavius Constantinus Pius Felix Invictus Augustus
308 to 324	Licinius	Valerius Licinianus Licinius / Imperator Caesar Gaius Valerius Licinius Pius Felix Invictus Augustus
308 to 313	Maximinus II	Gaius Valerius Galerius Maximinus Daia Augustus
337 to 340	Constantine II	Flavius Claudius Constantinus / Imperator Caesar Flavius Valerius Constantinus Augustus
337 to 361	Constantius II	Flavius Julius Constantius / Imperator Caesar Flavius Julius Constantinus Augustus

337 to 350	Constans I	Flavius Julius Constans / Imperator Caesar Flavius Julius Constans Augustus
350 to 353	Magnentius Accepted as Augustus of the west by Constantius II, but is considered by many to be a usurper.	Flavius Magnus Magnentius / Imperator Caesar Flavius Magnus Magentius Augustus
361 to 363	Julian I the Apostate	Flavius Claudius Julianus / Imperator Caesar Flavius Claudius Julianus Augustus
363 to 364	Jovian	Flavius Jovianus / Imperator Caesar Flavius Jovianus Augustus

Valentinian Dynasty

364 to 375	Valentinian I	Flavius Valentinianus / Imperator Caesar Flavius Valentinianus Augustus
364 to 378	Valens Declared emperor of the Eastern Roman Empire by his brother.	Flavius Julius Valens Augustus
367 to 383	Gratian	Flavius Gratianus / Imperator Caesar Flavius Gratianus Augustus
375 to 392	Valentinian II	Flavius Valentinianus / Imperator Caesar Flavius Valentinianus Augustus

Theodosian Dynasty

379 to 395	Theodosius I The Great The last emperor to rule over both the eastern and the western halves of the Roman Empire.	Flavius Theodosius / Imperator Caesar Flavius Theodosius Augustus

Emperors of the Western Roman Empire

395 to 423	Honorius Considered by historians as part of the Theodosian dynasty.	Flavius Honorius
421	Constantius III Co-emperor of the Western Empire with Honorius seven months in 421.	Flavius Constantius
423 to 425	Ioannes or Joannes Considered by many to be a usurper. Considered by historians as part of the Theodosian dynasty.	Ioannes or Joannes
425 to 455	Valentinian III Considered by historians as part of the Theodosian dynasty.	Flavius Placidus Valentinianus

Western Roman Empire—Non-Theodosian Dynasty

455	Petronius Maximus	Flavius Petronius Maximus
455 to 456	Avitus	Marcus Maecilius Flavius Eparchius
457 to 461	Majorian	Julius Valerius Majorianus
461 to 465	Libius Severus	Libius Severus
467 to 472	Anthemius	Procopius Anthemius
472	Olybrius	Ancius Olybrius
473 to 474	Glycerius	
474 to 475	Julius Nepos	.
477 to 480	Served as Emperor from 474 to 475. Resisted Odecoer's overthrow of Romulus and proclaimed himself Emperor again, but exercised no real power outside of Dalmatia. He was murdered in 480.	
475 to 476	Romulus Augustulus	.
	Deposed in the year 476 by Odoacer, considered by historians the last Roman Emperor. The fall of ancient Rome during his reign is considered the beginning of the Middle Ages in Western Europe.	

Emperors of the Eastern Roman Empire also known as the Byzantine Empire

395 to 408.	Arcadius	Flavius Arcadius Augustus
	Considered by many historians as part of the Theodosian dynasty.	
408 to 450	Theodosius II	Flavius Theodosius Junior Augustus
	Known as Theodosius the Younger, or Theodosius the Calligrapher. Considered by historians as part of the Theodosian dynasty.	
450 to 457	Marcian	Flavius Marcianus Augustus
	Considered by historians as part of the Theodosian dynasty.	

Leonid Dynasty

457 to 474	Leo I the Great	Flavius Valerius Leo / Imperator Caesar Flavius Valerius Leo Augustus
474	Leo II	Flavius Leo / Imperator Caesar Flavius Leo Augustus
474 to 475, 476 to 491	Zeno Originally named Tarasis.	Flavius Zeno / Imperator Caesar Flavius Zeno Augustus
475 to 476	Basiliscus	Flavius Basiliscus

491 to 518	Anastasius I	Flavius Anastasius

Justinian Dynasty

518 to 527	Justin I	Flavius Justinus Augustus
527 to 565	Justinian I	Flavius Petrus Sabbatius Iustinianus Augustus,
565 to 578	Justin II	Flavius Iustinus Iunior Augustus
574 to 582	Tiberius II Constantine	Flavius Tiberius Constantinus Augustus
582 to 602	Maurice	Flavius Mauricius Tiberius Augustus

Appendix C

The Popes

Popes	Antipope
	By definition an antipope is a bishop who claims to be the pope, but was not canonically elected as the Bishop of Rome.
1. St. Peter (32-67)	
2. St. Linus (67-76)	
3. St. Anacletus (Cletus) (76-88)	
4. St. Clement I (88-97)	
5. St. Evaristus (97-105)	
6. St. Alexander I (105-115)	
7. St. Sixtus I (115-125)	
8. St. Telesphorus (125-136)	
9. St. Hyginus (136-140)	
10. St. Pius I (140-155)	
11. St. Anicetus (155-166)	
12. St. Soter (166-175)	
13. St. Eleutherius (175-189)	
14. St. Victor I (189-199)	
15. St. Zephyrinus (199-217)	
16. St. Callistus I (217-222)	Natalius (200)
17. St. Urban I (222-230)	
18. St. Pontainus (230-235)	St. Hippolytus of Rome (reconciled with the church and died a martyr)
19. St. Anterus (235-236)	
20. St. Fabian (236-250)	

21. St. Cornelius (251-253)	Novatian (251-258)
22. St. Lucius I (253-254)	
23. St. Stephen I (254-257)	
24. St. Sixtus II (257-258)	
25. St. Dionysius (260-268)	
26. St. Felix I (269-274)	
27. St. Eutychian (275-283)	
28. St. Caius (283-296)	
29. St. Marcellinus (296-304)	
30. St. Marcellus I (308-309)	
31. St. Eusebius (309 or 310)	
32. St. Miltiades (311-314)	
33. St. Sylvester I (314-335)	
34. St. Marcus (336)	
35. St. Julius I (337-352)	
36. Liberius (352-366)	Felix II (355-365)
37. St. Damasus I (366-383)	Ursicinus (366-367)
38. St. Siricius (384-399)	
39. St. Anastasius I (399-401)	
40. St. Innocent I (401-417)	
41. St. Zosimus (417-418)	
42. St. Boniface I (418-422)	Eulalius (418-419)
43. St. Celestine I (422-432)	
44. St. Sixtus III (432-440)	
45. St. Leo I (the Great) (440-461)	
46. St. Hilarius (461-468)	
47. St. Simplicius (468-483) *He was the Pope when the last Roman Emperor of the west, Romulus Augustulus, was deposed in 476.	
48. St. Felix III (II) (483-492)	
49. St. Gelasius I (492-496)	
50. Anastasius II (496-498)	

51.	St. Symmachus (498-514)	Laurentius (498-501)
52.	St. Hormisdas (514-523)	
53.	St. John I (523-526)	
54.	St. Felix IV (III) (526-530)	
55.	Boniface II (530-532)	Dioscorus (530)
56.	John II (533-535)	
57.	St. Agapetus I (535-536)	
58.	St. Silverius (536-537)	
59.	Vigilius (537-555)	
60.	Pelagius I (556-561)	
61.	John III (561-574)	
62.	Benedict I (575-579)	
63.	Pelagius II (579-590)	
64.	St. Gregory I (the Great) (590-604)	
65.	Sabinian (604-606)	
66.	Boniface III (607)	
67.	St. Boniface IV (608-615)	
68.	St. Deusdedit (Adeodatus I) (615-618)	
69.	Boniface V (619-625)	
70.	Honorius I (625-638)	
71.	Severinus (640)	
72.	John IV (640-642)	
73.	Theodore I (642-649)	
74.	St. Martin I (649-655)	
75.	St. Eugene I (655-657)	
76.	St. Vitalian (657-672)	
77.	Adeodatus (II) (672-676)	
78.	Donus (676-678)	
79.	St. Agatho (678-681)	
80.	St. Leo II (682-683)	
81.	St. Benedict II (684-685)	
82.	John V (685-686)	
83.	Conon (686-687)	
84.	St. Sergius I (687-701)	Theodore (687), and Paschal (687)

85. John VI (701-705)	
86. John VII (705-707)	
87. Sisinnius (708)	
88. Constantine (708-715)	
89. St. Gregory II (715-731)	
90. St. Gregory III (731-741)	
91. St. Zachary (741-752)	
92. Stephen II (752) *He died of a stroke before being consecrated. The Second Vatican Council (1962-65) declared that he was not a pope. He is often omitted from listings of the popes.	
93. Stephen III (752-757) *When his predecessor is omitted he is called Stephen II	
94. St. Paul I (757-767)	
95. Stephen IV (767-772)	Constantine II (767) and Philip (768)
96. Hadrian I (772-795)	
97. St. Leo III (795-816)	
98. Stephen V (816-817)	
99. St. Paschal I (817-824)	
100. Eugene II (824-827)	
101. Valentine (827)	
102. Gregory IV (827-844)	
103. Sergius II (844-847)	John VIII (844)
104. St. Leo IV (847-855)	
105. Benedict III (855-858)	Anastasius III (855)
106. St. Nicholas I (the Great) (858-867)	
107. Hadrian II (867-872)	
108. John VIII (872-882)	
109. Marinus I (882-884)	
110. St. Hadrian III (884-885)	

111. Stephen VI (885-891)	
112. Formosus (891-896)	
113. Boniface VI (896)	
114. Stephen VII (896-897)	
115. Romanus (897)	
116. Theodore II (897)	
117. John IX (898-900)	
118. Benedict IV (900-903)	
119. Leo V (903)	Christopher (903-904)
120. Sergius III (904-911)	
121. Anastasius III (911-913)	
122. Lando (913-914)	
123. John X (914-928)	
124. Leo VI (928)	
125. Stephen VIII (929-931)	
126. John XI (931-935)	
127. Leo VII (936-939)	
128. Stephen IX (939-942)	
129. Marinus II (942-946)	
130. Agapetus II (946-955)	
131. John XII (955-963)	Leo VIII (956-963)
132. Leo VIII (963-964)	
133. Benedict V (964)	
134. John XIII (965-972)	
135. Benedict VI (973-974)	
136. Benedict VII (974-983)	Boniface VII (974; 984-985)
137. John XIV (983-984)	Boniface VII (974; 984-985)
138. John XV (985-996)	
139. Gregory V (996-999)	John XVI (997-998)
140. Sylvester II (999-1003)	
141. John XVII (1003)	
142. John XVIII (1003-1009)	
143. Sergius IV (1009-1012)	
144. Benedict VIII (1012-1024)	Gregory (1012)
145. John XIX (1024-1032)	

146. Benedict IX (1032-1045) *He appears on this list three times. He was twice deposed and restored (See also Pope # 148 and 151)	
147. Sylvester III (1045)	*Considered by some to be an antipope, he appears in the Official Roman Catholic Church listings as a legitimate Pope.
148. Benedict IX (1045)	
149. Gregory VI (1045-1046)	
150. Clement II (1046-1047)	
151. Benedict IX (1047-1048)	
152. Damasus II (1048)	
153. St. Leo IX (1049-1054)	
154. Victor II (1055-1057)	
155. Stephen X (1057-1058)	
156. Nicholas II (1058-1061)	Benedict X (1058-1059)
157. Alexander II (1061-1073)	Honorius II (1061-1072)
158. St. Gregory VII (1073-1085) *Gregory and the following three popes were opposed by Guibert ("Clement III"), antipope (1080-1100)	Clement III (1080-1100)
159. Blessed Victor III (1086-1087)	Clement III (1080-1100)
160. Blessed Urban II (1088-1099)	Clement III (1080-1100)
161. Paschal II (1099-1118)	Theodoric (1100), Adalbert or Albert (1101) and Sylvester IV (1105-1111), Maginulf, 1105
162. Gelasius II (1118-1119)	Gregory VIII (1118-1121)
163. Callistus II (1119-1124)	
164. Honorius II (1124-1130)	Celestine II (1124)
165. Innocent II (1130-1143)	Anacletus II (1130-1138) and Victor IV (1138)

166. Celestine II (1143-1144)	
167. Lucius II (1144-1145)	
168. Blessed Eugene III (1145-1153)	
169. Anastasius IV (1153-1154)	
170. Hadrian IV (1154-1159)	
171. Alexander III (1159-1181)	Victor IV (1159-1164), Paschal III (1165-1168), Callixtus III (1168-1177), and Innocent III (1178-1180)
172. Lucius III (1181-1185)	
173. Urban III (1185-1187)	
174. Gregory VIII (1187)	
175. Clement III (1187-1191)	
176. Celestine III (1191-1198)	
177. Innocent III (1198-1216)	
178. Honorius III (1216-1227)	
179. Gregory IX (1227-1241)	
180. Celestine IV (1241)	
181. Innocent IV (1243-1254)	
182. Alexander IV (1254-1261)	
183. Urban IV (1261-1264)	
184. Clement IV (1265-1268)	
185. Blessed Gregory X (1271-1276)	
186. Blessed Innocent V (1276)	
187. Hadrian V (1276)	
188. John XXI (1276-1277)	
189. Nicholas III (1277-1280)	
190. Martin IV (1281-1285)	
191. Honorius IV (1285-1287)	
192. Nicholas IV (1288-1292)	
193. St. Celestine V (1294)	

194. Boniface VIII (1294-1303)	
195. Blessed Benedict XI (1303-1304)	
196. Clement V (1305-1314) *Papacy moved to Avignon, France	
197. John XXII (1316-1334) *Papacy moved to Avignon, France	Nicholas V (1328-1330)
198. Benedict XII (1334-1342) *Papacy moved to Avignon, France	
199. Clement VI (1342-1352) *Papacy moved to Avignon, France	
200. Innocent VI (1352-1362) *Papacy moved to Avignon, France	
201. Blessed Urban V (1362-1370) *Papacy moved to Avignon, France	
202. Gregory XI (1370-1378) *Papacy moved to Avignon, France	
203. Urban VI (1378-1389) * Papacy returned to Rome, Italy.	Clement VII (1378-1394) Based in Avignon, also known as Robert of Geneva
204. Boniface IX (1389-1404)	Clement VII (1378-1394), Benedict XIII (1394-1423)*He started his papacy in Avignon and was expelled from there in 1403, and John XXIII (1400-1415)
205. Innocent VII (1404-1406)	Benedict XIII (1394-1417), and John XXIII (1400-1415)
206. Gregory XII (1406-1415)	Benedict XIII (1394-1417), John XXIII (1400-1415), and Alexander V (1409-1410)

207. Martin V (1417-1431)	Clement VII (1378-1394), Benedict XIII (1394-1423), and John XXIII) (1400-1415)
208. Eugene IV (1431-1447)	Felix V (1439-1449)
209. Nicholas V (1447-1455)	Felix V (1439-1449)
210. Callistus III (1455-1458)	
211. Pius II (1458-1464)	
212. Paul II (1464-1471)	
213. Sixtus IV (1471-1484)	
214. Innocent VIII (1484-1492)	
215. Alexander VI (1492-1503)	
216. Pius III (1503)	
217. Julius II (1503-1513)	
218. Leo X (1513-1521)	
219. Hadrian VI (1522-1523)	
220. Clement VII (1523-1534)	
221. Paul III (1534-1549)	
222. Julius III (1550-1555)	
223. Marcellus II (1555)	
224. Paul IV (1555-1559)	
225. Pius IV (1559-1565)	
226. St. Pius V (1566-1572)	
227. Gregory XIII (1572-1585)	
228. Sixtus V (1585-1590)	
229. Urban VII (1590)	
230. Gregory XIV (1590-1591)	
231. Innocent IX (1591)	
232. Clement VIII (1592-1605)	
233. Leo XI (1605)	
234. Paul V (1605-1621)	
235. Gregory XV (1621-1623)	
236. Urban VIII (1623-1644)	

237. Innocent X (1644-1655)
238. Alexander VII (1655-1667)
239. Clement IX (1667-1669)
240. Clement X (1670-1676)
241. Blessed Innocent XI (1676-1689)
242. Alexander VIII (1689-1691)
243. Innocent XII (1691-1700)
244. Clement XI (1700-1721)
245. Innocent XIII (1721-1724)
246. Benedict XIII (1724-1730)
247. Clement XII (1730-1740)
248. Benedict XIV (1740-1758)
249. Clement XIII (1758-1769)
250. Clement XIV (1769-1774)
251. Pius VI (1775-1799)
252. Pius VII (1800-1823)
253. Leo XII (1823-1829)
254. Pius VIII (1829-1830)
255. Gregory XVI (1831-1846)
256. Blessed Pius IX (1846-1878)
257. Leo XIII (1878-1903)
258. St. Pius X (1903-1914)
259. Benedict XV (1914-1922)
260. Pius XI (1922-1939)
261. Pius XII (1939-1958)

262. Blessed John XXIII (1958-1963)
263. Paul VI (1963-1978)
264. John Paul I (1978)
265. John Paul II (1978-2005)
266. Benedict XVI (2005-2013)
267. Francis (2013-Present)

Appendix D

Obelisks in Rome

Name	Location	Details
Agonalis	Piazza Navona	Moved from the Temple of Serapis to the Circus of Maxentius by Maxentius.
Dogali	Baths of Diocletian	Originally one of a pair of obelisks from Heliopolis that was constructed by Ramses II. The other is in the Boboli Gardens in Florence.
Esquiline	Piazza dell'Esquilino	Originally erected by the Mausoleum of Augustus. Moved to behind Santa Maria Maggiore in 1527.
Flaminio	Piazza del Popolo	Constructed at Heliopolis by Ramses II. Brought to Rome by Augustus in 10 BC.
Lateranense	Piazza di San Giovanni in Laterano	From the temple of Amun in Karnak, Egypt. This is the tallest obelisk in Rome and was brought to Rome by Constantius II.
Macuteo	Piazza della Rotonda	Constructed for Ramses II for the Temple of Ra in Heliopolis. Moved to its present location in 1711.
Matteiano	Villa Celimontana	This is the smallest obelisk in Rome and was originally one of a pair with the Macuteo obelisk. They were constructed for Ramses II for the Temple of Ra in Heliopolis.

Minerveo	Santa Maria sopra Minerva	This obelisk was brought to Rome by Diocletian for the nearby Temple of Isis. In 1667, it was placed on the elephant base by Bernini.
Pinciano	Pincian Hill	Originally constructed for Hadrian and erected in Tivoli over the tomb of Antinous, it was moved to its present location in 1822.
Quirinale	Piazza del Quirinale	Originally erected at the Mausoleum of Augustus, it was paired with the Esquiline obelisk until it was moved to this location.
Sallustiano	Trinità dei Monti (Spanish Steps)	This obelisk is a copy of the Flaminio obelisk of Ramses II in the Piazza del Popolo.
Solare	Piazza di Montecitorio	Originally from Heliopolis, this obelisk was brought to Rome by Augustus in 10 BCE.
Vaticano	St. Peter's Square	From the Forum Iulium in Alexandria, Egypt, it was constructed around 30-28 BCE.

Appendix E

Types of Churches

Abbey—An abbey is the home of an autonomous monastic community approved by the Vatican of not fewer than twelve religious brothers under the government of an abbot. The abbot does not answer to the local bishop. The term abbey is also applied to large churches that at one time may have had associated religious communities. For example: Westminster Abbey in London, England.

Baptistery—This term can mean a separate building in which the Sacrament of Baptism is held, a section of the church dedicated exclusively to baptisms, or the actual font used for the baptisms.

Basilica—The term basilica can apply to either the architectural style of a church or its canonical status.

- Architectural definition: A building in the shape of a parallelogram whose width was not greater than one-half of the length and not less than one-third of it. The internal area should be separated by columns from a lower cloister, gallery, or portico; the width of the lower cloister should equal the height of the columns and measure one-third of the width of the central space.
- Canonical definition: A formal designation given by the Vatican to a religiously important or historically significant church. Basilicas can be designated as either greater or patriarchal basilicas, or as thee lesser basilicas.
    - There are 4 greater basilicas in Rome: St. Peter's, St. John Laterano, St. Mary Major, and St. Paul Outside the Walls. Each is considered the property of the

Vatican and has a special "holy door". A visit to this door is one of the conditions for gaining the Roman Jubilee.

- These 4 basilicas also are given the designation of patriarchal basilicas and assigned as representatives of the great ecclesiastical provinces of the world. The patriarchal basilicas in Rome are: St. John Laterano is the cathedral of the pope, the Patriarch of the West; St. Peter's is assigned to the Patriarch of Constantinople; St. Paul's to the Patriarch of Alexandria; St. Mary Major to the Patriarch of Antioch; St. Lawrence Outside the Walls is attributed to the Patriarch of Jerusalem.
- Minor Basilicas are churches designated by the Vatican as having special significance, such as the Basilica of the Grotto at Lourdes. While considered special, these minor basilicas are subject to the jurisdiction of their local cathedral.

Cathedral—The main church of a diocese, in which the bishop has his throne or cathedra (seat). Roman Catholic ecclesiastical law, which is based on the constitution of the Church, provides that there shall be but one bishop for each diocese.

Chapel—By definition a chapel is an informal church or any place set aside for prayer. There are several different types of chapels.

- *Chapels within a larger church*—Any chapel that is under the main roof of the church itself. This includes lady chapels, side-chapels, ante-chapels, and subsidiary chapels.
- *Chevet Chapels*—These are chapels dedicated to important saints and are usually located inside the larger church.
- *Ambassadors' Chapels*—Roman Catholic ambassadors were permitted to have chapels attached to their embassies when serving in a Protestant Court. Principally these are found in London.
- *Bishops' Chapels*—These are often cited as the origin of the cathedral. However, church law permits all bishops the right

to have a private chapel in their house, and they retain this right even when traveling.

- *Cemetery or Mortuary Chapels*—a place for prayer near or in a cemetery. These are usually designated as such because they are at the burial place of a martyr or the common resting places of the faithful. The Roman catacombs are an example, as are Becket's Crown at Canterbury, England; Henry VIII's chapel at Westminster Abbey; and the tomb of Charlemagne at the Cathedral of Aachen in France.
- *Chantry Chapels*—A chantry chapel is a special chapel designated for celebration of Masses of requiem, in perpetuity. These chapels are usually attached to a larger church, but are privately or separately endowed. They have one or more specific priests appointed to their management. The priests say or sing Mass for the soul of the endower, or for the souls of persons designated by him. These chapels are usually blocked off from the main church by a screen. Examples can still be found in England, for example Prince Arthur's chantry at Worcester.
- *Charnel Chapels or Charnel-houses*—These are the same as cemetery chapels.
- *Chapels of Ease*—These structures were remote extensions of the parish church. They were built for parishioners in large geographic parishes that could not travel the long distance to the main parish church for services. The clergy who manage these chapels report to the parish priest.
- *Gatehouse chapels*—The enclosure wall of most medieval monasteries contained gatehouse chapels which could be used by the brothers or visitors for prayer.
- *Papal Chapels*—Chapels designated for the use of the pope and where he says Mass. There are several in Rome. The most famous of which is the Sistine Chapel in the Vatican.
- *Chapels of Repose*—An altar or chapel where the Blessed Sacrament is solemnly reserved between the Mass of Maundy Thursday and the Mass of the Pre-sanctified on Good Friday. Traditionally, these were movable wooden structures erected year by year in a niche on the north side of the sanctuary of a church. Some have been constructed of stone. One of the

few still existing examples of this is in the church of Arnold in Nottinghamshire, England.

- *Lady Chapel*—A lady chapel can also be called a Marian chapel. It is a chapel located inside a cathedral or basilica and is dedicated to the Blessed Virgin Mary. They are commonly found in France, Italy, and Spain, though one of the oldest is in the cathedral in Canterbury, England.
- *Radiating Chapels*—Radiating chapels are more an architectural designation than an ecclesiastical one. They are chapels that "radiate" or branch off from the main church. Believed to be French in origin, legend has it that Henry III introduced them to Westminster Abbey.
- *Royal Chapels*—These are private chapels for the use of the Royal Court. They can be free standing or inside a palace.
- *Ship Chapels*—Certain ships were allowed to carry consecrated hosts on board and to hold Mass for the crew. The host was kept in a separate area designated as the ship's chapel.
- *Votive Chapels*—These chapels were erected during the Middle Ages for devotion by private persons, to commemorate some special event, or to enshrine some valued relic. They can be freestanding or attached to a church.
- *Wayside Chapels*—These chapels were erected for the use of travelers and are usually found along pilgrimage routes. An example is the "Slipper Chapel" in Norfolk, England which is on the pilgrim's route to the shrine of Our Lady of Walsingham. These can sometimes be called Pilgrims' Chapels.

Convent—A convent by definition is a religious community of either sex. However, it is usually applied to a community of women and the term monastery is usually applied to a male community.

Diocese—(from the Greek *dioikesis*) a diocese is made of several local parishes and is subject to the jurisdiction of a particular bishop. Dioceses are further grouped into what is called an ecclesiastical province and are subject to the authority of the metropolitan archbishop.

- Suburbicarian dioceses (*diœceses suburbicariœ*) are six dioceses situated near Rome. Each of these is administered by one of the six cardinal-bishops. These form a special class of dioceses; the cardinal-bishops hold special rights and obligations within the Roman Catholic Church.

Parish Church—The smallest unit of a diocese, the parish church is usually at the neighborhood level. They are traditionally operated by canonical parish priests who report to the local bishop. (A canonical priest is one who has been ordained under church law which is also called canon law.)

Appendix F

The Portico of Santa Maria Trastevere

Parts of a Church

Ad Orientem—Facing east; the direction from which Jesus, as symbolized by the rising Sun, will come again.

Altar—Usually at the front of the church, this is the table-like area where the main activity of the service takes place. It is traditionally positioned so that the congregation is facing east when they are looking at the altar. (Also see: Sanctuary). The main altar in the church is called the high altar. Other altars, such as those located in chapels, are sometimes called devotional altars.

Altar Canopy—A square decorative covering that can be supported on columns or suspended and covers the altar area. The framework that is used to support it is called the "altar-herse". (Also see: Ciborium and Baldachino)

Altarpiece—This is a picture or sculpture suspended or framed and hung behind the altar of a church. (Also see: Reredos and Iconostasis)

Ambulatory—A place for walking. This term can be used to denote a cloister, gallery, or alley. It can also be applied to the side aisles of a church when they are used to form a continuous route or lap around the church.

Antimensium—In the Roman Catholic Church, this term is used to denote a portable altar usually made of a solid piece of natural stone which must be consecrated by a bishop or other authority before it can be used. In the Orthodox Church, it is a linen or silk cloth that is decorated with representations of Christ, the four Evangelists, and scriptural passages. It has a relic of a martyr sewn into it and the Eucharist cannot be celebrated without one.

Apse—A semi-circular recess in a church. The term is sometimes applied to a canopy over an altar or a domed or arched roof of a room. The bishop's throne is usually located in an apse.

Baldachin—An ornamental canopy over an altar, throne, or tomb. They can be supported by columns or suspended from the ceiling. The term can also be applied to a portable canopy carried in religious processions, usually to shield a statue, icon, or the relics of a saint.

Baptistery—This term can mean a separate building in which the sacrament of baptism is held; a section of the church dedicated exclusively to baptisms ceremonies; or the actual font used for the baptisms.

Bema—A raised platform or room set aside for teaching. In Judaism, the bema is located in the center of the synagogue.

Campanile—The Italian word for a bell tower. In English, it is used as an architectural term to denote a free standing structure (i.e. not attached to a church or other building).

Catafalque—A raised bier or platform, used to support a body when lying in state or sometimes for a funeral or memorial service.

Cathedra—The Bishop's seat, sometimes called a throne.

Chancel—The part of the church near the front where the choir or the deacons sit. It was originally closed off by *cancelli* or lattice work.

Choir—This term is used architecturally to denote the part of the church where the stalls for the clergy are. The term can also be used to indicate the eastern arm or wing of the church.

Choir stalls—The seats in a choir, they can be wholly or partly enclosed.

Ciborium—From the Latin word *cibus* which means "food". The term ciborium can be used to denote a container that holds the Blessed Sacrament or it can be used to indicate the canopy that surmounted and crowned the altar.

Concha—A shell-like, hemispherical space in church. (Also see: Apse)

Clerestory—Pronounced "clear story". This is a row of small windows along the sides at the top or upper level of a church. They add light to the structure.

Cloister—From the Latin word *clausura* meaning "to shut up or enclose". The cloister is a covered walkway usually surrounding a courtyard. The word can also be applied to a restricted area in a convent or monastery.

Diaconicum—See Sacristy.

Daily Divine Offices—This term does not apply to a space but to the services held every day. These are: Matins, Lauds, Prime, Terce, Sext, None, Vespers, and Compline.

Font—The basin used to hold the water for baptism.

Gospel Side of the Sanctuary—The left side of the church that has the Bible or New Testament that is used by the clergy for the gospel lesson.

Holy Doors—In the Roman Catholic Church, the 4 papal basilicas of Rome have "Holy Doors" which are closed and only opened during Jubilee years or at the will of the Pope. In the Orthodox Church, the iconostasis has three sets of doors. The Deacons' Doors are the single doors located on either side. These are used on regular occasions. The central double doors are the "Holy Doors" which are used at certain moments during the services, and only by the higher clergy.

Iconostasis—From the Medieval Greek word: *eikonostasion* which means "shrine". The Iconostasis is a screen or wall that runs from side to side across the entire church. It divides the sanctuary from the body of the church. This is the primary structural feature that differentiates an Orthodox church from a Roman Catholic one. It is usually made of stone, wood, or a solid material. (Also see: Altarpiece and Reredos)

Lectern Side of the Sanctuary—The right side of the church has a Bible that is used by lay readers for the Old Testament and epistle lessons.

Lychgate—A covered gateway at the entrance to a traditional English-style churchyard. In Medieval times, the dead were carried to the lychgate and placed on a bier, where the priest conducted the first part of the funeral service.

Misericords—From the Latin for "mercy seat". Misericords are small wooden shelves on the underside of a folding seat in the choir stall which the monks can lean on when standing for long periods of time. They can be elaborately carved.

Monstrance—A case or container used to display a relic or the Blessed Sacrament. It can be fixed in a church or carried in a procession. Also called an Ostensorium or Tabernaculum.

Narthex—The entry or front foyer of the church.

Nave—The main body or central part of the church. From the Latin: *navis* meaning a "ship". The ceiling above the nave often looks like the inside of the hull of a ship and is sometimes said to symbolize Noah's Ark.

Oculus—A circular window; the name of the round opening in the top of the dome.

Ostensorium—A case or container used to display a relic or the Blessed Sacrament. It can be fixed in a church or carried in a procession. Also called a Monstrance or Tabernaculum.

Predella—From the Italian *predalla* which means "kneeling bench", this is the platform or step on which an altar stands.

Presbytery or Presbyterium—The part of the church reserved for use by the high clergy (priests, bishops, cardinals, etc).

Prie-dieu—An individual kneeling bench that may be found in a chapel. In the Orthodox Church a prie-dieu is provided for the bishop when he kneels.

Reredos—From the Middle English *areredos* meaning "behind". The reredos is a panel behind the altar that depicts a religious scene. Introduced in the beginning of the twelfth century, the oldest existing example is the Pala d'Oro in St. Mark's in Venice. It can also be called an altarpiece. (Also see: Altarpiece and Iconostasis)

Rooster Weathervanes—Rooster weathervanes are often found on the roofs of Protestant churches in Europe. Crosses are found on the top of Roman Catholic churches. There are many explanations as to why. One thought is that it is a reminder of Jesus Christ's prophecy in Luke 22:34: "I say to you, Peter, the rooster will not crow today until you have denied three times that you know Me." Another is that the rooster represents the dawn and a rebirth of the light of day.

It is therefore an allegory for the rebirth of Christianity (through Protestantism).

Sacristy—This is the room where the vestments are kept and where the clergy dress for the service. It is usually located behind or adjacent to the Sanctuary. It can also be called the *secretarium* or *diaconicum.*

Sacrarium—A special sink that bypasses the traditional drainage system, but instead goes straight into the earth. Used for washing the holy vessels used at Mass.

Sanctuary—Another name for the altar. The word sanctuary is from the Latin: *sānctuārium* meaning "some place safe". Tradition has it that people were not allowed to be arrested in the sanctuary. This does not mean that they could not be arrested in the aisles or other parts of the church.

Secretarium—See Sacristy.

Tabernacle—The receptacle or case placed upon the altar in which the vessels containing the Blessed Sacrament are kept.

Tabernaculum—A case or container used to display a relic or the Blessed Sacrament. It can be fixed in a church or carried in a procession. Also called a Monstrance or Ostensorium.

Transept—The aisle that bisects the church close to the altar or front of the church and makes the church cross-shaped. It is said to be symbolic of Jesus' cross.

Vestibule—An entrance hall or passage between the entry and the interior of the church.

Appendix G

Map of Rome

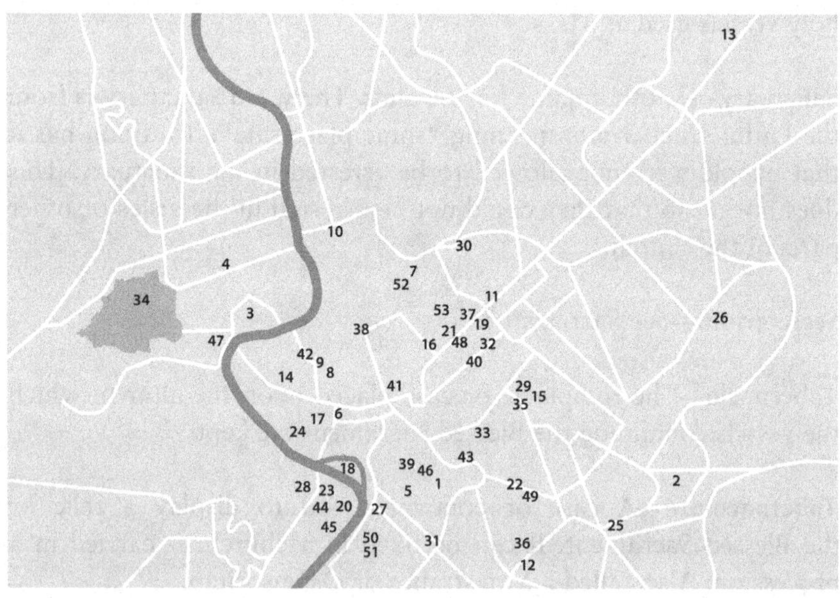

Legend

1. Ancient Church of St. Mary at the Forum
2. Basilica of the Holy Cross in Jerusalem
3. Castle of the Holy Angel (Castel Sant'Angelo)
4. Church of the Sacred Heart of Suffrage/ Museum of the Souls in Purgatory
5. Mamertine Prison/ St. Joseph of the Carpenters
6. Most Holy Name of Jesus
7. Most Holy Trinity at Monte Pincio
8. Our Lady above (over) Minerva

9. Our Lady and the Martyrs (The Pantheon)
10. Our Lady of the People
11. Our Lady of Victory
12. Sanctuary of Our Lady of Divine Love
13. St. Agnes Outside the Walls and St. Costanza
14. St. Agnes in Agone
15. St. Alphonsus Liguori / Shrine of Our Lady of Perpetual Help
16. St. Andrew's at the Quirinal
17. St. Barbara of the Books
18. St. Bartholomew on the Island
19. St. Bernard's at the Baths
20. St. Cecilia in Trastevere
21. St. Charles at the Four Fountains
22. St. Clemente in Laterano
23. St. Crisogono
24. St. Ignatius of Loyola at Campus Martius
25. St. John Laterano
26. St. Lawrence Outside the Walls
27. St. Mary in Cosmedin
28. St. Mary in Trastevere
29. St. Mary Major
30. St. Patrick's at the Villa Ludovisi
31. St. Paul Outside the Walls
32. St. Paul Within the Walls
33. St. Peter in Chains
34. St. Peter's/ The Vatican
35. St. Prassede
36. St. Sebastian Outside the Walls
37. St. Susanna
38. St. Sylvester at the Head
39. St. Teodoro at the Bottom of the Palatino
40. St. Vitalis, Valeris, Gervase, and Protase
41. Archaeology and Art History Library
42. Bernini's Elephant
43. Coliseum
44. Excubitorium of the Firemen
45. Forty Hour Device

46. Forum
47. Italian Clocks and Italian Time
48. Piazza of the Four Fountains
49. Pope Joan
50. Protestant Cemetery
51. Pyramid of Cestius
52. Spanish Steps
53. Trevi Fountain

Map Illustration by Cara Bufanio

Appendix H

Map of Vatican City

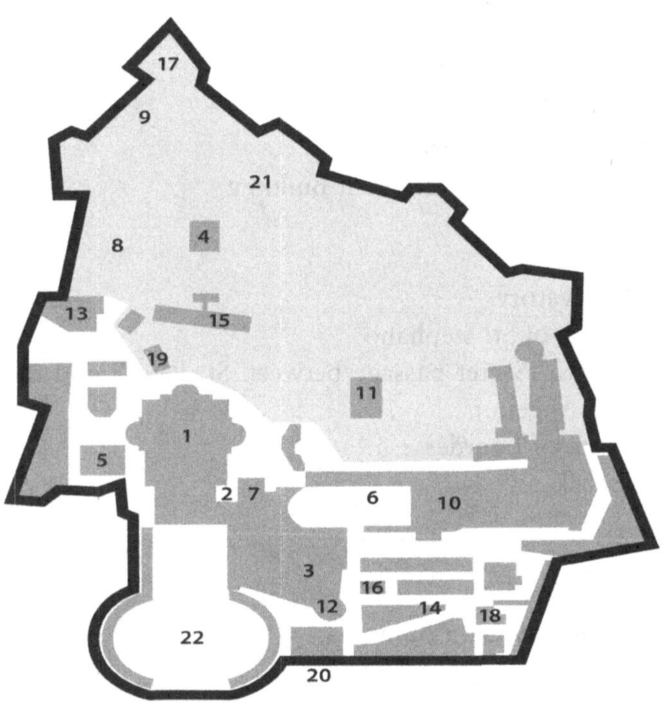

Legend

1. The Papal Basilica of St. Peter

2. The Vatican Grottoes and the Clementine Chapel
3. The Vatican Palace
4. The Ethiopian College
5. Sacristy and Treasury Museum
6. The Vatican Museums
7. The Sistine Chapel
8. The Vatican Gardens
9. St. John's Tower
10. The Vatican Library and Secret Archives
11. Casina of Pius IV
12. The Vatican Bank
13. Railroad Station
14. Vatican Supermarket
15. Vatican City Government Building
16. Post Office
17. Heliport
18. Observatory
19. Church of St. Stephano
20. Passetto (Secret passage between St. Peter's and the Castel Sant' Angelo.)
21. Grotto of Lourdes
22. Obelisk

Map Illustration by Cara Bufanio.

Appendix I

Pilgrimage Routes in Rome

The Seven Pilgrimage Churches of Rome:

1. San Pietro in Vaticano
2. San Paolo Fuori le Mura
3. San Giovanni in Laterano
4. Santa Maria Maggiore
5. Santa Croce in Gerusalemme
6. San Lorenzo Fuori le Mura
7. Santuario della Madonna del Divino Amore*
8. San Sebastiano Fuori le Mura*

Ferragosto (Feast of the Assumption) Pilgrims Path—August 15th

1. San Giovanni in Laterano
2. San Clemente
3. The Coliseum
4. Saints Cosmas and Damian
5. Santa Prassede
6. Basilica di Santa Maria Maggiore

---

* San Sebastiano Fuori le Mura was one of the original seven pilgrimage churches declared in the first Jubilee Year (1300). It was replaced by Pope John Paul II for the Great Jubilee of 2000 with Santuario Della Madonna Del Divino Amore. Some people prefer to visit the original seven churches.

Pilgrimage of Divine love

The Pilgrimage of Divine Love takes place every Saturday night, from Easter until the end of October. Pilgrims leave from the Passeggiata Archeologica in the Piazza di Porta Capena at midnight. They walk along the Via Appia Antica (old Appian Way) to the church: Quo Vadis; then turn on to the Via Ardeatina and continue to the Catacombs of St. Callisto walking past the Mausoleum of the Ardeatin Caves (Fosse Ardeatine). They arrive at the Sanctuary of Our Lady of Divine Love at 5 am in time for Mass. The walks were traditionally only for men, though this has changed in recent years.

Appendix J

The Seven Hills of Rome are:

1. Aventine Hill (Italian: Aventino)
2. Caelian Hill (Italian: Celio)
3. Capitoline Hill (Italian: Campidoglio)
4. Esquiline Hill (Italian: Esquilino)
5. Palatine Hill (Italian: Palatino)
6. Quirinal Hill (Italian: Quirinale)
7. Viminal Hill (Italian: Viminale)

Appendix K

Pollo all' Arrabbiati (Angry Chicken)

Just for fun, here is the Angry Chicken recipe. If you don't understand why this is included, please read the introduction. In Italy, anything cooked in a tomato sauce with pepper is called an "angry" dish.

1 whole chicken (3-4 lbs), cut into 8 pieces or 3 lbs of legs and thighs.
¼ cup olive oil
1 red onion, chopped
2-3 garlic cloves, minced
¾ cup red wine
1 teaspoon crushed red pepper flakes or 1 fresh chopped small chili pepper (use less if you don't like spicy food)
1 can (28 ounces) peeled whole tomatoes, crushed or 1 pint fresh cherry tomatoes cut in half
1-2 slices of pancetta (whole-this will be chopped later into smaller pieces.)
Salt and pepper to taste
Polenta—(cooked per package)

Sauté pancetta in olive oil in a large skillet at medium to low heat for 4-6 minutes or until the pancetta is slightly crisp. (The pancetta is flavoring the oil.) Remove the pancetta and set aside. Turn heat up and brown chicken in the same skillet. Chop pancetta into small sprinkle sizes.

Place all the other ingredients in a Dutch oven (or slow cooker). Add chicken and chopped pancetta. Simmer on medium heat for 1 hour or until chicken juices run clear. Add salt and pepper to taste after the chicken is cooked. Serve over polenta.

Hints:

- The longer the chicken simmers the more tender it will be, but don't cook it all day; the onions and tomatoes will disintegrate.
- If using a slow cooker, you may need to add a little water towards the end. There should be a broth to spoon over the polenta, but it isn't soup.
- I was taught to leave the pancetta whole as you are flavoring the oil. It is easier to fish out of the pan and you can chop it later.
- If you forget to add the pancetta to the Dutch oven or slow cooker, you can also sprinkle it in as you serve it. It's fine and adds a nice crunch. (Like bacon bits in a salad.)

Bibliography

Alighieri, Dante. *The Divine Comedy*. Whitefish, MT: Whitefish, Montana Kessinger Publishing, LLC. 2010.

Almagno, R. Stephen, O.F.M. ed. *Mary Our Hope: A Selection from the Sermons, Addresses, and Papers of Cardinal John J. Wright*. San Francisco, CA: Ignatius Press, 1984.

Anderson, Robin. *Roman Churches for English Speaking People*. Vatican City: Liberia Editrice Vaticana, 1982.

Aquilina, Mike. *The Fathers of the Church*. Huntington, IN; Our Sunday Visitors Publishing, 2006.

Basilica San Clemente—Official Website. Collegio San Clemente.n.d. Web. 24 Apr. 2012. <http://www.basilicasanclemente.com>.

Benedictine Monks of St. Augustine's Abbey. *The Book of Saints: A Dictionary of Servants of God Canonized by the Catholic Church*. 7th Revised ed. London: A & C Black Publishers Ltd., 2002.

Beny, Roloff and Peter Gunn. *The Churches of Rome*. New York: Simon and Schuster, 1981.

Bettenson, Henry, ed. *Ignatius of Loyola, Spiritual Exercises. Documents of the Christian Church*. 2nd ed. London: Oxford University Press, 1963.

Bokenkotter, Thomas. *A Concise History of the Catholic Church*. New York: Doubleday Religious Publishing Group, 2004.

Boyle, Leonard. *A Short Guide to St. Clement's, Rome*. Rome, Italy: Collegio San Clemente Via Labicana, 1989.

Catholic Encyclopedia. Vol. 3. New York: Robert Appleton Company, 1908. 24 Dec. 2010. Web. 24 Apr. 2012. <http://www.newadvent.org/cathen/>.

Claridge, Amanda. *Rome (Oxford Archaeological Guides)*. 2nd ed. New York: Oxford University Press, 2010.

Collins, Michael. *The Vatican*. London: DK Adult Publishers, 2011.

Cornwell, Hilarie, and James Cornwell. *Saints, Signs and Symbols*. New York: Morehouse Publishing, 2009.

Cross, FL and Elizabeth A. Livingstone. *Oxford Dictionary of the Christian Church*. 3rd Revised ed. New York: Oxford University Press, 2005.

Cruz, Joan Carrol. *Miraculous Images of Our Lady*. Rockford, IL: Tan Books & Publishers, 1993.

Degni, Paola, et al. *San Carlino alle Quattro Fontane: The Restoration of the Cloister*. Rome, Italy: Gangemi, 1996.

Di Carlantonio, Lisa. *La Basilica Sotterranea Di San Crisogono in Trastevere*. Rome, Italy: Available at the church in Trastevere.

Duffy, Eamon. *Saints and Sinners: A History of the Popes*. New Haven, CT: Yale University Press, 2006.

Ferguson, George. *Signs and Symbols in Christian Art*. London: Oxford University Press, 1961.

Gizzi, Federico. *Le Chiese Barocche di Roma*. Rome, Italy: Newton Compton, 1994.

Graziano, A, et al. *Michelangelo and Raphael in the Vatican: with Botticelli, Perugino, Signorelli, Ghirlandaio, and Rosselli.* Rome, Italy: Treasures Inc., 1996.

Grotowski, Piotr L. *Arms and Armour of the Warrior Saints: Tradition and Innovation in Byzantine Iconography*. Leiden, The Netherlands: Brill Press, 2010.

Haddan, Arthur, et al. *Councils and Ecclesiastical Documents Relating to Great Britain and Ireland II*. Oxford: Oxford University Press, 1873.

Healy, John. *Insula Sanctorum et Doctorum: Ireland's Ancient Schools and Scholars*. 6th ed. Dublin, Ireland: Sealy, Bryers & Walker, 1912.

Hannah, Robert and Guilio Magli. "The Role of the Sun in the Pantheon's Design and Meaning." *Numen* 58 (2011): 486-513.

Heater, James and Colleen Heater. *The Pilgrims Guide to Italy*. Inner Travel Books. Nevada City, California, USA. 2008.

Hicks, Sandy Burton. "The Anglo-Papal Bargain of 1125: The Legatine Mission of John of Crema." *Albion: A Quarterly Journal Concerned with British Studies* 8.4 (1976): 301-310.

Kah-Red, M, Franciolli, M. ed. *The Young Borromini: From his Debut to San Carlo alle Quattro*. Geneva-Milano, Italy: Fontane, 1999.

Lacouture, Jean. *Jesuits, a Multibiography*. Washington, DC: Counterpoint Press, 1995.

Lugli, Guiseppe, *The Pantheon and Adjacent Structures*. Rome, Italy: Giovanni Bardi Publisher, 1971.

MacDonald, William L. *The Pantheon: Design, Meaning, and Progeny*. Cambridge, MA: Harvard University Press, 1976.

Male, Emile. *The Early Churches of Rome.* London: Ernest Benn Limited, 1960.

Mancinelli, Fabrizio. *Catacombs and Basilicas: the Early Christians in Rome.* Florence, Italy: Scala Books, 1989.

Martin, Christopher. *The Philosophy of Thomas Aquinas: Introductory Readings.* London: Routledge, Kegan, and Paul, 1988.

Martin, F.X. "Archives of the Irish Augustinians, Rome: A Summary Report." *Archivium Hibernicum.* 18 (1955): 157-163.

McDermott, Timothy. *Aquinas Selected Writings.* New York: Oxford University Press, 1993.

McGurn, Barrett. *The Pilgrims Guide to Rome for the Millennial Jubilee Year 2000.* New York: Viking Penguin, 1998.

Morley, Henry. *Memoirs of Bartholomew Fair.* London: Tansill Press, 2008.

Newall, Christopher. "Jones, Sir Edward Coley Burne-, First Baronet (1833-1898), Painter." *Oxford Dictionary of National Biography.* Oxford: Oxford University Press, 2004.

Newman, Barbara. "The Heretic Saint: Guglielma of Bohemia, Milan, and Brunate." *Church History.* 74.1 (2005): 1-38.

Nes, Solrunn. *The Mystical Language of Icons.* Grand Rapids, MI: William B. Eerdmans Publishing Company, 2005.

O'Malley, John. *The First Jesuits.* Cambridge, MA: Harvard University Press, 1993.

Oxford Dictionary of the Christian Church. New York: Oxford University Press, 2005.

Pardoe, Rosemary and Darroll Pardoe. *The Female Pope: The Mystery of Pope Joan. The First Complete Documentation of the Facts behind the Legend.* New York: Crucible, 2004.

Pupillo, Marco. *St. Bartholomew's on the Tiber Island: a Thousand Years of History and Art.* Milan: Italy: Edizioni Angelo Guerini e Associati, 1998.

Rendina C. *Le Chiese di Roma.* Milan, Italy: Newton and Compton, 2000.

Santa Barbara dei Librai Church Circular. Rome, Italy: The Comunita di Santa Barbara, 2010.

St. John Calibita Hospital Website. 24 Dec 2010. Web. 24 Apr. 2012. <http://www.oh-fbf.it/Objects/Pagina.asp?ID=640>.

St. Maria in Cosmedin. Rome, Italy: Santa Maria in Cosmedin. 2012.

Sturgis, Michael. *When in Rome: 2000 Years of Roman Sightseeing.* London: Frances Lincoln Publishers, 2011.

Semes, Steven W. "Pantheon Inside." *Architecture Week* 254: 2005. Web. 24 Apr. 2012. <http://www.architectureweek.com/2005/0831/culture_1-1.html>.

Staccioli P. *Museum of Purgatory in The hidden museums of Rome.* Rome, Italy: Newton and Compton, 1996.

Taylor, Richard. *How to Read a Church.* Mahwah, NJ: Paulist Press, 2005.

The Capitoline Museums: Exhibition "The Capitoline She-Wolf." *The Capitoline Museums: Exhibition.* June-October 2000. Web. 4 Apr. 2012. <http://www.museicapitolini.org/>.

The Jesuit Curia in Rome Home page. n.d. Web. 4 Apr. 2012. < http://www.sjweb.info/>.

Tiber Island. Encyclopædia Britannica. Encyclopædia Britannica Online. 24 Dec 2010. Web. 4 Apr. 2012. <http://www.britannica.com/EBchecked/topic/594852/Tiber-Island>.

Ward-Perkins, J.B. *Roman Imperial Architecture (The Pelican History of Art)*. New Haven, CT: Yale University Press, 1992.

Webb, Matilda. *The Churches and Catacombs of Early Christian Rome: A Comprehensive Guide*. Ontario, Canada: Sussex Academic Press, 2010.

Index

G

H

I

J

M

O

P

R

S

T

V

W

Z